International Transfer Pricing in Asia Pacific

International Transfer Pricing in Asia Pacific

Perspectives on Trade between Australia, New Zealand and China

Jian Li and Alan Paisey

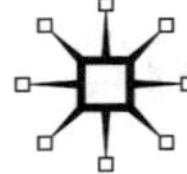

First published 2005 by
PALGRAVE MACMILLAN
Houndmills, Basingstoke, Hampshire RG21 6XS and
175 Fifth Avenue, New York, N. Y. 10010
Companies and representatives throughout the world

PALGRAVE MACMILLAN is the global academic imprint of the Palgrave Macmillan division of St. Martin's Press, LLC and of Palgrave Macmillan Ltd. Macmillan® is a registered trademark in the United States, United Kingdom and other countries. Palgrave is a registered trademark in the European Union and other countries.

ISBN-13: 978–1–4039–9167–6   hardback
ISBN-10: 1–4039–9167–7   hardback

This book is printed on paper suitable for recycling and made from fully managed and sustained forest sources.

A catalogue record for this book is available from the British Library.

Library of Congress Cataloging-in-Publication Data
Li, Jian, 1967 Feb. 25–
    International transfer pricing in Asia Pasific : perspective on trade between Australia, New Zealand, and China / Jian Li and Alan Paisey.
        p. cm.
    Includes bibliographical references and index.
    ISBN 1–4039–9167–7 (cloth)
    1. Transfer pricing–Australia. 2. Transfer pricing–New Zealand. 3. Transfer pricing–China. 4. International business enterprises–Taxation–Australia. 5. International business enterprises–Taxation–New Zealand. 6. International business enterprises–Taxation–China. 7. Transfer pricing–Law and legislation–Australia. 8. Transfer pricing–Law and legislation–New Zealand. 9. Transfer pricing–Law and legislation–China. I. Paisey, Alan. II. Title.

10   9   8   7   6   5   4   3   2   1
14 13 12 11 10 09 08 07 06 05

Printed and bound in Great Britain by
Antony Rowe Ltd, Chippenham and Eastbourne

Contents

List of Figures

List of Tables

Acknowledgements

We are grateful for the use of material from the following sources: Australian Bureau of Statistics (ed.) (1999, 2000, 2001, 2002, 2003); Yearbook Australia. Canberra, Australia: Author; Ernst & Young. (2001; 2004). Transfer Pricing Global Reference Guide; Ernst & Young. (2002). Worldwide Corporate Tax Guide (2002); International Monetary Fund. (2003). Balance of payments statistics yearbook. WA: Author; Ministry of Commerce of the People's Republic of China. (2004). Retrieved January 15, 2004 from http://www.mofcom.gov.cn; Statistics New Zealand. (ed.) (1999, 2000, 2002). New Zealand official yearbook. Wellington: Author.

Foreword

*Dr Michael Heimert, Chief Executive Officer, Ceteris Inc.,
United States*

The subject of transfer pricing is discussed little in academic circles, and even less so in the popular press. As a practitioner in this field, I accept the latter omission. After all, any matter that deals with tax and accounting issues will never be as exciting to the general public as the dating lives of Hollywood actresses. In fact, I am grateful for this omission, because I cannot imagine any excitement in a world where paparazzi are following the lives of accountants. But on the academic front, I must express some consternation. Transfer pricing is a matter of major importance to governments and multinational firms around the world, as it is a fundamental mechanism for shifting tax revenues from one country to another.

The major question is whether this lack of academic discussion is due to disinterest or lack of awareness. My untested hypothesis is that it is the latter. In interviewing newly minted students in economics and finance, many of whom have earned PhDs from leading universities, I find that their textbook experiences have dealt only with the managerial accounting aspects of transfer pricing. The lessons learned from this subject are that an incorrectly designed transfer pricing system can cause inefficient resource allocations and wasted managerial effort among the operating divisions of a company. Yet, this is not why companies spend a great deal of time and effort on transfer pricing, and why companies even hire professionals whose full-time jobs deal with transfer pricing. Companies are concerned about transfer pricing because they can create serious tax complications when not dealt with appropriately.

Why is there a lack of academic interest? Very likely because it is a multidisciplinary exercise. To examine and answer the many questions that arise in transfer pricing, one needs, at the least, an understanding of international tax law, accounting, industrial organisation, mathematical modeling and business practice. This knowledge rarely resides in one individual, and it takes many years to become conversant in the fundamentals of these subject areas. Yet, to those who are willing to tackle the issue, either alone or jointly, there is much fruitful research to be explored from both the theoretical and applied perspectives.

Perhaps 'International Transfer Pricing in Asia Pacific' will serve as a catalyst to the academics and students who read this book.

Because it is my conjecture that many readers may be uninitiated into transfer pricing, a simple example might be helpful to highlight the fundamental issues:

> Multinational Company (yes, that is its name and it obviously does not have a very clever marketing department) has two subsidiaries named Manufacturer and Distributor. Manufacturer is located in Country A, and Distributor is located in Country B. The tax rate in Country A is 35% and the tax rate in Country B is 50%. Let us also assume that it costs $25 to make the firm's product in Country A, and that it sells it in Country B's market for $100. Now, unencumbered by any international laws restricting transfer prices, what is the transfer price that Multinational Company will set between Country A and Country B?

As the reader can plainly see, if the transfer price were set at *$25* (italicised for easy observation), the total taxes paid by Multinational Company would be .35*(*25*-25) + .50*(100-*25*) = $37.50, while if Multinational Company set its transfer price at *$100* its total taxes would be .35* (*100*-25) + .50*(100-*100*) = $26.25. Thus, Multinational Company will set its transfer price at $100, thereby shifting its taxable income from Country B to Country A. In fancier parlance, Multinational Company has a tax arbitrage opportunity, and can gain $0.15 for every $1.00 it raises its transfer price from Country A to Country B. (This is to ignore another possibility – setting different transfer prices in each country by reporting a transfer price of $100 in Country B and $25 in Country A).

Let's continue with this example, for it has deeper implications. Even the most casual of observers will notice that Country B will be none too pleased with a transfer price of $100, since it has no tax revenues being generated by Distributor. What can it do?

A couple of strategic alternatives immediately come to mind. One possibility is for Country B to reduce its tax rate to something less than Country A's. For example, lowering its tax rate to 25% would cause Multinational Company to change its transfer price from $100 to $25. Of course, this lowering of the tax rate becomes a game of ruinous tax competition, because Country A would then have reason to retaliate and lower its tax rate further.

Another possibility is for Country B to simply 'force' a transfer pricing requirement on Distributor. For instance, it might require that all distribution companies operating within its borders set a transfer price at 60% of its market sales price. Country B would now be assured of tax revenue of $20 (.5*(100-*60*)). Of course, such an arbitrary policy could cause inefficiencies on two fronts. To see this, assume unrelated distributors in Country B could purchase the same product at $45. Then Distributor may find itself at a significant disadvantage in the marketplace and shut down operations. This policy has a more dire consequence to Country B than simply letting Multinational choose a transfer price to minimise taxes. A less extreme outcome might be that Multinational would divest itself of its operations in Country B, creating a loss in any economic benefits from efficiencies of vertical integration between the manufacturing and distribution operations in Countries A and B.

Another problem with the transfer pricing policy of Country B arises in Country A. Would Country A be satisfied with the tax revenue arbitrarily thrust upon itself by the policies of Country B? Provided with a $60 sales price, maybe Country A would be satisfied. However, think about the situation if the market price in Country B were $30. Now the transfer price under Country B's arbitrary policy would be $18 and the Multinational would report a tax loss in Country A.

Rather than by unilateral action, there are other solutions to this game. Country A and Country B might decide to agree jointly to a new set of rules to prevent the arbitrary shifting of profits via transfer pricing. In fact, in practice this is precisely one solution that has been arrived at by governments. Many countries have adopted the "arm's length standard" as the general principle by which transfer prices are to be set by multinationals.

The arm's length standard requires Multinational Company to set its transfer prices as if the operations in Country A and Country B were completely independent of each other. In other words, the multinational must determine a theoretical market price for dealings between its two related entities. In a perfect world, the multinational will choose an arm's length price and simultaneously satisfy the requirements of Country A and Country B. Country A and Country B will not play a game of ruinous tax competition, and Multinational Company will not be able to shift profits arbitrarily between the countries.

Going back to our example again, if independent distributors in Country B pay $45 for the same product that Distributor distributes in the market, then the transfer price will also be $45 and all parties (Country A, Country B and Multinational) should have reason to agree, by virtue of the observation of objective information.

If only it were that easy! Practitioners in the area are keenly aware that determining an arm's length transfer price is a subjective exercise. There is not enough strong benchmark information by which to determine an arm's length price truly. Many assumptions are often required, and transfer prices are generally investigated by tax auditors in hindsight – so that a transfer price that appeared arm's length at the outset might create losses in one country because of interim changes in market conditions. This still might be what would be arm's length, but proving it becomes a much more difficult exercise for Multinational Company.

This problem is further compounded when one realises that the realm of transfer pricing goes far beyond transactions involving the sale of tangible products. The types of transactions between related entities are at least as varied as those between unrelated parties, and they are often under different economic circumstances than transactions between unrelated parties.

For instance, suppose that Manufacturer in Country A has developed a secret manufacturing process that gives it significant advantage in its market. Now, let's assume that Multinational Company has another manufacturing subsidiary in Country C, and that Manufacture in Country A has provided the Country C manufacturer with its secret manufacturing process. There is now a need to make a determination of what an arm's length price would be for the sale or the license of intellectual property from Country A to Country C. Messy accounting data, the lack of true third party comparables, and other factors make this a difficult exercise. If two objective parties were independently asked to determine the value of the intellectual property, it is quite likely that both parties would arrive at very different values. Thus, the arm's length standard, while providing a starting point and some boundaries for what is reasonable, does not give complete certainty. This is a troubling point to many taxpayers and governments, and much time and energy is still spent by both sides in their attempt at proving what constitutes an arm's length payment.

In addition, related party entities can be different economic characters than unrelated entities. Companies sometimes set up legal entities that only hold intellectual property. General management, future R&D activities and other activities might be contracted out for this entity. The pricing of such transactions, which are legally allowed, requires economic analysis that often cannot resort to benchmarks because there are no companies of a 'stand alone' nature that are perfectly comparable to the activities of the related entity. Nonetheless, the arm's length standard requires the benchmarking of the transaction and thus requires detailed economic analysis and assumptions for which there is not a detailed body of commonly accepted techniques.

Let's return to the example once more. Another possible solution to the game played between Multinational Company, Country A and Country B would be for all parties to agree to a transfer price upfront, versus having Country A or Country B challenge the transfer price under audit. This also has a 'real world' parallel, as many countries allow for Advanced Pricing Agreement (APA) negotiations on a multilateral basis. APAs allow for taxpayers to receive approval of their transfer prices, free of audit, for a number of years in the future, and in some instances, for past years. This is a compelling choice to some companies, but it is also extremely time consuming (not everyone is audited, while you guarantee an upfront investigation under an APA). As would be expected, because of the time investment required by a multinational company, this route has typically been chosen by companies only when entering into transactions that are difficult to value, that might be construed as tax-shifting by an uninformed party, and that have significant tax dollars at stake.

Li and Paisey's book is a welcome addition to the transfer pricing literature. The example I have provided is too simple for anyone who really wants to explore the transfer pricing field in more depth. "International Transfer Pricing in Asia Pacific" serves as a better introduction to the specifics of transfer pricing in general, and a detailed survey of the transfer pricing practices of multinationals operating in Australia, New Zealand and China. Of particular interest is that the book surveys the transfer pricing practices of multinationals in Australia, New Zealand and China from the perspective of the host country. This also is an important change in many surveys, as surveys have often been conducted at the parent level of a multinational. But as one might expect, for many subsidiaries, Rome is far and the hills surrounding it are high. Thus, when a survey participant is a parent company answering questions for activities it delegates to its operating subsidiary, there is the possibility that what is policy and what is procedure are different, causing erroneous conclusions to ensue.

Another area of new ground in this book is its survey and discussion of Chinese tax authorities, and their insight into transfer pricing. Foreign direct investment in China, and the level of international trade with China, has substantially increased over the last decade, and so have concerns over how to deal with transfer pricing issues in China. The observations and survey results by Li and Paisey should therefore be of extensive interest to many transfer pricing practitioners dealing with China.

Finally, this book also shows the differences and similarities of the transfer pricing practices of companies located in different tax jurisdictions. Much of this information does confirm what many practitioners know – practices and methods to set transfer pricing do not, in general, often differ across countries. However, audit practices across countries do differ. This also implicitly confirms an issue that is at the heart of one of the biggest problems with the current arm's length regime: there is an inordinate amount of time and energy devoted to setting and auditing transfer prices, much of which would not matter but for the determination of taxable income in any given country.

In conclusion, Li and Paisey's book helps push us along the learning curve, as it investigates and elucidates some of the areas where policy makers and practitioners would welcome additional transfer pricing and international tax research. To the interested academic community, I will also add my personal laundry list of additional research opportunities:

1. *What is the theoretically most appropriate transfer pricing governance system?* The arm's length standard and a standard of formulary apportionment (dividing global profits of a multinational firm amongst the countries in which it operates using some formula that uses as inputs total assets, employees or sales in each country) are currently the two standards most commonly debated among policy makers. Is either standard appropriate, or is a better standard available? What is the optimal formulary apportionment rule? Given the possibility of gaming a system, is the arm's length standard the only viable standard?

2. *What are appropriate benchmarks by which to set arm's length standards?* There are currently many ways in which taxpayers are required to arrive at an arm's length value for their intercompany transactions. These differ slightly in application among tax authorities, and sometimes greater priority is given to one valuation method over another. These standards, such as the comparable uncontrolled price method, resale price method, cost plus method, comparable profits method or transactional net margin method, are discussed within Li and Paisey's book. But, are some of these standards more effective at determining a true transfer price, given the fuzziness of information by which objectively to arrive at a conclusion? Are other valuation standards that are currently not explicitly discussed

in OECD Guidelines more appropriate in some circumstances? What would those circumstances be?

3. *What is the true economic loss due to transfer pricing manipulation?* Some studies have attempted to evaluate the amount of tax revenues lost by transfer pricing manipulation. But, they often fall short of bringing a conclusion as to whether transfer pricing manipulation is the actual culprit, or other economic factors at work. Further, the question of how much expenditure is undertaken by multinationals and tax authorities to audit and prove arm's length pricing has not been adequately addressed. Finally, lost revenues are often calculated in a vacuum, ignoring differences in functions, risks, and intangible property ownership between related party transactions and market price benchmarks used as the starting point to determine arm's length prices.

4. *What are the appropriate methods by which to examine and adjust benchmark evidence to set arm's length transfer prices?* The applied problems of transfer pricing are numerous and there have been no universally accepted solutions yet. For instance, in determining arm's length pricing between a manufacturer and a distributor, third party benchmark information may not be adequate because that information ignores savings from vertical integration synergies. Which party would receive the savings from the synergy. What are the rules for a more objective determination and sharing of the savings? Also, how might prices be adjusted for foreign exchange rate risk, market risk, or other factors?

There are many other questions that are too numerous to list in this Foreword. It is hoped that academics, after reading Li and Paisey's book, will be persuaded to take up transfer pricing as an area of academic research. A system with less conflict and uncertainty, with fairness to all parties involved, would be welcome by all of us.

Michael Heimert
Chief Executive Officer
Ceteris, Inc.
USA
February 2005

Preface

With the advent of China's appearance as a major power in international trade and its repercussions for Asia Pacific countries such as Australia and New Zealand, the subject of trade between these countries in general suggested itself as a field of research. Owing to the perennial difficulties or obstacles over language, access, the practices of government agencies and business, and interpersonal exchanges in any studies involving China, Jian Li's own native experience in business and government in China has been an important asset for such research, allied to the research, publishing, economics, and management interests of Alan Paisey.

In particular, the expectations of Australia and New Zealand to extend their international trade with China have created the potential for an increase of indigenous new or existing enterprises that are seeking to establish subsidiaries in these other economies. The subsequent intent to formulate free-trade arrangements between these three countries has added to the impetus. Inevitably, the deportment of companies over their level of probity in their dealings with taxation, duties, and value transfers will become a consideration between the three governmental authorities and business people.

For many years the subject of International Transfer Pricing has attracted the attention of governments, has been a regular and absorbing pre-occupation of international companies that try to use it for advantage, and has provided a prominent study base for scholars world-wide. Since scant if any attention has been given specifically to Asia Pacific countries, it seemed apt and opportune to focus on this subject in relation to those countries.

On completion of the research for Jian Li's doctoral degree, we decided to use the data freely to prepare this book in a form that may be read by practitioners in all fields of interest related to the subject of International Transfer Pricing – including government officials, the senior staff of firms which operate in more than one country, and financial and accounting professionals, but also scholars and students of accounting and economics who have an interest in the subject.

The complications involved in designing and executing the research itself were overcome by the generosity of many bodies and individuals. In the first place, Lincoln University, New Zealand offered a founding scholarship grant and followed it up with a subsidiary grant in 2001. The substantial costs of travel and postage charges put a large strain on the research but they were relieved by two generous grants from the New Zealand Institute of Chartered Accountants, respectively in 2002 and 2004. Thanks are extended for these crucial grants and to all the following persons who assisted in a variety of ways.

Qualitative help over the design, validity and presentation of the Questionnaires was elicited from many who showed patient interest in the project. They include Wang Cao, Sales Manager, Chang Sha Appliances Limited, Hunan, China; Tom Davies, the Director for Professional Support at the New Zealand Institute of Chartered Accountants; Dr Jamie Elliott, Transfer Pricing Advisor, Deloitte LLP, United Kingdom; Dr Michael Heimert, formerly of Ernst & Young LLP, and currently of Ceteris, Inc., United States; Richard Mercer, formerly of New Zealand Wool Services International; Leslie Prescott-Haar of Ernst & Young LLP, New Zealand; Robyn Russell, Partner, Transfer Pricing Services, Deloitte LLP, New Zealand.

Administrative support and help were afforded throughout the time taken to complete the research, notably at Lincoln University by Dr Ross Cullen, Professor and Post-Graduate Coordinator, Commerce Division; Annette E. Brixton, Secretary to the Commerce Division; Kristene Broad, Administator to the Commerce Division; and Lindley Turnbull, the University's Assistant Librarian for Information Studies.

The assistance received in China was critical for the research. It particularly relied on the help given by Yang Wei, Manager, and Tian Zheng, Vice-Manager, of the Bright Consultancy Company, Beijing, and Bei Zong, Manager, of the Wang Long Hotel, Beijing.

Overall, the research had the inestimable benefit of advice and supervision from Dr Peter Oyelere, formerly Senior-Lecturer in the Commerce Division, Lincoln University, New Zealand, and Professor Fawzi Laswad, Head of the School of Accountancy, Massey University, New Zealand.

The subsequent preparation of this book on the basis of the data gathered for the research project was accomplished with the expert help of Sheila Smurthwaite, Administration Manager at ChambersPR of Christchurch, New Zealand. We are grateful for her many suggestions and practical computer work.

1
Global Trading Issues

Introduction

The world economy has been significantly internationalised since the end of World War II. This phenomenon is revealed in the fact that a large percentage of the world's economic products is generated by international business activity, mostly undertaken by multinational enterprises.

A multinational enterprise is an organisation that engages in the production or service activities in two or more countries. Multinational enterprises engage in international operations mainly through foreign direct investment. In contrast with exporting and importing, where a stake is taken in an overseas business without operational control, foreign direct investment requires the establishment of a subsidiary or branch by a company from one country in the territory of another country, at which point the investing company becomes a parent company.

A substantial part of international trade now consists of high volumes of intercompany sales, or commercial transactions between parent companies and their foreign affiliates or between their several subsidiaries. These transactions by multinational enterprises with related parties may take various forms, such as transfers of goods and services, transfers or uses of intangible property, the use of tangible property loans, and intercompany financing and licensing. The internal charges for these related party transactions take a variety of forms, such as management fees, service charges, royalties, licensing fees, rents, and interest. The actual prices attached to a transaction between a parent company in the home country and its subsidiary or between two subsidiaries of the same company – when they are located in different countries, as host countries, with their own tax jurisdictions – are referred to as International Transfer Pricing.

Multinational enterprises

It is estimated by the World Trade Organisation that intercompany transactions among multinational enterprises now account for about one-third of total world trade. This significant amount of intercompany transactions has important tax implications for both the multinational enterprises themselves and the agencies of governments of the countries in which they operate. Since such a large proportion of international trade consists of transfers between related business entities located in different tax jurisdictions, a small change in the transfer prices adopted for such intercompany trade can have a considerable potential for saving substantial tax payments for the multinational enterprises involved but by the same token it can deny tax revenues to the interested governments concerned.

Consequently, tax authorities in many countries have intensified their surveillance and investigation of multinational transfer pricing practices to counter actual or suspected International Transfer Pricing manoeuvres. Hence, a major challenge facing multinational enterprises today lies in the effective management of International Transfer Prices – an activity that has been and continues to be of central managerial concern for them.

The use of transfer pricing can occur domestically as well as internationally. It is needed when a company structures itself into divisions which are able to make independent decisions, as profit-making units, and can sell their products or services to each other within the company.

From a domestic company's point of view, transfer pricing is the price used for the internal sales of goods and services transferred from one profit centre to another within the same firm. In this regard, transfer pricing is at the heart of interprofit centre relations. The prices adopted for the transfer of goods or services between such related parts of the same firm may be fixed at sharply different levels from that which would apply to the same transactions between unrelated parties.

At the domestic level, transfer prices are designed to accomplish the following objectives:

- To provide each part with the relevant information required for determining the optimum trade-off between company costs and revenues.

- To promote goal congruence
- To preserve divisional autonomy
- To enhance managerial motivation
- To help in the evaluation of the performance of various profit centres.

If a company located wholly within a single national boundary, albeit in the form of numerous independent units, grows to the point of being able to contemplate the establishment of overseas units, the firm becomes by definition thereby a multinational enterprise. The intercompany pricing processes which then have to take place between its constituent parts for involving movements across national borders within the multinational enterprise group as International Transfer Pricing activities are of a critically different order from those previously and exclusively conducted within a single national boundary.

Compared with intercompany pricing practices for domestic firms, International Transfer Pricing is thus of great significance for multinational enterprises. They are faced with an 'economic environment...much more complex and perplexing than that for domestic transfers...' (Wu and Sharp, 1979, p. 83).

Within the host country they are focused on minimising tax liabilities, reducing tariffs on imports and exports, avoiding restrictions on the repatriation of profits, minimising foreign exchange risks, enhancing the competitive position of subsidiaries in international markets, and improving the relations between subsidiaries and foreign host governments. At the international level, the objectives and motivations associated with transfer pricing revolve around issues of taxation and duties.

Taxation issues

Multinational transfer pricing and international taxation are two highly interrelated issues. From the point of view of taxation, International Transfer Pricing can be defined as the pricing process of goods and services transferred between related companies of a multinational enterprise system across different tax jurisdictions. The amount of taxes paid in each jurisdiction is therefore subject to the internal price that is assigned to the goods involved.

A multinational enterprise engages in international operations involving the shipments of goods and services among its foreign subsidiaries or between the parent company and its foreign subsidiaries. Charges by the parent company for specific services rendered to its subsidiaries are levied by headquarters. Since corporate income tax rates vary across countries, and the foreign subsidiaries are theoretically subject to control by the parent company, the parent company may have considerable discretion in setting its transfer prices when one subsidiary – or the parent company itself – transfers an asset or provides a service to another subsidiary, and vice versa, as a means for manipulating tax liabilities. This process is modelled in Figure 1.1.

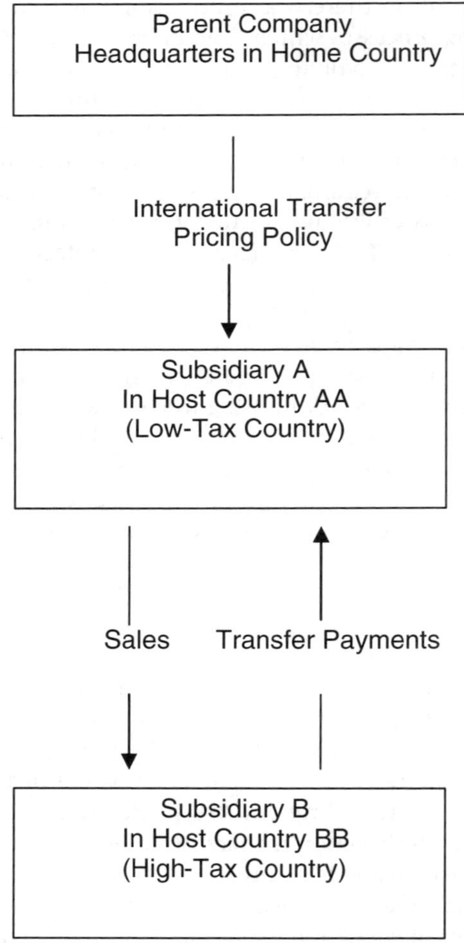

Figure 1.1   Simplified International Transfer Pricing Model

In this simplified International Transfer Pricing model, the parent company in the home country has two subsidiaries A and B, located respectively in the host countries AA and BB. Subsidiary A sells its product to its sister subsidiary B. The International Transfer Pricing policy is set by the parent company with its headquarters in its home country. The corporate tax rate in host country AA is 20%, but 33% in the other host country BB.

It follows, for example, that subsidiary A can produce an intermediate product to be sold to subsidiary B, the latter processing the intermediate goods into a final product for sale in its local market. The products transferred have an open market price. The parent company sets an International Transfer Pricing policy based on a chosen currency.

All other factors being equal, then in this case the parent company would like to allow its subsidiary A in the low tax country AA to sell its products to its related subsidiary B in the high tax country BB at a high price – one that exceeds the market selling price – ignoring constraints imposed by tax laws in the host country. The resultant loss in subsidiary B's high tax jurisdiction country BB is more than offset by the profits of subsidiary A in low tax jurisdiction country AA. The overall effect is that the multinational enterprise as a whole can minimise its total tax payments by shifting its profits to the lower tax jurisdiction country AA.

It is worth noting, however, that in addition to tax rate differences among nations affecting International Transfer Pricing, resulting in income shifting, the extent and magnitude of cross-border profit shifting also depend on which tax system – either the exemption system or the credit system – multinational residence countries use to avoid double taxation. International double taxation occurs whenever the same taxable base such as income is subject to an identical tax such as income tax in at least two separate tax jurisdictions.

The gains from profit shifts are largest if the multinational enterprise resides in a home country that uses the exemption system. Once the firm has been taxed abroad, foreign income is exempted from home-country taxation. Examples are France and the Netherlands. Other countries, amongst them the United States, the United Kingdom and Japan, use the so-called credit system, which provides for a tax credit for corporate taxes already paid abroad, and defers home tax payments until income is repatriated from the source country – the host country – to the residence country – the home country. Under the credit system, the gains from profit shifting primarily arise from deferring the timing of profit repatriations from foreign subsidiaries to a residence country with a higher tax rate.

Considerable evidence has accumulated concerning the tax-motivated International Transfer Pricing strategies adopted by multinational enterprises. Studies focus on examining whether tax rates affect taxable income reported by multinational enterprises operating in different foreign locations. Substantial attention has been given to income shifting activities by firms with tax haven affiliates. Tax havens are often defined as locations with the following four attributes: low corporate tax rates; legislation that supports banking and business secrecy; advanced communications facilities; and self-promotion as an offshore financial centre (Hines and Rice, 1994).

Consistent research results show that the reported income of multinationals' foreign affiliates is significantly higher in those countries with low corporate income tax rates whilst that of affiliates in high tax rate jurisdictions is reported as being at lower levels of before-tax profitability, implying the aggressive International Transfer Pricing behaviour of the multinational enterprises involved.

Grubert and Mutti (1991) examined the relationship between profit margins and tax rates to see whether profits were shifted from high-tax countries to low-tax countries. They examined profit/equity and profit/sales ratios of affiliates of United States companies in thirty-three foreign countries. Their results revealed that before-tax profitability is negatively correlated with local tax rates, and that high taxes reduce the reported after-tax profitability of local operations. The fact that tax rates are a significant determinant of reported profits may indirectly be evidence of international tax avoidance activities by the multinational enterprises.

Hines and Rice (1994) examined the ability of United States multinationals to shift their reported profits and real business activities between high-tax foreign countries and low-tax foreign tax havens. By analysing the aggregated reported profitability of United States firms in different tax locations in 1982, they found that reported profit rates were sensitive to local tax rates. A one percentage point higher tax rate reduced reported profits by three percent in their data. This elasticity may have been partly the consequence of profit shifting activities.

Grubert and Slemrod (1998) investigated the impact of taxation in the context of United States corporate investment in Puerto Rico, as a low-tax foreign tax haven favoured by many United States multinationals. Their results showed that income shifting advantages were the predominant reason for United States investment in Puerto Rico.

This finding is an echo of the prevalent allegation that a significant function for tax havens is to facilitate international tax avoidance.

The above studies focused on multinationals of United States origin. They provide evidence that United States multinationals shift profit out of high-tax countries into the United States, and from the United States to low-tax countries as tax havens.

Profit shifting can take place in two ways. One way to shift profits is through the capital structure of multinational enterprises. For example, a multinational can use debt to finance foreign affiliates in high-tax countries and equity to finance subsidiaries in low-tax countries. Another way is by the manipulation of transfer prices for cross-border intercompany deliveries of goods and services (Bartelsman, 2000). The second type of profit shifting activity – International Transfer Pricing – is the subject of this book and formed the central concern of the research undertaken for it.

Models and methods

International Transfer Pricing methods can directly affect the amount of profit reported in a country by a multinational enterprise, which in turn affects the tax revenues of that country. Multinational enterprises use a large variety of pricing methods for dealing with intercompany transfers across international boundaries. The methods actually used in practice, however, may be very different from the theoretically based recommendations in the accounting literature.

In the transfer pricing literature, three different theoretical research frameworks have been developed to explain multinational transfer pricing strategies. These are the economic model, mathematical programming, and behavioural approaches.

Economic Model. The economic model includes market and marginal (incremental) pricing. In the economic model, if the intermediate market is competitive, the transfer price should be the market price; but if the intermediate market is imperfectly competitive – as it always is in the real world – then marginal pricing replaces market pricing (Hirshleifer, 1956). These methods, however, are open to criticism in that they ignore factors such as uncertainty and risk aversion by managers (Kanodia, 1979). Critics of these economic methods also cite their defects as ignoring both the divergence of preferences among division managers and information asymmetries. The latter occur when upper management does not possess the complete information which lies in the hands of lower management.

The consequence of this is that upper management cannot choose an optimal International Transfer Pricing method for the firm as a whole (Borkowski, 1990).

The Mathematical Programming Model. The mathematical programming model equates transfer price with the opportunity cost of the intermediate product. It deals with multiple divisions and multiple products, and allows for the inclusion of realistic production constraints. In the study of the mathematical programming model, both linear and non-linear approaches are developed (Abdel-Khalik and Lusk, 1974). Critics of this method cite its defects as including the underlying assumption of certainty, the neglect of managerial motivation and its complexity in implementation (Kanodia, 1979; Ismail, 1982).

The Behavioural Model. Both the economic and mathematical programming models place high importance on production efficiency, cost minimisation and profit maximisation. Although these analyses have provided useful insights, both models fail to take into account the human dimensions in transfer pricing decisions. To correct this deficiency, the behavioural model has been developed to incorporate the human dimension in transfer pricing.

Rather than relying on market forces or cost structures for determining transfer prices, the behavioural model recommends the use of negotiated transfer pricing for achieving organisational goals. Watson and Baumler (1975) argued that successful firms resolve interdepartmental conflicts through negotiated transfer prices. Acklesberg and Yukl (1979) suggested that negotiated transfer prices could result in better relations and co-operation among divisions of a multinational enterprise. Cited defects of this method have included the necessity for a higher claim on management time, the possible increase in divisional conflict, and evaluations based more on a manager's negotiating ability and handling of the process and less on his or her ability to control economic factors (Kaplan, 1982).

In contrast to these three alternative transfer pricing models, many firms are in favour of cost based methods in practice, though the cost based methods do not have as much theoretical support as the three listed above.

Empirical research on International Transfer Pricing has found a substantial difference between the actual methods used in practice and the theoretical models discussed above. The findings of those studies support the contingency theory approach to management accounting, in which multinational enterprises choose methods which seem entirely appropriate for the specific set of circumstances in which they find themselves.

Wu and Sharp (1979) investigated the dominant transfer pricing policies adopted by sixty-one firms based in the United States when the market price was unavailable. They reported that, when a market price exists for an intermediate product, market pricing was the prevalent method, followed in descending order by negotiated pricing, full cost plus profit margin, adjusted market price, full cost, marginal cost, variable cost plus profit margin, and mathematical programming. In the absence of a market price, the top three transfer pricing methods were full cost plus profit margin, negotiation, and full cost. Their finding is an echo of the approach encompassed in the economic model for explaining transfer pricing strategies.

Tang (1979) reported on transfer pricing methods employed in the United States and Japan. Of the 133 firms surveyed in the United States, 56% used cost based methods, rather than market, negotiated, mathematical programming or other non-cost based methods, as their dominant transfer pricing mechanisms. A relationship between firm size and transfer pricing method chosen was not found.

PriceWaterhouse (1984) surveyed the 148 largest of the Fortune 500 companies. Of the seventy-four firms responding, fifty-one companies (69%) used transfer pricing, with sixteen (31%) using full cost methods and twenty-two (44%) using cost plus methods, adopted either alone or in conjunction with a market based technique. Larger firms tended to use what PriceWaterhouse termed 'value added transfer pricing'.

Benvignati (1985) used the Federal Trade Commission's (FTC) data for 466 manufacturing firms in the United States, organising the sample into 3,186 'lines of business', of which 674 reported the undertaking of foreign transfers. Benvignati investigated whether or not transfer pricing methods were associated with firm and, or industry characteristics. Her study found that a firm's features were more likely to influence internal pricing decisions than that of the type of industry. Of the firm's characteristic variables investigated, advertising intensity, volume of foreign transfers, and the number of different countries where firms operated, were found to be strongly associated with non-market pricing, while larger multinational enterprises and those with a large number of foreign subsidiaries tended towards market based methods.

Academic research has tended to focus on the pricing methods used from a managerial or motivational point of view. Surveys for academic purposes are directed at uncovering whether market based, cost based or negotiated prices are in operation (Atkinson and Tyrrall, 1999). In contrast to academic research, Ernst and Young (2001), in their global survey of activity on transfer pricing, interviewed multinational companies in twenty-two countries on the use of arm's length pricing methods as the legally oriented transfer pricing methods. The survey results presented in Table 1.1 show that Cost Plus and Comparable Uncontrolled Price dominate the legally oriented pricing methods used by firms for all types of transaction.

Comparable uncontrolled price uses the market price for transferred goods and services and is often thought of as the 'best pricing method' (Atkinson and Tyrrall, 1999, p. 216). In practice, however, it can be extremely difficult to account for all the material differences in terms that exist between intergroup and third party transactions (Radebaugh and Gray, 1997; Atkinson and Tyrrall, 1999).

The cost plus method involves the costs of manufacturing the product plus a normal profit margin that would accrue from the sales of similar products. The cost plus method is generally simpler to administer and understand. Furthermore, the data are more readily available. The disadvantages are that the system does not create incentives for manufacturing companies to reduce costs and that accordingly it often reduces the profit margin for the final selling firm (Arpan, 1972; Radebaugh and Gray, 1997).

The resale price minus method is used to determine the transfer price that a controlled sales and marketing company as distributor should pay for goods which it sells on to unrelated parties. The resale price minus method works best when the distributor does little to add value to the product other than normal sales, marketing and distributive activities. Hence, there is less concern with the comparability of products than in the comparable uncontrolled price method. The resale price minus method is probably most useful where it is applied to marketing operations (OECD, 1995; Atkinson and Tyrrall, 1999).

The profit split method is based upon the economic notion of joint venture or partnership relationship. It divides profits between associated companies according to the relative economic value of each firm's contribution to that transaction. The profit split method depends on profit comparisons rather than price or transaction comparisons and functional analysis.

Previous studies have provided some insight into International Transfer Pricing practices. Some studies have reported International Transfer Pricing methods according to distinct categories, such as

Table 1.1   Legally Oriented Pricing Methods Used by Types of Transaction for International Transfer Pricing in Twenty-Two Countries

Pricing Methods	CUP	RPM	Cost Plus	CPM	Profit Split	CUT	TNMM	Historic Practice	Cost	Others
	%	%	%	%	%	%	%	%	%	%
Sale of finished goods	25	24	35	9	5	2	8	4	2	4
Sale of raw materials	26	12	48	7	3	2	4	4	2	5
Administrative or managerial services	11	1	62	4	3	2	2	7	<1	5
Technical services	18	2	55	4	3	4	3	7	<1	8
Commission for sales of goods	27	10	25	8	3	4	5	11	–	7
Technology cost sharing	17	<1	45	5	6	3	2	8	–	6
Royalties	33	5	16	7	4	11	1	12	–	8
Intercompany financing	37	3	24	4	2	7	2	9	1	10

CUP = Comparable Uncontrolled Price, RPM = Resale Price Minus, CPM = Comparable Profit Method, CUT = Comparable Uncontrolled Transaction, TNMM = Transactional Net Margin Method full cost, variable cost, market, and negotiated, while others have lumped negotiated and market together as market based methods. The finding of Ernst and Young (2001) was that cost plus and comparable uncontrolled price dominated the use of arm's length pricing methods by firms for all types of transaction. Although economic theory suggests that marginal cost pricing and mathematical programming are the most appropriate policies for many International Transfer Pricing situations, they are rarely used in practice.

Summary

Globalisation requires and facilitates the growth of multinational intercompany trade. The disparity in tax rates across countries creates an obvious incentive for the members of a multinational enterprise to try to minimise their tax liability in home or host countries, and in return, to maximise joint profits within the multinational enterprise as a whole. For a multinational enterprise this effect can be accomplished by artificially shifting taxable income from affiliates incorporated in high-tax jurisdictions to subsidiaries in low-tax jurisdictions to reduce total worldwide tax payments.

The emergence of the multinational enterprise has been one of the most significant economic phenomena of the contemporary world. The activities of multinational enterprises have an important impact on international trade. Multinational enterprises tend to integrate their operations globally, rather than within the boundaries of individual countries. As a result, multinational enterprises transfer large quantities of goods and services among operating subsidiaries in different countries. The pricing at which such items are transferred across borders within corporate networks and especially between foreign affiliates and the parent company creates considerable managerial and taxation problems, owing to its direct effects on the profits of both parties and the revenues of host and home countries. For this reason, International Transfer Pricing is a crucial component of corporate strategy, commanding the attention of managers of multinational enterprises.

Multinational transfer pricing strategies generally involve method choices. Corporate internal pricing methods can be classified into a number of categories. Some methods – such as marginal cost, opportunity cost, and mathematical programming models – are theoretically effective but are rarely used in practice. Empirical studies of International Transfer Pricing methods concentrate on three major categories: market based, cost based and negotiated prices. Contingency theory offers a better explanation of a firm's choice of transfer pricing methods in practice. The contingency theory approach states that firms choose the International Transfer Pricing systems that are perceived as optimal for their particular situation. In other words, each company selects a method that offers the best fit for its needs and circumstances.

2
Company and Government Interests

Introduction

From the point of view of multinational enterprises, International Transfer Pricing is an instrument to manage internal markets efficiently. It serves their goals to maximise global profits and minimise their business risks. Yet, from the viewpoint of a host government, International Transfer Pricing itself is a potential problem in that it can create losses of taxation revenue, and therefore negatively affect the national economy. For developing countries, owing to their lack of institutional frameworks and administrative expertise to analyse complex transfer pricing situations, their economies are more vulnerable to transfer pricing manipulation than those of developed countries.

Transfer opportunities

The core reason for the existence of an organisation can be identified in its vision and mission statement, and can be more specifically defined by its corporate goals and objectives. Corporate goals and objectives can be directly and indirectly linked to different corporate strategies and, in turn, to different organisational structures.

Since organisations exist in different shapes and sizes, their organisational structures can be categorised in different ways. The traditional organisational alternatives are functional, divisional and matrix in macro form. In a multinational context, corporate structures can be grouped into three categories: vertically integrated businesses, horizontally integrated businesses and conglomerates (Ward, 1992; Rugman, 1985b; Anthony and Govindarajan, 1998). Each of these three organisational structures may be considered in association with issues for multinational intercompany transfer pricing, as follows.

Vertically integrated businesses. A popular industrial structure of multinational enterprises is vertical integration. In terms of Porter's (1980; 1985) strategic management concept of vertical integration, vertically integrated businesses tend to operate with a relatively undifferentiated product. This business strategy can be used as a competitive weapon against non-integrated firms. The form of vertical integration enables an organisation to take advantage of economies of scale, and enables it to use an internal market to minimise its transaction costs (Dunning and Rugman, 1985).

For reasons of size, most of a vertically integrated company is broken down into a variety of geographic and functional divisional units located in different countries. The divisions often trade with each other within the integrated group, and each division is given responsibility for a specified set of activities in recognition of the superior information regarding resource use and labour effectiveness it might command compared with that of central management. To measure financial performances at the divisional level effectively, the group must set transfer prices for those goods and services that are exchanged between any two divisions or between the divisions and their parent company. This regime is well established in the case of the oil industry, which is normally a single focus industry, as an example of the vertically integrated business (Figure 2.1).

Aliber (1970, pp. 19–20) has presented the rationale of vertical integration structure for oil companies on an international scale. 'Efficiencies may be realized by co-ordinating activities that occur in several different countries within the firm. Thus, an oil company co-ordinates the production, transport, refining, and the distribution of petroleum at lower costs than individual firms at each stage might be able to by using the market. The economies of vertical integration involve a reduction in transaction costs, the costs of research, and the costs of holding inventories.'

As shown in Figure 2.1, there are four levels of vertical integration for the oil company – extraction, transportation, refining and distribution. The upstream and downstream operations of the group are separately run by the four divisions. The corporate office coordinates and integrates their competitive strategies. Their performances are evaluated by a variety of financial indicators such as profits and return on investment (ROI). This divisional structure within the vertical integration enables divisional managers to focus attention on their own divisions.

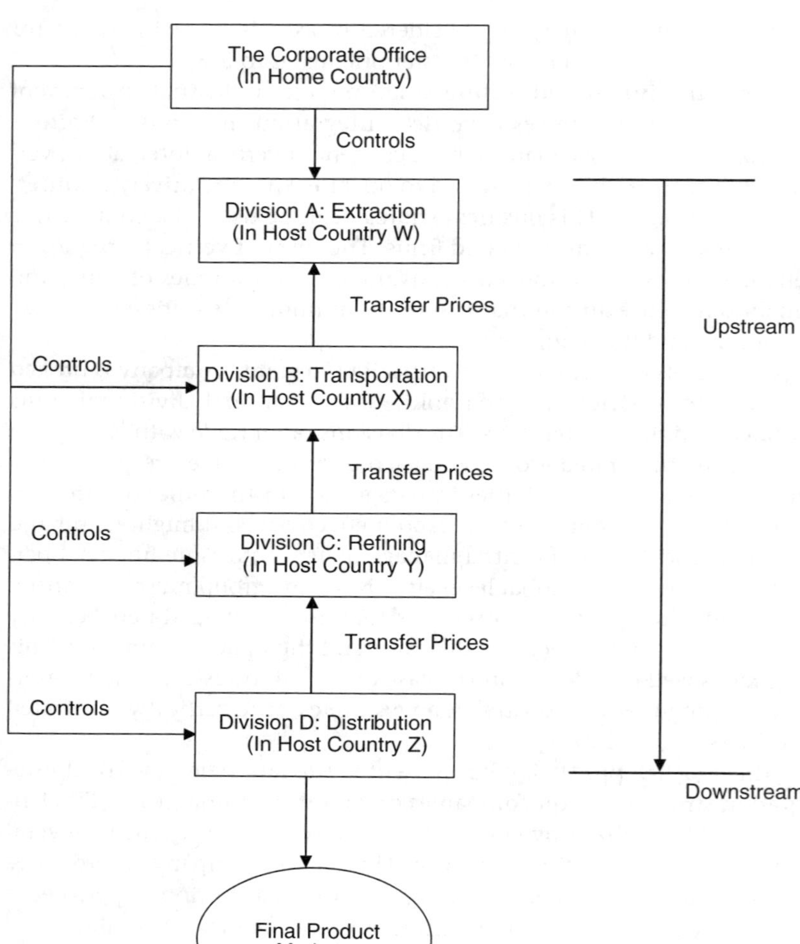

Figure 2.1   Vertical Integration of a Multinational Enterprise in the Oil Industry
Notes: Dotted lines represent transfer payments between the divisions of the business
enterprise (Adapted from Rugman, 1985a, p. 178).

For intercompany trade between the divisions, internal transfer
prices are used for the upstream division to attach a price to products
transferred to the downstream division located in a different country.
Thus, the crude oil to be processed by division C in the refining stage is
supplied by the upstream transportation division B. Because divisional

managers are held responsible for both revenues and costs in their own respective profit centres, and are often measured and rewarded on the basis of divisional profits, they take considerable interest in the price they pay or receive because this intercompany pricing plays a major part in showing a profit or a loss for their divisions (Eccles, 1985; Ward, 1992; Iqbal, Melcher and Elmallab, 1997; Hansen and Mowen, 2000).

As an example, in the case of the oil company, when division A sells a product to division B, it would try to receive the highest possible price from division B that would raise its own operating income. Conversely, division B would favour paying the lowest price that would raise its operating income. To ensure objectivity, these prices are normally set at externally established and quoted spot market prices, or are negotiated between the managers of the two divisions. Otherwise, disputes and controversy between divisional managers over transfer prices may incur, with damaging effects on employee morale. If this happens, their conflicts are often resolved arbitrarily at the corporate head level (Rugman, 1985b; Rugman and Eden, 1985; Ward, 1992).

Horizontally integrated businesses. An alternative structure to vertical integration for industrial multinational enterprises is horizontal integration. Horizontal integration involves two or more subsidiaries located across national boundaries. These subsidiaries operate in the same line of business and are controlled by the same parent company, headquartered in the home country. Like vertical integration, a horizontally integrated multinational enterprise has a transactional advantage in using a hierarchical administrative structure to control the allocation and distribution of resources and goods within the multinational enterprise group (Rugman, 1985b).

Horizontal integration is common in many industries. An example of the horizontally integrated form of multinational enterprises may be taken from the pharmaceutical industry. The pharmaceutical industry, characterised by high technology applications and expensive research, which is of central importance to it, engages in horizontal integration to protect its technical know-how. A viable multinational drug company must engage in research and development to remain competitive with new products. High research and development costs contribute to the high costs of innovative drugs.

An alternative way to recover the costs would be to place a patent on the products. This gives the firm exclusive property rights over the manufacture and distribution of the products in the domain of the patent. However, in host nations where patents are not respected, or when the firm fears that licensing or joint ventures can lead to the dissipation of its firm-specific advantage, the parent company has an incentive to keep the proprietary knowledge within the firm, rather than patent its products. This can be accomplished by making an internal market through organising a horizontally integrated structure.

Internal prices are set for the transfer of innovative pharmaceutical products from one subsidiary to another within the same horizontally integrated business. Another reason to set an internal price is that it is relatively difficult to establish the proper market price for intangibles involving research and development costs and intellectual property (Rugman, 1985b; Anthony and Govindarajan, 1998; Horngren et al., 1999).

Such an example of the horizontally integrated drug business is shown in Figure 2.2. It is to be noted that there are three divisions in each of the three subsidiaries. Intercompany transfers occur when

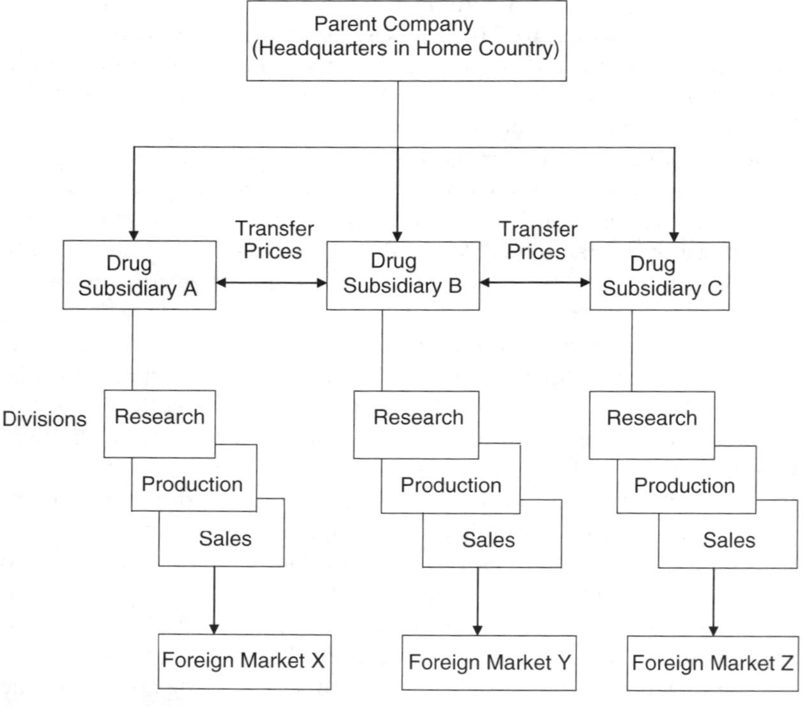

Figure 2.2   Horizontal Integration of a Pharmaceutical Multinational Enterprise Group

tangible and intangible property is transferred from the research division to the production division and, in turn, to the sales division. On the higher level, intercompany transfers occur between the subsidiaries or between the parent and its affiliates. Internal prices are set for both kinds of intercompany transfers within the pharmaceutical group.

Conglomerates. Distinct from the other two business structures, vertical integration and horizontal integration, is the third resultant of growth to characterise many large multinational enterprises called conglomerate structure. A conglomerate is the result of an action by an enterprise to acquire any number of distinct industries or types of business operation that are not organically related to one another as far as production and the market place are concerned. Each business is controlled from headquarters but operates as a relatively autonomous subsidiary. The connection between the subsidiaries is purely financial.

Textron is an example of a conglomerate firm. It operates in such diverse businesses as wiring instruments, helicopters, chainsaws, aircraft engine components, forklifts, machine tools, speciality fasteners, and gas turbine engines (Rugman, 1985a; Ward, 1992; Anthony and Govindarajan, 1998).

The organisational structure of a conglomerate is depicted in Figure 2.3. It may be noted that the three subsidiaries sell different products to

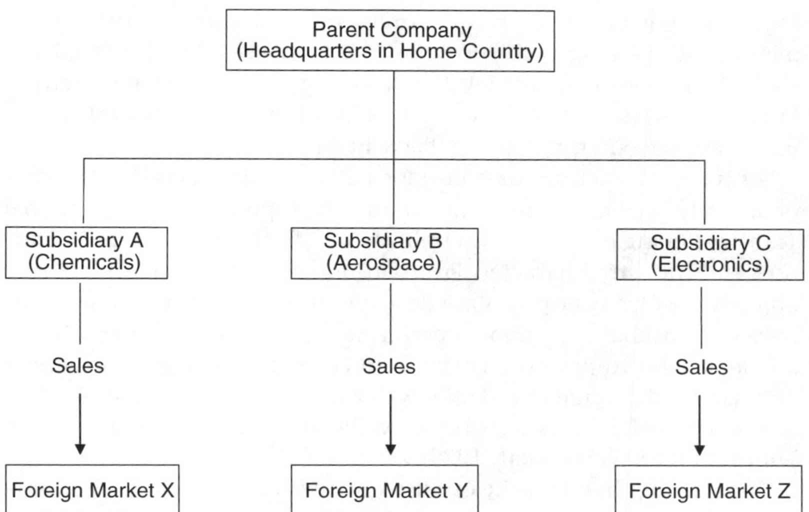

Figure 2.3   A Conglomerate Multinational Enterprise

each of their particular foreign markets. They share a certain support service provided by the parent company. The parent company would devise an internal pricing regime to charge each division for its usage of such shared services and to allocate indivisible overhead costs among the various members of the group.

The organisational form of conglomerates is partly justified by generating and using the economies of scale, which are mostly gained through shared common services by the individual subsidiaries at the group level. These services include such assets as information technology, research and development, market research, and financial departments. The efficiency of these services is centrally controlled at the group level. However, the subsidiary managers can control the amount of services that they receive. As these subsidiaries are highly autonomous businesses, in some cases they may be tempted to seek to maximise their own benefits to the detriment of the multinational enterprise as a whole.

For instance, if a subsidiary pays less than it should be charged, it will be motivated to use more of the service in self-interest than it should. This behaviour could then be disadvantageous to the company as a whole. In another instance, if a subsidiary is required to pay more than it should be charged, it might avoid using certain services that are worthwhile from the point of view of headquarters. To achieve goal congruence and effectively to evaluate their financial performances, senior management at headquarters must devise an appropriate method of charging each subsidiary for its usage of such shared services. This is normally achieved by creating an International Transfer Pricing system to ensure the efficient allocation of resources within the multinational enterprise group (Plasschaert, 1979).

For trade transactions or non-trade payment flows between affiliates of a multinational enterprise group, an appropriate International Transfer Pricing policy can be established to fit the organisation's structure and industry character. From an organisation's perspective, the objectives of transfer prices are designed to provide reasonable measures of subsidiary economic performances, to motivate subsidiary managers and to promote goal congruence. This group of objectives emphasises the behavioural effects of the pricing of an organisation's internal transfers as is also the case for domestic and International Transfer Prices (Plasschaert, 1979; Ward, 1992).

On the other hand, at the exclusively international level, additional factors must be taken into account by multinational enterprises. Compared with domestic firms composed of a number of divisions that trade with each other within a single nation state, foreign affiliates of a multinational enterprise are usually further removed geographically from central headquarters. Subsidiaries may face very different economic conditions, political forces and contrasting cultures from those of their home countries. International Transfer Pricing policies of the multinational enterprise are therefore far more affected by differing foreign environmental factors than by organisational variables such as size and internal structure. Among various areas related to multinational International Transfer Pricing objectives and motivations in the host countries, income tax tends to attract the greatest attention (Plasschaert, 1979; Hansen and Mowen, 2000).

The disparity in tax rates across countries creates an obvious incentive for the members of a multinational enterprise to try to minimise taxation liabilities in home or host countries, but, in turn, to maximise joint profits within the multinational enterprise as a whole. For a multinational enterprise this effect can be accomplished by artificially shifting taxable income from affiliates incorporated in high tax jurisdictions to subsidiaries in low tax jurisdictions to reduce total worldwide tax payments (Grubert and Mutti, 1991; Ghosh and Crain, 1993). These possibilities are illustrated in Figure 2.4.

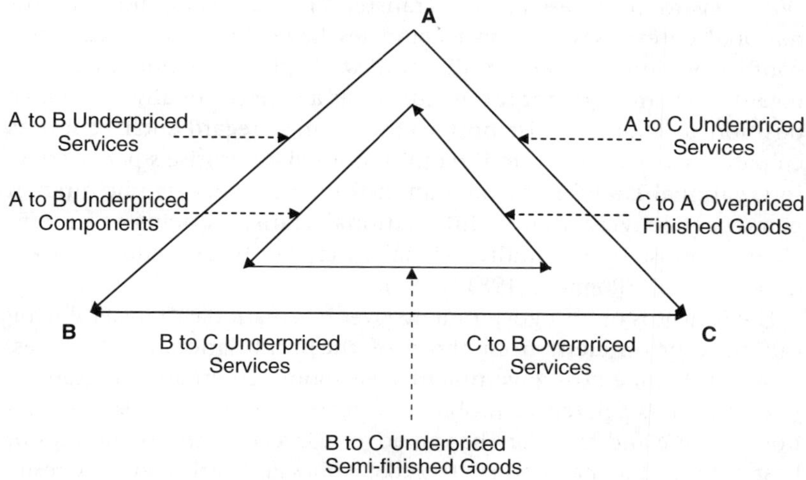

Figure 2.4 International Transfer Pricing Model for Three Company Units Each Located in a Different Country

International Transfer Pricing Triangular Model. This model depicts the possibilities of International Transfer Pricing manipulations that could accrue to a multinational company consisting of three units, as follows.

Unit A is the parent company manufacturing component parts, located in a home country with a higher tax rate than that of either of its two subsidiaries

Unit B is a subsidiary company for assembling component parts into semi-finished goods, located in a **host** country with a higher tax rate than that of the other subsidiary

Unit C is a subsidiary company for completing the manufacture of semi-finished goods and packaging them to market quality, located in a **host** country with a lower tax rate than that of either the other subsidiary or the parent company.

In this model, the movements of goods and services from Unit A to Unit B and from Unit B to Unit C are charged at low prices, whereas high prices are charged from Unit C to Unit B and from Unit C to Unit A. By taking advantage of the tax rate differences among countries, the multinational enterprise as a whole can minimise its total tax payments.

Government viewpoints

With regard to International Transfer Pricing issues, both multinational enterprises and host countries have their own, frequently conflicting interests and philosophies. Typically, companies may regard their strategies for tax avoidance as a conventionally acceptable position to adopt, whilst host countries may regard such action as culpable tax evasion. From the multinational enterprise's perspective, International Transfer Pricing is an instrument to manage the internal markets effectively, that is, International Transfer Pricing is an 'efficient response by the multinational enterprise to exogenous market imperfections' (Rugman, 1981, p. 83).

The concerns of host governments over International Transfer Pricing can be very different from those of the multinational enterprises, however. From a host government's viewpoint, International Transfer Pricing itself is a potential problem, which may result in losses of taxation revenue and therefore has an adverse effect on the economies of host nations (Rugman and Eden, 1985; Nobes and Parker, 2000; Gresik, 2001). International Transfer Pricing manipulation may be a more serious problem in developing countries (and especially least developed countries) where the governments of developing economies do not have the capacity or resources to identify the profit-shifting effects of International Transfer Pricing gambits. Another possible motive is that multinational enterprises, as a risk-averse strategy, may consider it preferable to remit their profits out of a developing country into related companies, notably parent companies, in developed countries.

Most multinational enterprises are headquartered in the wealthy, industrialised nations such as the United States, Japan, Germany, the United Kingdom and France. These countries have enacted sophistic-ated International Transfer Pricing regulations and have their own highly qualified professional tax experts to deal with the issues gener-ated by it in practice.

On the other hand, developing countries are often host countries. International Transfer Pricing is likely to be more detrimental to devel-oping countries (typically the source countries) than to developed coun-tries (typically the residence countries). It is generally easier to cream off the profits that would accrue to the subsidiary than that of the parent company. This may be simply for the reason that the developed coun-tries usually have, and can afford, more sophisticated administrations that are more experienced in identifying International Transfer Pricing abuses, whereas developing countries lack an institutional framework and administrative expertise to analyse complex International Transfer Pricing situations, and are therefore more vulnerable to International Transfer Pricing manipulations. Conceivably, the threat to fiscal sover-eignty through multinational transfer pricing manoeuvres is more prominent and imminent for developing countries than for developed economies (Easson, 1991; Chan and Chow, 1997a,b).

The next section examines the economic impact of International Transfer Pricing manipulations on the economies of host countries, into which category a great majority of developing countries fall.

Effects on host nations

A few studies have attempted to provide empirical evidence by way of trading statistics to assess the extent of income shifting out of developing countries by International Transfer Pricing abuses. These studies reveal the significant over-pricing of imports or under-pricing of exports by multinational enterprises in certain industries.

Lall (1973) used data from the Colombian Planning Office and the Import Control Board to investigate the extent of Internatio-nal Transfer Pricing abuses in Colombia. The results showed that, compared with world market prices, multinational enterprises in Colombia overpriced their imports from 33% to over 300% in the pharmaceutical sector, and from 24% to 81% in the rubber and electrical industries. It could be suggested from the findings of this study that the Colombian tax base had been eroded as a result of profit shifting by multinational enterprises.

Natke (1985) used data on imports collected from 141 manufacturing firms – both domestic firms and multinational enterprises – operating in Brazil during 1979. These data were used to test the hypothesis that import prices paid by multinational enterprises would be higher than those of Brazilian firms for the same products because of International Transfer Pricing behaviour.

The findings revealed that, in the aggregate, all sampled multinational enterprises paid higher prices than Brazilian firms with the degree of overpricing ranging from a high of 39% in the full sample (127 products) to 21% in the narrow sample (26 products). The import prices of multinational enterprises exhibited even greater variability. These results may be caused by multinational transfer pricing behaviour, though they must be interpreted with caution.

Rahman and Scapens (1986) investigated the International Transfer Pricing practices of multinational enterprises in Bangladesh. In the early 1980s there were twenty multinational manufacturing enterprises operating in Bangladesh. This study compared the reported profitability of the multinational enterprises with those of their local counterparts. The results showed that multinational enterprises were less profitable than those of the local enterprises – a finding that was inconsistent with the market power of the particular multinational enterprises in Bangladesh, which local enterprises did not possess.

The authors therefore asserted that International Transfer Pricing manipulation accounted for the low profitability of multinational enterprises in the country. In order to get specific evidence, they further investigated the import prices of ten pharmaceutical items in Bangladesh in the study. Their finding was that the over-pricing of imports by multinational enterprises from affiliates varied by 78% to 600% in the pharmaceutical industry and could be cited as evidence of income shifting activities by multinational enterprises in the country.

Chan and Chow (1997a) examined the business environment in China and used import and export data to test the hypothesis that foreign investment enterprises in China overpriced their imports and underpriced their exports to shift profits out of the country. In aggregate, foreign firms in China both paid higher prices for imports and charged higher prices on exports than their domestic counterparts. This result failed to justify International Transfer Pricing abuses by multinational enterprises in China. Outward profit shifting was detected, however, in certain industrial sectors, such as the manufacture of audio/video equipment, garments, and plastics raw materials and products. Both the overpricing of imports and the underpricing of exports were detected in these three industries. This implies that multinational enterprises had shifted profits out of the three businesses in China.

While International Transfer Pricing may maximise profits or minimise operational risks for multinational enterprises, the abusive nature of it has far-reaching implications for the economies of countries where multinational enterprises operate.

The conceivable costs of International Transfer Pricing manipulations to the host countries can therefore be summarised as follows:

1. **Tax losses.** Through International Transfer Pricing manipulation, the host governments are forced to reduce the tax revenue imposed on corporate income, import duties, and withholding taxes.
2. **Difficulty in auditing and evaluating firms.** International Transfer Pricing manipulations can distort a company's operating and financial results. To evaluate and audit the financial reports, the local government must attempt to identify and adjust for the effects of International Transfer Prices. This can be very inefficient and costly especially to the developing economies that are poorly equipped.
3. **Monopolised market.** The International Transfer Pricing mechanism can be used by a multinational enterprise to protect its monopoly position as a supplier. It is often the case that a foreign subsidiary needs some components or parts from the parent company. The parent company therefore can use International Transfer Pricing manipulations to keep its monopoly position as a supplier. For example, when there is no competition, the supplier can overprice, but as soon as competition appears, the parent can supply the service by underpricing International Transfer Pricing (Lin et al., 1993).

Host Country Verbatim Complaints. The following statements were obtained in response to a Questionnaire from the United

Nations Conference on Trade and Development (UNCTAD). Government officials in their responses echoed the above theoretic analyses and reflected the concerns of the governments of developing nations over International Transfer Pricing manipulations (Borkowski, 1997b).

- Instead of paying taxes on income earned in the country, the use of pricing manoeuvres could cause substantial foreign income or currency to leave the country. (Grenada)
- It is at times an unfair way of competing with local companies. (Malawi)
- It is difficult to ascertain the true profit or loss of the transactional corporation resident in this country. Hence, the ascertainment of their tax liabilities in this country also becomes difficult. (Nigeria)
- Profit correctly belonging to our country is moved offshore and out of our tax jurisdiction. (Papua New Guinea)
- Problems exist because it is aimed at the reduction in income tax and import duties, and avoidance of exchange rate control. It is a major concern as price manipulation seriously affects the tax revenues of host countries. Through the tax evasion by multinational enterprises, the full potential of the host nation's revenues is not realised, and the legal interests of these countries are undermined. (Solomon Islands)
- It is important for our national multinational enterprises to disclose validly the results of their operations. Transfers at below market prices increase the risk for creditors and lenders, and are detrimental to government fiscal interests. (Zimbabwe)
- It results in capital flight and an underpayment of tax, resulting in both shortfalls of government revenue and foreign exchange reserves. Both are vital for a developing country. (South Africa)
- There must be full disclosure of transfer pricing policies in the multinational enterprise's annual reports, which can then be audited to determine if the declared policy is fair and reasonable, and is being followed. (Bangladesh)
- We must develop guidelines and policies to prevent transfer prices which damage tax revenue. (Indonesia)
- Transfer pricing methods must be standardised regarding free market commodities and services to prevent undesirable adjustments, tax evasion, and hidden unauthorised increases in profit. (Czech Republic).

Summary

With the pace of the globalisation of economic activity and the internationalisation of a good part of world trade, more multinational enterprises are engaging in transfers involving larger monetary amounts with affiliates that are located in more and more countries, transfers that also take place between the affiliates themselves. The prices at which goods, services or other assets are transferred determine the profits of multinational enterprises and therefore the tax base of the countries involved. Tax underpayments caused by the movement of profits out of a country can result in shortfalls in government revenue and in foreign exchange reserves.

In past years, the number of multinational enterprises operating in developing countries has increased significantly. Items of anecdotal evidence suggest that multinational enterprises operating in developing countries have considerable income shifting opportunities by International Transfer Pricing. One explanation for this is the lack of institutional frameworks and administrative expertise in host countries to deal with the situation. Another important explanation is that some developing countries are so eager to attract foreign investment that they have little interest in International Transfer Pricing controls (Rahman and Scapens, 1986; Chan and Chow, 1997a,b, 1998). Developing countries 'have long relied on corporate income taxes as a principal means of revenue. These taxes account for up to a third of revenue in some developing countries' (Cohen, 1995, p. 11). Therefore, the nature of International Transfer Pricing can have significant tax implications for their developing economies.

3
Influential Regulations

Introduction

As more and more of the world's trade is conducted through multi-national intercompany networks, the temptation for multinational enterprises to indulge and contrive price manipulation is high. The tax authorities of many governments have begun to expand their concern with respect to the abusive nature of multinational transfer pricing practices. Consequently, they are intensifying their surveillance of the International Transfer Pricing practices of multinational enterprises.

Some of the most rigorous and efficient tax authorities in the world are the United States, Germany, France, the United Kingdom and Canada. Many governments have issued transfer pricing legislation and guidelines to preserve the integrity of their own taxation systems. In this regard the United States leads the way in the world. It has enacted the world's toughest and perhaps the most comprehensive transfer pricing rules and regulations – as may be appreciated by reference to Section 482 of its Internal Revenue Code.

Since the United States is the major trading partner of all three national economies which form the subject of the study which is presented in this book, the policy and practice of the United States regarding International Transfer pricing are of the utmost relevance and significance.

The other centre of world-wide importance in the field of controls over International Transfer Pricing is the Organisation for Economic Cooperation and Development (OECD). A report entitled *Transfer Pricing and Multinational Enterprises* was released by the OECD Committee on Fiscal Affairs in 1979. It was influenced a great deal by the extensive experience of the United States. Later reports addressed related issues, in particular those of *Transfer Pricing and Multinational Enterprises – Three Taxation Issues* (1984), and *Thin Capitalisation* (1987). In 1995, the OECD adopted major modifications to the 1979 Report and issued *Transfer Pricing Guidelines for Multinational Enterprises and Tax Administrations*. This document has become a substantial benchmark worldwide for the practice and control of International Transfer Pricing, being referred to in this book hereafter as the OECD Guidelines.

OECD Guidelines

The OECD, formed in 1960, is an influential international governmental organisation. The objectives of the OECD are to promote, in general, worldwide economic development, and in particular the growth and stability of the economies of its member countries. The work of the OECD focuses primarily on providing financial accounting and reporting guidelines for multinational enterprises and making information available to multinational enterprises regarding their host countries.

The membership of the OECD consists of thirty countries, most of which are Western industrial nations. At present, the member countries of OECD include: Australia, Austria, Belgium, Canada, Czech Republic, Denmark, Finland, France, Germany, Greece, Hungary, Iceland, Ireland, Italy, Japan, Korea, Luxembourg, Mexico, Netherlands, New Zealand, Norway, Poland, Portugal, Slovakia, Spain, Sweden, Switzerland, Turkey, the United Kingdom and the United States.

The OECD Guidelines in current use represent an international consensus on the application of the arm's length standard to test the appropriateness of particular transfer pricing practices for intercompany transactions. They express a strong preference for the use of traditional transaction based methods. The Guidelines were issued in loose-leaf format to accommodate the addition of future revisions as required by the ongoing experience of developing international trade.

The main points set forth in the OECD Guidelines involve the following.

1. The adoption of the arm's length principle and a strong preference for the use of traditional transaction based methods
2. Setting out the levels of comparability that emphasise functions performed, assets employed, and risks assumed
3. The introduction of a profit based method called 'transactional net margin method'

4. An acknowledgement of the need for taxpayer documentation of the arm's length character of its transfer pricing
5. A description of the role played by penalties for encouraging compliance.

In most OECD countries, transfer pricing legislation was enacted during the late 1980s and early 1990s. Except for the United States, which has opted for legislation based on its own methods and principles, most countries – both within and outside the OECD membership countries – have enacted legislation that has largely followed the OECD approach.

In determining that an enterprise's transfer pricing constitutes a manipulation of prices, the existence of 'fair' or 'correct' prices, that is, the arm's length price, is implied. The arm's length principle is stated in Paragraph 1 of Article 9 of the OECD Model Tax Convention. The need for it is manifest '[when] conditions are made or imposed between …two [associated] enterprises in their commercial or financial relations which differ from those which would be made between independent enterprises, [so that] any profits which would, but for those conditions, have accrued to one of the enterprises, but, by reason of those conditions, have not so accrued, may be included in the profits of that enterprise and taxed accordingly.' (OECD Guidelines 1–3)

The significance of the arm's length principle is justified because the implementation of the principle is to provide a 'broad parity of tax treatment for multinational enterprises and independent enterprises. Because the arm's length principle puts associated and independent enterprises on a more equal footing for tax purposes, it avoids the creation of tax advantages or disadvantages that would distort the relative competitive positions of either type of entity'.

The application of the arm's length principle requires that the transfer price adopted by the associated enterprises – the member units of a multinational enterprise – must be compared with the price adopted by independent firms operating in the open market. The focus of the principle is to ensure that the same price is charged to the multinational as that between independent firms for similar transactions under similar circumstances.

The arm's length principle as a standard uses the pricing behaviour of an independent firm in an uncontrolled transaction as the benchmark for determining a transfer price in a similar transaction between members of a multinational enterprise. By applying this benchmark to the multinational enterprise, the arm's length principle seeks to remove the effect of any ownership relationship between members from the transfer price they use when members deal with each other.

In international practice, several pricing methods have been developed in calculating the arm's length price. These methodologies lay the foundation for considering the theory underpinning the arm's length principle. The OECD Guidelines prescribe that the arm's length price is determined using one or more of the following intercompany pricing methods.

The Comparable Uncontrolled Price Method. The comparable uncontrolled price method compares the price charged for property or services transferred in a controlled transaction to the price charged for property or services transferred in a comparable uncontrolled transaction in comparable circumstances. Under this method the price charged between independent enterprises in a comparable uncontrolled transaction forms the basis for determining the arm's length price. When it is possible to seek comparable uncontrolled transactions, the comparable uncontrolled price method is preferable over all other methods.

The Resale Price Method. The resale price method determines an arm's length price for transactions between associated enterprises by comparing the gross margin earned on that transaction with the gross margin earned in similar uncontrolled transactions. The resale price method begins with the price at which a product, purchased from an associated enterprise, is resold to an independent enterprise. This resale price is then reduced by an appropriate resale price margin to determine the arm's length cost of the product payable by the associated supplier. The resale price margin can be established by reference to the arm's length gross margin that a reseller, purchasing from an independent supplier and selling to non-associated customers, would have secured in comparable circumstances. The resale price method is probably most useful when it is applied to marketing operations.

The Cost Plus Method. As with the resale price method, the cost plus method uses an arm's length gross mark-up to determine an arm's length price for transactions between associated enterprises. The cost plus method begins with the costs incurred by the supplier for making the product or performing the service. A cost plus mark up is then added to the cost – for an appropriate profit earned in the light of functions performed and the market conditions – to determine the arm's length price to charge the associated purchaser. The cost plus mark up may be determined by reference to the cost plus mark up that the same supplier could earn in comparable uncontrolled transactions. The cost plus method probably is most useful when semifinished goods are sold between related parties, when related parties have concluded joint facility agreements or long-term buy-and-supply arrangements, or when the controlled transaction is the provision of services.

The Profit Split Method. The profit split method is based upon the economic notion of a joint venture or partnership. The method calculates an arm's length net profit for each of the associated enterprises by determining the combined profit attributable to the associated enterprises in the controlled transaction, and then splitting that profit according to the relative economic value of the contribution that each enterprise made to that transaction. The contribution of each enterprise is based on a functional analysis. The functional analysis is an analysis of the functions performed, taking into account the assets used and risks assumed by each enterprise. To avoid the use of hindsight, the OECD Guidelines state that the expected profits should be used as the touchstone rather than actual profits.

In addition, the transfer pricing report outlines two alternative approaches to the allocation of the combined profit – the contribution analysis and the residual analysis. These two approaches are not necessarily exhaustive or mutually exclusive. The OECD Guidelines acknowledge other possible ways – depending on the circumstances of the case and the information available – for splitting a profit that makes for a reliable arm's length result.

The Transactional Net Margin Method. The transactional net margin method determines an arm's length profit by comparing the net profit margin obtained by an associated enterprise against that which is attained by a comparable independent firm. It is to be relative to an appropriate base of such variables as the costs, sales and assets that the associated enterprise makes from a controlled transaction. In the application of the transactional net margin method a functional analysis of the associated enterprise on one side, and the independent enterprise on the other, is required to determine whether the transactions are comparable and what adjustments should be made to obtain reliable results. Since the transactional net margin method, along with the profit split method, tends to be less reliable than methods of the traditional transactional methods – the comparable uncontrolled price method, the resale price method, and the cost plus method – the adoption of either of the two profit based methods is considered in practice to be a method of last resort.

A Non-Arm's Length Approach: Global Formulary Apportionment. In addition to the foregoing transfer pricing methodologies, the

OECD Guidelines discuss the use of 'global formulary apportionment', which is a non-arm's length approach. A global formulary apportionment method allocates the global profits of a multinational group on a consolidated basis among its associated enterprises in different countries, using a pre-set formula. Compared with other methods, the advantage of the global formulary apportionment is that it provides greater administrative convenience and certainty for taxpayers. However, given that using a predetermined formula is unlikely to reflect accurately the economic substance of the transactions entered into, as a theoretical, rather than a realistic alternative, to the arm's length principle which it represents, global formulary apportionment as a method is discouraged in the report.

OECD Method Summary. To recapitulate, the comparable uncontrolled price method is primarily concerned with the product being transferred, whereas the resale price method and the cost plus methods focus on the functions being performed. The OECD Guidelines refer to them as traditional transactional methods. The OECD Guidelines favour the use of these approaches. The comparable uncontrolled price method is regarded as preferable over all other methods as it is the most direct and reliable in cases where it is possible to locate a comparable uncontrolled transaction.

In a perfectly competitive market, all three approaches would separately result in the determination of the same arm's length price. In international practice, however, the application of the transaction based methods is subject to the limitation of the availability of comparable data. In those exceptional cases in which comparable data are unavailable or are difficult to obtain, the profit based methods – the profit split method and the transactional net margin method – may be the alternative approaches for use in determining the arm's length pricing of associated party transactions.

The OECD transfer pricing report refers to them as the transactional profit methods as these kinds of method examine the profits that arise from particular controlled transactions among associated enterprises. They specifically prescribe that the profit based methods should be methods of last resort. The global formulary apportionment method is seen as arbitrary and contrary to the arm's length principle and therefore is generally unacceptable.

Advance Pricing Agreement. The 1995 OECD Guidelines advocate advance pricing agreements as one of several administrative approaches for resolving transfer pricing disputes. The OECD Guidelines define an advance pricing agreement as an agreement in advance of controlled transactions, that determines an appropriate set of criteria concerning methods, comparables and appropriate adjustments to them, and critical assumptions regarding future events, for the determination of the transfer pricing for those transactions over a fixed period of time (OECD, 1995, G–1).

Advance pricing agreements can be unilateral, bilateral or multilateral. The OECD Guidelines suggest, wherever possible, the negotiation of bilateral and multilateral advance pricing agreements between the tax authorities of the home country of a multinational enterprise and the host countries of its subsidiaries.

Categories of Intercompany Transfers. Intercompany transactions include the transfer of tangible property and intangible property, the provision of services and finance as well as rentals and leasing arrangements. While an international consensus regarding the application of the arm's length principle to tangibles is lacking, the determination of arm's length prices for intangibles poses even greater difficulties, as the value of intangibles lies in their unique qualities.

For the transfer of technology, the 1979 and 1984 OECD reports suggest that payments should be allowed as a deduction for tax purposes only if a real benefit has been conferred or could be reasonably expected. It may be possible to use the comparable uncontrolled price method if the same or similar technologies are licensed to unrelated parties. A cost oriented method may not be appropriate as the value of intangible property may have no predictable or reliable relationship with the costs of developing it. For the provision of intercompany services, an open market value of the services would have to be established. A cost oriented method may be helpful in providing an approximation to arm's length prices.

The 1995 OECD Guidelines have not yet been completed regarding intangibles and intercompany services. The OECD Guidelines have provided no provision regarding on which party – the taxpayer or the tax authority – the burden of proof should fall.

Documentation Requirements and Penalties. Over the question of documentation requirements, the OECD Guidelines suggest a flexible approach, recommending the maintenance of a level and detail of documentation that allows a verification of compliance while avoiding the imposition on firms of burdensome time and cost demands. For example, the Guidelines suggest that each taxpayer should try to determine transfer pricing 'in accordance with the arm's length principle, based upon information reasonably available at the time of the determination'. In this regard, the information needed will vary depending upon the facts and circumstances of the case. As with documentation requirements, the OECD Guidelines do not suggest specific penalties but recommend that each country sets penalties such that 'tax underpayments and other types of non-compliance are more costly than compliance' (OECD, 1995, pp. IV–7).

Cost Sharing Arrangement. A cost sharing arrangement is an agreement whereby two or more persons or organisational units agree to share the costs and risks of research and development of new, intangible property as they are incurred, in exchange for a specified interest in any such property that is developed. The OECD Guidelines emphasise the arm's length nature of any cost sharing allocations, and the requirement for defined prospective benefits to participate in a cost sharing arrangement.

United States regulations

In the United States, Section 482 of the Internal Revenue Code authorises the Internal Revenue Service to allocate income or deductions among related companies to prevent tax evasion and clearly reflect the income of each company. As stated in Section 482 of the 1954 Internal Revenue Code: 'In any case of two or more organisations, trades, or businesses (whether or not incorporated, whether or not organised in the United States, and whether or not affiliated) owned or controlled directly or indirectly by the same interests, the Secretary or his delegate may distribute, apportion, or allocate gross income, deductions, credits, or allowances between or among such organisations, trades, or businesses, if he determines that such distribution, apportionment, or allocation is necessary in order to prevent evasion of taxes or clearly to reflect the income of any such organisations, trades, or businesses'.

Over recent decades, the United States has revised its transfer pricing regulations and initiated new rules to strengthen the power of the Internal Revenue Service to control transfer pricing practices. The development of the United States transfer pricing rules can be summarised as follows.

- In 1968, the Internal Revenue Service issued rules and regulations relating to Section 482. In these regulations, the Internal Revenue Service explains in detail the scope and methods applying to Section 482.
- In 1986, the super royalty provision was added to Section 482 of the Internal Revenue Code by the Tax Reform Act. This provision

provides the Internal Revenue Service with the means to collect royalties commensurate with the economic values of intangibles. At the same time, Congress directed the Treasury Department and the Internal Revenue Service to conduct a comprehensive study of inter-company transfer pricing issues to determine whether and how the existing regulations should be modified. The Treasury Department and the Internal Revenue Service responded to that directive by issuing a discussion draft entitled '*A Study on Intercompany Pricing*' (a White Paper) in October 1988. The proposed rules in the White Paper have had a significant impact on transfer pricing practices for intangible property.

- Between 1988 and 1992 Congress added or amended Sections 982, 6038A, 6038C, and 6503(k) to impose on taxpayers a higher demand for information and record keeping requirements, and to provide Internal Revenue Service agents with greater access to that information and those records. In addition, Congress added Sections 6662(e) and (h) to impose penalties for significant transfer pricing adjustments, and Section 6621(c) to provide for higher interest payments for under-payments of tax resulting from transfer pricing adjustments.

- In 1992, the Internal Revenue Service issued new proposed regula-tions under Section 482. These regulations were implemented to establish the 'commensurate with income' standard for the transfer of intangible property and introduced significant new procedural rules and pricing methods. These proposed regulations also included significant new rules for cost sharing arrangements.

- In 1993, the Internal Revenue Service revoked the 1992 proposed transfer pricing regulations, except for those relating to cost sharing, and issued temporary regulations that were effective for taxable years beginning after 21 April 1993 and before 6 October 1994. These regulations emphasised the use of comparable transactions between unrelated parties, and a flexible application of pricing methods to reflect specific facts and circumstances. However, these regulations imposed substantial obligations on taxpayers to create contemporary documentation with the transactions. In 1993 the Internal Revenue Service also issued proposed regulations under Sections 6662(e) and (h). The regulations specified the nature of the contemporaneous documentation that must be maintained to avoid the imposition of penalties. They also explained how the pricing methods specified in the Section 482 regulations had been applied. Congress amended Section 6662 to codify these contemporaneous documentation requirements.

- In 1994 the Internal Revenue Service issued temporary and proposed regulations under Sections 6662(e) and (h) applicable to all tax years beginning after 31 December 1993. The Internal Revenue Service also issued final regulations under Section 482 that became effective for tax years beginning after 6 October 1994 and amended the temporary and proposed Sections 6662(e) and (h) regulations retroactively to 1 January 1994. Final Section 482 regulations were also issued in 1994. They are generally effective for tax years beginning after 6 October 1994. However, taxpayers may elect to apply the final regulations to any open year and to all subsequent years.
- In 1995 final regulations on cost sharing were issued, subject to minor modification in 1996. These regulations became effective for taxable years beginning on or after 1 January 1996. Existing cost sharing arrangements were not grandfathered and had to be amended to conform to the final regulations. If an existing cost sharing arrangement met all the requirements of the 1968 cost sharing regulations, participants had until 31 December 1996 to make the required amendments. Revised competent authority procedures were issued in 1995.
- In 1996, final transfer pricing penalty regulations under Section 6662 were issued on 9 February with effect from that date, subject to a taxpayer's election to apply them to all open tax years beginning after 31 December 1993 (Rolfe, 1997).

The Acceptable Pricing Methods. The Internal Revenue Code, Section 1.482–1(d)(3) of the United States regulations defines the 'arm's length price' as 'the amount which was charged or would have been charged in independent transactions with unrelated parties under the same or similar circumstances.'

The most recent version of the United States regulations under Section 482 released in 1994 adopts the comparable uncontrolled price method, the resale price method and the cost plus method. As for the profit based methods, the only difference from the OECD approach is that the United States' regulations stipulate the use of the comparable profit method as a replacement for the transactional net profit margin method.

The comparable profit method determines an arm's length result using the amount of operating profit that the tested multinational enterprise unit would have earned on related party transactions with other multinational enterprise entities if its profit level indicator were equal to that of an uncontrolled comparable transaction – the comparable operating profit which the multinational enterprise entity would have earned in a transaction with an independent customer. The comparable profits method deals with income, whereas the transactional net profit margin method deals with pricing. In this regard, the OECD Guidelines concentrate on how prices are set – which is generally viewed as a subjective test focusing on behaviour – whereas the United States regulations require an arm's length result which is an objective test that focuses on taxable income, reflecting the Internal Revenue Service's concern over the correctness of the tax base.

The comparable profit method and profit split method remain viable alternatives when adequate comparability is unavailable for transaction based methods. The strict priority hierarchy of these methods is removed. The United States legislation introduces the 'Best Method Rule', under which the method which provides the most reliable measure of an arm's length result in the light of the facts and circumstances of the transaction under review should be used. The selection of the best method must be supported by the best level of comparable data. To establish comparability between companies, an in-depth functional analysis of the risks borne and functions performed by related entities is required by the Internal Revenue Service.

Factors which should be taken into account in selecting the best method include:

- the degree of comparability between controlled and uncontrolled transactions
- the completeness and accuracy of the underlying data
- the reliability of the assumptions
- the sensitivity of the results to deficiencies in the data and assumptions.

Advance Pricing Agreement. In 1991, the United States Internal Revenue Service introduced the advance pricing agreement procedures. They are similar to that of the OECD. The Internal Revenue Service Rev. Proc 96-53 Section 482 defines an Advance Pricing Agreement as 'an agreement between the service and the taxpayer on the transfer pricing methodology to be applied to any apportionment or location of income, deductions, credits, or allowances between or among two or more organisations, trades, or businesses owned or controlled, directly or indirectly, by the same interests'. A taxpayer can initiate in advance an agreement with the tax authorities, for a fixed number of years, on the transfer pricing method to be applied to particular international transactions.

The United States regulations contain a more detailed and formalised advance pricing agreement programme with specific and detailed disclosure procedures and restrictions than is implemented in any other country which follows the OECD approach. For instance, to obtain the advance pricing agreement, the taxpayer has to submit detailed information along with a $5,000 user fee. Once the advance pricing agreement is approved, the taxpayer must maintain sufficient books and records to enable the Internal Revenue Service to examine the taxpayer's compliance with the advance pricing agreement in force. In addition, the taxpayer has to submit an annual report to the Internal Revenue Service describing advance pricing agreement activities.

Advance pricing agreements might help to alleviate some transfer pricing problems. However, multinational enterprises typically appear uninterested in participating in advance pricing agreement programmes. One survey (Borkowski, 1996a) found that, depending on the home country, the percentage of multinational enterprises with no plans to pursue advance pricing agreements with either their home or host country tax authorities ranged from 71% to 96%. The reasons for their lukewarm attitude were obvious. Canadian multinational enterprises asserted that the cost to provide the volume of information and the documentation required, and the fee for advance pricing agreements, exceeded the benefits derived from such agreements. German multinational enterprises ranked the volume of information required and the difficulty of concluding multilateral advance pricing agreements as the most important deterrents. Japanese multinational enterprises were concerned over the volume of information required and issues of confidentiality. Multinational enterprises in the United States ranked cost and volume of information required as the chief drawbacks to advance pricing agreements.

While the United States tax authority has been a leading proponent of the advance pricing agreement programme, multinational enterprises based in the United States were apparently wary of the programme. Only 10% of the multinational enterprises canvassed had or planned to pursue an advance pricing agreement with their own United States tax authority, while only 4% were considering taking up advance pricing agreements with host country tax authorities.

Categories of Intercompany Transfer. The intercompany business dealings covered by the United States regulations include the following.

1. Loans and advances
2. Performance of services

3. Use of tangible property
4. Transfer or use of intangible property
5. Sales of tangible property.

For transfers of tangible property, the regulations emphasise comparability of products under the comparable uncontrolled price method, and the comparability of functions under the resale price and cost plus methods. There is no order of priority to these methods, the 'best method' rule applying. For the provision of services, the arm's length charge is equal to the costs or deductions incurred for the services by the uncontrolled party providing the services.

According to the 'super royalty' provision added to the code of the United States Internal Revenue Service Section 482 in 1986, income with respect to the transfer or license of intangible property must be commensurate with the economic value of it. For the transfer of intangible property, the 1994 United States regulations stipulate the use of the comparable uncontrolled transaction method as a replacement for the comparable uncontrolled price method. The resale price method and the cost plus method are not available for the transfer of intangible property.

Burden of Proof. According to the United States regulations, the allocation of income between related parties made by the Internal Revenue Service will be sustained by the courts, unless the taxpayer can establish that the allocation is 'arbitrary, capricious or unreasonable'. In this regard, the burden of proof lies squarely with the taxpayer who must prove that his prices are charged at arm's length.

Documentation and Penalties. The Internal Revenue Service has stated that the objective of the United States penalty regime is to encourage taxpayers to make reasonable efforts to determine and document the arm's length character of their intercompany transfer prices. Therefore, a taxpayer can avoid a detailed transfer pricing audit and the risk of a transfer pricing penalty by preparing and maintaining contemporaneous documentation to establish that its selection and application of a pricing method provide the most accurate measure of an arm's length result.

Contemporaneous documentation includes the following.

- An overview of the taxpayer's business
- A description of the taxpayer's organisational structure covering all related parties engaged in controlled transactions
- Any documentation explicitly required under Section 482

- A description of the transfer pricing method selected; this description should include an explanation of why it was selected
- A description of the transfer pricing methods considered; this description should include an explanation of why they were not selected
- A description of the controlled transactions
- A description of the comparables used; this description should include an explanation of how comparability was evaluated
- An explanation of the economic analysis and projections relied upon in developing the method
- A description of any relevant data obtained between the end of the year and the filing of the tax return
- A general index of the principal and background documents (Section 1.6662(e)).

A complex and tough transfer pricing penalty regime can be observed in United States. Section 6662 imposes transactional and net adjustment penalties for misstatements. These penalties are not deductible in determining gross income.

1. **The Transaction Penalty.**
   - The regulations impose a 20% non-deductible transactional penalty on a tax underpayment attributable to a transfer price claimed on a tax return which is 200% or more, or 50% or less, than the arm's length price.
   - The penalty is increased to 40% if the reported transfer price is 400% or more, or 25% or less, than the arm's length price. Where these thresholds are met, the transfer pricing penalty will be imposed unless the taxpayer can demonstrate reasonable cause and good faith in the determination of the reported transfer price.
2. **The Net Adjustment Penalty.**
   - The regulations also impose a 20% net adjustment penalty on a tax underpayment attributable to a net increase in taxable income caused by a net transfer pricing adjustment that exceeds the lesser of US$5 million or 10% of gross receipts.
   - The penalty is increased to 40% if the net transfer pricing adjustment exceeds US$20 million or 20% of gross receipts.

International comparisons

To prevent international tax avoidance activities by the multinational companies, more and more revenue authorities are now focusing legislative, regulative and enforcement efforts on multinational transfer pricing practices. Among them, the most rigorous and efficient tax authorities in the world are the seven predominant industrialised nations – Canada, France, Germany, Italy, Japan, the United States and the United Kingdom. They have unanimously adopted the arm's length standard as the most principled approach to deal with the transfer pricing issue. Yet, owing to different legal and tax systems, transfer pricing regulations among them vary in various respects, such as the pricing methods used and documentation requirements.

Tables 3.1 to 3.9 summarise the similarities and differences of the key features between the OECD Guidelines, the United States Regulations and these other main industrialised countries. Table 3.10 summarises those that exist between the OECD and the United States (Ernst and Young, 2004).

Table 3.1   Tax Authority and Tax Law

OECD	Not applicable
Canada	Canada Customs and Revenue Agency (CCRA), Canadian Income Tax Act Section 247
France	French Tax Administration: Articles 57 and 238A. French Procedure Code: Articles L13B and L188A. Case Law Abnormal Management Act Theory
Germany	Federal Ministry of Finance;
	General arm's length principle: Section 1 Foreign Tax Act.
	Hidden profit distribution: Section 8 para. 3 Corporate Income Tax Act. Hidden capital injection: Section 36a Corporate Tax Directives
Italy	Administration of Finance; Presidential Decree n. 917. Article 110 (7) and Article 9 (3)–(4)
Japan	National Tax Administration; Special Taxation Measures Law Article 66–4
United Kingdom	Inland Revenue; Schedule 28AA, Income and Corporate Taxes Act of 1988 and Section 12B Taxes Management Act 1970; Section 108–111 and Schedule 16 Finance Act of 1988
United States	Internal Revenue Service. Internal Revenue Code § 482, §6038A, §6038C, §6662 (e)–(h)

Table 3.2   Regulations, Rules and Guidelines

OECD	Transfer Pricing Guidelines for Multinational Enterprises and Tax Administrations
Canada	CCRA Information Circular 87 – 2R
France	Administrative Doctrine on Articles 57 and 238A of the French Tax Code, and Article L13B of the French Procedure Code
Germany	Administration principles, Circular of the Federal Ministry of Finance.
	Principles for the Review of Income Determination through Cost Allocation Agreements among internationally Related Parties, Circular of the Federal Ministry of Finance.
	Administrative Principles relating to the Examination of Apportionment of Income in the Case of Permanent Establishments of internationally operating Enterprises.
	Principles for the Examination of Allocation of Expenses between internationally affiliated Enterprises for the cross-border Secondment of Employees, Circular of the Federal Ministry of Finance
Italy	Circular Letters 32/9/2267 and CL 42/12/1587
Japan	STML – Enforcement Order 39–12, STML – Circular 66–4–(1)–1to 66–4–(7) 2. Enforcement Regulation 22–10. Administrative Guideline issued on June 1, 2001 and partly revised on June 20, 2002
United Kingdom	"Guidelines Notes" in Inland Revenue Tax Bulletins 37 and 38
United States	§ 1.482, § 1.6662; § 1.6038A, §1.6038C; Rev.Proc. 96–53 and Rev. Proc. 99–32

Summary

Determining multinational transfer prices is one of the most complex and closely monitored decisions by multinational enterprises. Many governments and the supra-national governmental authorities have also scrutinised the International Transfer Pricing policies of multinational enterprises. The OECD Guidelines are characterised by flexible application, moderate documentation requirements, avoidance of double taxation and a non-adversarial relationship between

Table 3.3   Acceptable Methods

Countries	CUP	Cost Plus	Resale Price	Profit Split	CPM	TNMM	Global Formulary Apportion-ment
OECD	Yes	Yes	Yes	Yes	No	Yes	No
Canada	Yes	Yes	Yes	Yes	No	Yes	No
France	Yes	Yes	Yes	Yes	No	Yes	No
Germany	Yes	Yes	Yes	Yes	No	No	No
Italy	Yes	Yes	Yes	Yes	Unclear	Unclear	Unclear
Japan	Yes	Yes	Yes	Yes	No	No	No
United Kingdom	Yes	Yes	Yes	Yes	No	Yes	No
United States	Yes	Yes	Yes	Yes	Yes	No	No

Table 3.4   Priority of Methods

OECD	Transaction-based preferred over profit-based
Canada	Most appropriate method. Transaction-based preferred over profit-based
France	Transaction-based methods have priority over other methods.
Germany	Transaction-based methods preferred over profit-based methods. Profit split as a method of last resort
Italy	Transaction-based methods preferred over profit-based methods
Japan	Transaction-based methods preferred over profit-based methods
United Kingdom	Most reasonable method. Transaction-based preferred over profit-based
United States	Best method

tax authorities and the multinational enterprises. Currently, they serve as the foundation of most countries' transfer pricing regulations except for the United States where different opinions have prevailed.

It can be concluded that, while both the OECD and the United States fully support and are committed to the arm's length principle, there

Table 3.5   Transfer Pricing Penalties

OECD	Civil monetary penalties are frequently calculated as a percentage of the tax understatement, with the percentage ranging from 10 to 200%
Canada	A 10% penalty on total transfer pricing adjustment to transaction, plus non-deductible interest
France	Penalties for failure to produce requested documents. Late payment interest levied on assessments. Penalties of 40% for bad faith and 80% for fraud
Germany	If taxpayer fails to submit transfer pricing documentation or if the documents are insufficient or in case that the documentation for extraordinary business transactions is not prepared contemporaneously: Surcharge of 5%–10% on income adjustment. Late filing penalty: Up to 1 million Euros. Interest is assessed on taxpayments
Italy	General penalties for underpayment apply. New tax criminal law (Lgs. Decree 74/2000) includes valuations for possible tax frauds
Japan	General tax penalty provisions apply, but no specific transfer pricing penalty provision
United Kingdom	Up to 100% of any additional tax due as a result of a transfer pricing adjustment (where the taxpayer was negligent in complying with the transfer pricing legislation)
United States	20 and 40% penalties for underpayment of tax

Table 3.6   Reduction in Penalties

OECD	No provision
Canada	No penalty if reasonable effort to determine arm's length price, including contemporaneous documentation
France	No provision
Germany	Penalties may not be imposed, if the taxpayer is not or only insignificantly responsible for the lack of appropriate documentation
Italy	N/A
Japan	No provision in the law for reductions in penalties
United Kingdom	A transfer pricing policy fully documented evidencing due consideration to the "arm's length" principle
United States	No penalty if transfer pricing method reasonably applied and documented. Contemporaneous obligation

Table 3.7   Documentation Requirements

OECD	Pricing decisions should be documented in accordance with prudent business practices. Reasonable for tax authorities to expect taxpayers to prepare and maintain such material. No contemporaneous obligation
Canada	Contemporaneous documentation required
France	No formal obligation to document transfer prices. However, given the short delay granted by the law to submit the documentation, the large scope of documentation to be provided and the new modifications of the corporate law to French companies, a de facto documentation obligation exists in France
Germany	Section 90 of the Fiscal Code contains transfer pricing documentation requirements
Italy	No specific documentation requirements are provided. Documentation should adhere to OECD guidelines. All income and deduction items should be adequately substantiated
Japan	Not required by statute (no additional penalty). List of documentation that will be examined during the transfer pricing audit is disclosed in the Administrative Guideline issued on June 1, 2001 and partly revised on June 20, 2002
United Kingdom	Contemporaneous documentation expected; Documentation is important for audit defence and to refute neglect arguments
United States	Extensive contemporaneous documentation required

are differences of opinion on several important issues: the methods that are preferred, the profit based methods that are acceptable – the transactional net profit method versus the comparable profit methods – the extent of documentation requirements, the identity of the party on whom the burden of proof lies, and the type and severity of penalties imposed for non-compliance.

Because business environments and tax systems are distinctly different among nations, transfer pricing regulations vary as to how to apply the arm's length principle. As a consequence, tax authorities in different countries may hold different views on what price should be attached to the same transaction. In addition, there may be difficulties

Table 3.8   Return Disclosures/Related Party Disclosures

OECD	No provision
Canada	Form T106
France	In the case of specific request from the French Tax Administration provided by Article L13B of the French Procedure Code, there is an obligation to disclose the nature of the relations with the related parties, i.e., the links of dependence between the French audited entity and the related parties. This article states also an obligation to disclose the activities of the related parties. Annual report required if filing an APA
Germany	No specific disclosure
Italy	Detailed statement concerning related parties. The tax returns should detail transactions with tax havens concerning costs/expenses
Japan	Schedule 16–4: Detailed Statement Concerning Foreign Affiliated Persons and related party transactions
United Kingdom	No return disclosures except that required in statutory accounts and that annual reports are to be filed in compliance with any current APAs
United States	Forms 5471 and 5472

Table 3.9   Advance Pricing Agreement Available

OECD	Unilateral and bilateral available
Canada	Unilateral and bilateral/multilateral available
France	Unilateral unavailable formally, but an informal process is developing
Germany	Generally available, but restricted to 'big' cases
Italy	Not available
Japan	Unilateral and bilateral available
United Kingdom	Bilateral APAs are preferred, but unilateral also possible
United States	Unilateral and bilateral available

in getting one country to accept adjustments initiated by another country. These practical considerations can result in an audit controversy, that is, transfer pricing adjustments by tax authorities under different transfer pricing rules could create tax conflicts between revenue

Table 3.10 Comparison of the Key Features of the OECD Guidelines and the United States Regulations

	OECD	United States
Tax authority and Tax law	Not applicable	Internal Revenue Service. Internal Revenue Code § 482, §6038A, §6038C, §6662 (e)–(h)
Regulations, rules and guidelines	Transfer Pricing Guidelines for Multinational Enterprises and Tax Administrations	Reg. § 1.482, § 1.6662; § 1.6038A, §1.6038C, Rev.Proc. 96–53; Rev. Proc. 99–32
Priorities/ pricing methods	Transaction-based preferred over profit-based. CUP, Resale price, Cost plus, Profit split, TNMM	Best method. CUP, Resale price, Cost plus, CPM, split or other Profit unspecified method
Documentation requirements	Pricing decisions should be documented in accordance with prudent business practices. Reasonable for tax authorities to expect taxpayers to prepare and maintain such material. No contemporaneous obligation	Extensive contemporaneous documentation required
Transfer pricing penalties	Civil monetary penalties are frequently calculated as a percentage of the tax understatement, with the percentage ranging from 10 to 200%	Penalty of 20 or 40% for underpayment of tax
Reduction in penalties	No provision	No penalty if transfer pricing method is reasonably applied and documented. Contemporaneous obligation
Return disclosure-related party disclosure	No provision	Forms 5471 and 5472
Advance pricing agreement	Unilateral and bilateral	Unilateral and bilateral

authorities and, in the end, lead to double taxation (Ernst and Young, 2001). In order to minimise disagreements on transfer pricing, to avoid potential transfer pricing penalties and to mitigate the extent of double taxation, it is important for both the Commissioners of tax authorities and taxpayers to be aware of the disparities which exist regarding national transfer pricing rules and regulations.

4
Determining Factors

Introduction

Multinational enterprises are organisations which engage in production or service activities outside the country in which they are incorporated. The maximisation of global profit and minimisation of risk are their major objectives. These objectives are largely achieved through the exploitation of market imperfections. Market imperfections arise from differentials in a country's labour costs, educational levels, technology and political stability. International Transfer Pricing could be employed by multinational enterprises to ensure profit maximisation and risk minimisation from market imperfections.

The effects of market imperfections consist of a broad set of elements that differ from one country to another. These elements include international tax differentials, customs duties, trading restrictions imposed by host governments and the like. In the International Transfer Pricing literature, the elements of market imperfections are referred to as environmental factors (Natke, 1985; Leitch and Barrett, 1992). From a multinational enterprise's point of view, the particular environment of a host country may well be one of the most important factors influencing the long-term use of the International Transfer Pricing mechanism (Lall, 1973).

Motivational variables

Tax Rate Differentials. Tax minimisation and correlative profit maximisation are important objectives of International Transfer Pricing decisions. Yet the full range of objectives and motives behind the International Transfer Pricing manoeuvres of a multinational enterprise are far more complex than these two objectives taken by themselves imply. Multinational enterprises have simultaneous multiple objectives and goals in the global market. At all times, multinational enterprises engaging in international operations usually face huge financial risks. Taxation may not necessarily be the sole reason for the use of International Transfer Pricing as a means to move income by multinational enterprises (Radebaugh and Gray, 1997).

The motive to evade or minimise taxes may not necessarily be even of great importance in multinational enterprise transfer price manipulations. Evidence suggests that obtaining a tax advantage is not the primary reason for International Transfer Pricing abuses in some host countries, especially when these particular host countries are developing nations (Chan and Chow, 1997a). Non-tax factors probably play an equally important role in the motives for International Transfer Pricing gambits. These non-tax factors along with tax considerations themselves are generally grouped together as the environmental variables in the transfer pricing literature.

Subsidiaries of a multinational enterprise family are geographically distant and operate in different jurisdictions and cultural environments. Their overseas operations are subject to the laws and regulations of host countries. Apart from international tax differentials, many other environmental factors, both naturally and governmentally generated, need to be considered in dealing with problems of International Transfer Pricing in the multinational environment (Leitch and Barrett, 1992).

If the assumption is made that a parent company sells an intermediate product to its foreign subsidiaries, an International Transfer Pricing manoeuvre can take place in its simplest form by overpricing (also called overinvoicing or overcharging) or underpricing (also called underinvoicing or undercharging). Apart from tax considerations, the fundamental environmental factors likely to influence the parent company's pricing behaviour variously will include the following.

Customs Duties. In industrialised nations, import and export duties in essence serve as protective devices rather than serve distributive objectives. By contrast, some developing country governments still regard import duties as a major source of fiscal revenue, and import duties tend to be substantially higher than in developed countries. Tariffs can be reduced by making transfers at an arbitrarily low price. If goods are transferred at low prices, the resulting tariffs they attract will be lower. In this case, there must be some inducement for the parent company to underprice goods by using International Transfer Pricing means to gain fiscal savings at the expense of the host government. On the other hand, low import duties are often associated with high income tax rates. The saving resulting from the underinvoicing for customs purposes may be more than offset by higher income tax liabilities because income taxes are typically a larger imposition than tariffs (Lecraw, 1985; Belkaoui, 1991; Lin et al., 1993; Chan and Chow, 1997a; Anthony and Govindarajan, 1998).

Currency Fluctuation and Inflation. A country suffering from balance-of-payments problems may decide to devalue its national currency. Currency devaluation often results in an inflationary environment. The devaluation could substantially reduce the corporate profits of foreign subsidiaries if they did not take measures to hedge against the devaluation. Furthermore, inflation in a host country weakens the purchasing power of any return on investment. By setting a high International Transfer Pricing on goods imported into the host country, the parent company may transfer funds out of this uncertain foreign environment (Lin et al., 1993; Plasschaert, 1985).

Foreign Currency Exchange Control and Risks. In some developing nations, foreign exchange is stringently constrained by government, local currencies being only semi-convertible. In this situation, a multinational enterprise would face problems in converting profits into its own currency. Moreover, when the local currency unit is devalued, exchange losses may rise. Multinational enterprises usually view exchange uncertainties as their most pervasive risk in foreign environments. In most cases, they tend to hedge this risk by changes in the timing of the payments, that is, by leading (anticipatory moves) or lagging (delaying techniques). For instance, a buying company may pay a selling company before the due date (leading) and thereby anticipate a fall in the currency of the buyer's country. In this way, an exchange loss can be averted.

International Transfer Pricing practices can enhance the exchange-risk-avoiding virtues of leading or lagging. A multinational enterprise faced with exchange rate risks can use a higher transfer price to move funds out of the countries with weak currencies into countries with strong ones. In this particular case, the perceived exchange loss risk may induce the parent company to transfer profits out of the host country by overpricing (Lin et al., 1993; Plasschaert, 1985).

Pricing Controls of Host Governments. In some industries, host governments control prices in relation to the costs and profits of foreign companies to a large extent, requiring that all price increases be approved by government agencies in advance. High import prices can reduce profits and increase costs, thereby justifying increased prices. In this case, the parent company may allow its subsidiaries to record a low profit by overpricing to resist the introduction of price controls (Lecraw, 1985).

Restrictions on Remittance of Income. Limits imposed on the remittance of profits create a strong inducement for a multinational enterprise to use the International Transfer Pricing mechanism. In some less developed countries, notably those that often suffer from balance-of-payment problems, local governments introduce a number of regulations or policies to restrict profit and capital repatriations. When foreign subsidiaries face the difficulties of profit remittance to their home countries, they can circumvent such constraints by way of International Transfer Pricing. In this case, the parent company can artificially raise its sale prices to the foreign subsidiary to avoid the restrictions on the remittances. In addition, International Transfer Pricing could be used to minimise withholding tax on dividends. By artificially setting high prices for transferred-in goods, cash is funnelled to the parent company in the form of a sales price. This leaves less profit in the subsidiary's country, reducing the need to transfer funds to the parent through dividends (Belkaoui, 1991; Lin et al., 1993; Plasschaert, 1985).

Existence of Local Partner. Multinational enterprises conduct business in foreign environments usually via joint ventures for political, legal or cultural reasons. For example, some host governments in developing countries require that a local firm must be a partner in the business venture of a foreign-based company. Multinational enterprises themselves may use the strategy of local presence for bridging cultural gaps and fostering local cultural understanding. In most arrangements of this type, both sides – foreign investors (subsidiaries) and local partners in joint ventures – share the profits, costs and management. This means that a foreign investor has only a part profit share, the rest being distributed to the local partner who has legal rights to a fair share of the profit of the business. To restrict the profits accruing to the partner, and in return, to increase its own interest and benefit, the parent company has a high motivation to shift profits out of the joint venture by International Transfer Pricing (Lin et al., 1993; Lecraw, 1985; Iqbal et al., 1997).

Political and Social Pressure. Political and social pressures as determinants appear to be related to some of the aforementioned factors. For example, volatile fluctuations in the value of currencies, high inflation rates, foreign exchange controls and restrictions on remittances increase financial risks and uncertainty. A lack of political stability increases the political risk for foreign investors. In some developing countries the threat of expropriation and nationalisation is often a concern for multinational enterprises. All of these factors impose political and social pressures on business operations. Consequently, multinational enterprises tend to transfer profits out of the host country to avoid these risks (Belkaoui, 1991; Lin et al., 1993; Plasschaert, 1985). In fact, a host country which tries to control or limit the activities of multinational enterprises may be considered by them as a more or less undesirable area in which to retain high profits with safety for the long-term. The multinational subsidiaries may use the International Transfer Pricing mechanism to send profits abroad (Lall, 1973).

Wage increase demands. In some countries, labour unions exercise significant influence. They may impose pressures on subsidiaries to raise wages for local workers in response to high operating earnings of the foreign firms. To nullify claims for higher wages by local labour unions, the parent company may overprice to reduce the profits of the subsidiaries (Belkaoui, 1991).

Maintenance of Good Relationships with Host Governments. The practice of shifting profits out of the host countries by multinational enterprises has attracted considerable attention from host governments. Concerned about the potential adverse effects on their economies when International Transfer Pricing is abused by multinational enterprises, the tax authorities of host countries have adopted an increasingly aggressive attitude towards the audit of multinational enterprise transfer pricing practices, and have placed some economic restrictions on their operations. These actions can impose intense pressures upon multinational enterprises. If disputes with local tax officials arise, they can be costly to foreign subsidiaries. Multinational enterprises have realised the importance of maintaining positive relations with host governments. In justifying their International Transfer Pricing methods, some subsidiaries are even willing to sacrifice some profits by transfer pricing in order to satisfy the host governments. Their end purpose is to forestall any government action that may have potentially detrimental effects on them (Plasschaert, 1979).

Enlarged Market Share of the Subsidiary and Support for an Infant Subsidiary. Frequently, International Transfer Pricing is used as an instrument to facilitate the penetration of an overseas subsidiary into foreign markets, or to support an infant subsidiary abroad in its competition with local firms. In these cases, the parent company may temporarily underprice to provide support to its subsidiaries in another country where they want to increase market share (Plasschaert, 1979; Belkaoui, 1991).

The Need to Maintain Adequate Cash Flows in the Subsidiary. A multinational enterprise may prefer to accumulate its funds at a particular foreign location for one reason or another. Transfer prices could then be employed as a means of shifting funds into a subsidiary at that location (Anthony and Govindarajan, 1998).

Avoiding Anti-Dumping Charges. When goods are transferred from a parent company to an overseas subsidiary in a foreign country, the host government may impose anti-dumping charges on the multinational company to protect its home industries against the dumping of excess production of the companies of other countries. In this case the parent company may overprice to escape charges of anti-dumping practices (Belkaoui, 1991).

Performance Evaluation. Corporate policies regarding International Transfer Pricing for tax purposes may be in conflict with the performance evaluation of subsidiary managers. For example, arbitrarily shifting profits from a foreign subsidiary through International Transfer Pricing, while enhancing overall corporate profitability, may affect the measured profitability of that subsidiary and, in turn, distort the performance of the subsidiary's managers which is frequently evaluated on the basis of net income and return on investment. To resolve this conflict, multinational enterprises often separate managerial performance from that of the subsidiary's performance. An alternative is to set a 'fair' transfer price – an intercompany price that managers can perceive as equity in performance evaluation, based on an externally established market price (Yunker, 1983; Hansen and Mowen, 2000).

Table 4.1 lists the environmental factors that can affect International Transfer Pricing policy decisions of a multinational company, on the basis that the parent company sells to the subsidiary.

This list of environmental factors is not exhaustive. The maximisation of overall corporate profits is an important objective of International Transfer Pricing, related to tax differentials existing among national tax jurisdictions. The concepts of environmental factors (also called variables or determinants), transfer pricing motivations, and transfer pricing objectives are often used interchangeably in the International Transfer Pricing literature.

The foregoing analysis adopts the deductive line of reasoning, that is, a parent company would have the incentive to shift profits out of the host country through the overpricing of its exports, if one or more

Table 4.1   Environmental Factors and Their Possible Effect on International Transfer Pricing Decisions

Environmental Factors	Analysis	Action Taken by Parent Company
Tax rate differentials	Host country tax is lower	Underpricing
	Host country tax is higher	Overpricing
Customs duties	High import duties in host country	Underpricing
Currency fluctuation	Devaluation of the foreign currency	Overpricing
Inflation	High inflation in host country	Overpricing
Foreign exchange control and risks		Overpricing
Pricing control		Overpricing
Restrictions on repatriation of income		Overpricing
Existence of a local partner		Overpricing
Political and social pressures		Overpricing
Wage increase demands by trade unions in host country		Overpricing
Maintenance of good relationships with host government		Fair Pricing
Enlarge market share of the subsidiary		Underpricing
Support an infant subsidiary		Underpricing
The need to maintain adequate cash flows in the subsidiary		Underpricing
Avoid anti-dumping charges		Overpricing
Performance evaluation		Fair Pricing

(Adapted from Plasschaert, 1985, p. 265; Chan and Chow, 1997a, p. 1278).

particular condition applied when all other factors remained the same. These conditions include when:

- the effective tax rates in the host country are higher than in the home country
- the exchange rates of the two currencies fluctuate frequently
- the host government imposes restrictions on foreign investors who are repatriating their share of profits to their home country
- the political and social situation is uncertain in the host country.

A multinational enterprise would take advantage of market imperfections by transfer pricing as expressed in the words of one American multinational enterprise manager: 'If I cannot get my dividends out, and my royalty rate is fixed, and I want to remit more money, then I do this by an uplift [sic] of my transfer prices on commodities' (Robbins and Stobaugh, 1973, p. 91). At first glance, the foregoing explanation is straightforward and intuitively obvious. And yet the deductive line in assessing multinational enterprise transfer pricing practice is debatable in the real world.

Actual conditions are seldom as clear-cut as that shown in Table 4.1. International Transfer Pricing objectives are interactive. One motivation may conflict with other inducements during the formulation of a multinational enterprise's transfer pricing policies. Therefore, it is difficult to manipulate transfer prices to achieve all corporate objectives simultaneously. For instance, while overpriced exports reduce the taxes on profits in the importing country (the host country), it may enhance the burden of import duties of the foreign subsidiary. Another dilemma is that, arbitrarily taking out profits from the foreign subsidiary for purely tax avoidance purpose may have a distorting effect on subsidiary performance evaluation (Plasschaert, 1979). The pros and cons of any particular level of transfer prices must therefore be considered.

Multinational enterprises are exposed to a wide variety of environmental conditions that affect their international operations. As the host environments remain in a state of flux, a multinational enterprise's transfer pricing objectives and policies must also constantly change to adapt to changing foreign environments, since the changing environments may affect management's perception of the relative importance of various factors of transfer pricing decisions in a foreign country over time (Cunningham, 1978; Tang, 1993; Lin, et al., 1993; Borkowski, 1996b; Oyelere, et al., 1999).

Governmental constraints

Facing the growth of multinational business, national governments have become increasingly aware of the losses of tax revenues as a result of International Transfer Pricing abuses. Over the years, the tax authorities of many governments have developed regulations to limit the ability of multinational enterprises to use International Transfer Pricing for the purpose of reducing their tax payments. In addition, tax authorities have intensified their efforts to investigate multinational transfer pricing practices.

A global survey conducted by Ernst and Young (2001) revealed that in 2001, nearly two-thirds of multinational respondents reported having suffered a transfer pricing audit in their organisations. Sixty-one per cent of the respondent parent companies and 94% of their subsidiaries regarded International Transfer Pricing as the most important international tax issue facing them. A tax audit is an expensive process in terms of time, resources, and tax at risk, not to mention the potential penalties and interest charges incurred. To be effective, an International Transfer Pricing system must be designed not only to achieve internal corporate objectives, but also to meet the requirements of interested tax authorities. This suggests that International Transfer Pricing tax auditing may be an increasingly important consideration governing multinational transfer pricing decisions.

Summary

The issue of transfer pricing has long been a source of frequent managerial concern and frustration (Rushinek and Rushinek, 1988). Compared with domestic business, pricing considerations for multinationals in international business are far more complicated and perplexing. Multinational enterprises are exposed to a greater variety of environmental disturbances than domestic firms. The constantly changing international environment can have a great impact on multinational transfer pricing practices (Tang, 1982; Ghosh and Crain, 1993). The general theoretical analysis of environmental factors affecting International Transfer Pricing is bound to be controversial in actual practice. Empirical evidence concerning the number of factors actually considered in transfer pricing decisions and the relative importance of various factors in national settings are therefore of practical significance.

As International Transfer Pricing practice can have such an adverse effect on the tax base of the countries involved, it has captured the attention of governmental tax authorities. The tax authorities of many countries have increasingly scrutinised the International Transfer Pricing policies of multinational enterprises. Accordingly, International Transfer Pricing audits now carry significant tax implications for the multinational enterprises involved.

5
Preparing for Research

Introduction

The pacific region is home to a majority of the world's population. Within it, China is developing as one of the world's largest economies. Elsewhere in the pacific region, Australia and New Zealand are two countries which have substantially expanded their trade with China and are set to develop that trade further. The examination and contrasting of International Transfer Pricing practices among the companies of the three nations have a practical value.

In contemplating how to collect the data required for a study of International Transfer Pricing involving Australia, New Zealand and China as the three countries of the Pacific chosen for it, the full range of possibilities were considered. The great distances, the disparate languages and the costs that are characteristic of such an undertaking created potential difficulties and affected the eventual choice of research methods from the panoply of methods potentially available.

These consist of various instruments such as self-administered questionnaire surveys, personal or telephone interviews, field studies and the analysis of archival information. There is no one best survey method. Each has its strengths and weaknesses but must be subjected to a consideration of its suitability as a method of data collection, depending on the research objectives and the physical factors involved.

In the event, for the research required for this book, the primary information about company characteristics, environmental variables and International Transfer Pricing methods used by companies were obtained by means of a Questionnaire. Chapter 4 has generally examined the various environmental variables that are theoretically likely to determine the pricing manipulation behaviour of multinational enterprises. Based on prior research, seventeen environmental variables were selected in designing the data collection Questionnaire.

This chapter describes both empirical and case based research approaches, noting the comparative strengths and weaknesses of them, and why and how they were employed.

As part of the development of a Questionnaire that would prove effective for the purposes of the research, a review of existing literature on the subject of International Transfer Pricing was first carried out, with particular attention being paid to various management and tax issues relating to multinational transfer pricing, such as issues concerning the administration of an International Transfer Pricing system, International Transfer Pricing method choices, contingency theory, and environmental variables which may bear on International Transfer Pricing.

Another information source for the research was archival data. This included finding essential information relating to important aspects of the business environments and their recent changes in the three countries, transfer pricing regulations, guidelines or policies issued by government agencies and the OECD, and the transfer pricing legal frameworks for the three countries concerned.

In the end, the primary data were gathered by two methods – direct from the subsidiary companies of multinationals in the three countries by Questionnaire, and from personal contact, in-depth interviews with Chinese tax authorities.

Selecting the unit of study

Predominantly, previous studies of International Transfer Pricing practices have focused on the headquarters, the parent companies, of the multinational enterprises subjected to research. The rationale for their selection was based upon the notion that the freedom for subsidiary managers to take independent, decisive action was incomplete, the assumption being made that corporate policies in general and transfer pricing policies in particular were frequently set or directly affected by the headquarters of the parent companies located in the home countries.

Hence, the reasoning has prevailed that data about corporate transfer pricing practices should be taken directly from the headquarters of the parent unit (Yunker, 1983; Hansen and Mowen, 2000). However, it can be argued that corporate headquarters may not have all the facts about their foreign subsidiaries and that the information which they do have may be inaccurate, while a subsidiary's managers may have different or more realistic perspectives of what business operations are intended to achieve and how they might be affected by the environmental factors prevailing in a host country (Arpan, 1972).

As their overseas operations expand, large multinational enterprises often become highly decentralised. A highly decentralised structure propels decision-making down to the local managers on the basis that they have more accurate information than their parent companies about the external environments relevant to the local daily operations and management of their companies (Chan and Chow, 1998). Philips, the global electronics company with its headquarters in the Netherlands, for instance, delegates marketing and pricing decisions for its television business in the Indian and Singaporean markets to its local managers (Horngren et al., 1999).

Members of senior management are obliged to use divisional reports in arriving at policy decisions. In the establishment of corporate policies such as transfer pricing policies, a parent company often heavily relies on the information that is typically supplied and periodically reported by the subsidiary firms, located in the local markets of their host countries.

Most importantly, an effective host country corporate policy should provide for timely responses to local economic conditions and changes in the political climate. Foreign managers of subsidiaries have keener perceptions and specialised knowledge of local environments than higher-level management. They are more familiar with the local political, economic and cultural environment (Hansen and Mowen, 2000).

In short, whilst investigations carried out on the headquarters of parent units in their home countries are valid in reflecting the impact of home country environmental variables on International Transfer Pricing policies, they fail to address the foreign host country environmental aspects of International Transfer Pricing, which should be registered by the subsidiaries located in overseas countries.

Consequently the research presented in this book takes account of these deficiencies, and is thereby differentiated from previous studies as well as by its focus on the particular choice of three countries in the Pacific – Australia, New Zealand and China.

It is concerned with the impact of environmental factors according to a company's geographic area of operation, not the location of the firm's headquarters or home country. This approach to a study of International Transfer Pricing is based on the notion that multinational enterprises generally adapt their foreign operations to local cultural environments rather than the firm's home country environment. Hence, the target research units of study for this book are foreign subsidiaries of multinational companies operating in Australia, New Zealand and China.

Developing the Questionnaire

The questionnaire itself was divided into three sections as follows:

- Section 1 General Information on the Company and its Related Party Transactions
- Section 2 International Transfer Pricing Methods Used
- Section 3 Environmental Variables of International Transfer Pricing.

The contents of these sections took account of and adopted or adapted items from previous studies including Al-Eryani et al. (1990), Tang (1993) and Borkowski (1997a,b). The survey used closed structured questions in most cases. A five-point Likert Scale was used by the responding firms to rate the importance of each variable.

Section I of the Questionnaire was designed to collect general information of the company and related party transactions – its type of industry, nationality, size, and the volume, nature and frequency of intercompany international transfers, International Transfer Pricing auditing, and company status regarding advance pricing agreements. These are detailed as follows.

Industry Classification. The first question in the survey sought to establish the industry type of the respondent companies. The analysis later in this book will examine whether certain types of industry are more prone to investigation by host country tax authorities than others.

The industry classifications of respondent firms in the three national groups are shown in Table 6.1. The ten classifications of industry adopted were initially based on the Australian and New Zealand Standard Industrial Classification (ANZSIC) codes. The industry information of Chinese firms was obtained from archival sources.

Nationality of Companies. The second question sought to establish the nationality of the respondent companies. The analysis later in this book will examine whether certain companies are looked at in more detail by the host country tax authorities on account of the nationality of their parent companies than others.

For the New Zealand sample, information about the nationality of companies was collected by asking where their ultimate parent companies were located. The same information was obtained from archival sources in the case of the Australian and Chinese firms.

Company Size. The third question asked about the size of the respondent companies. The analysis in later chapters will examine whether larger companies tend to be subject to more attention by the tax authorities of host countries than smaller companies. The firm's size is measured in terms of total sales/total revenue. Information on the size of Australian and Chinese companies was obtained from archival data.

Nature and Frequency of Intercompany Transactions. The fourth question addressed the nature and frequency of intercompany international transfers, which generally can involve up to four types of transaction. These are the payments arising from the transfer of

- tangible goods such as raw materials, trading stock, plant and equipment
- intangible goods such as the use of brand names and patents, and manufacturing processes
- financial assets and services such as intercompany accounts, loans, and loan guarantees
- services such as management, technical assistance, marketing, insurance, and training.

The respondents were asked to rank the frequency of the four types of intercompany transfers of their companies on a Likert Scale, assessed as being either 'always', 'often', 'sometimes', 'rarely' or 'never'. The analysis in a later chapter will examine whether certain types of intercompany transfers will attract more attention by the tax authorities in host countries than others.

The Volume of Intercompany Transactions. The fifth question asked the respondents to estimate the percentage which the value of intercompany transfers – the transfers of tangible goods, intangibles, financing and services involved in either Australia, New Zealand or China as the case might be – formed of the total transfers for the entire company year in 2002, meaning a company's worldwide transactions with related or unrelated parties. Jacob (1996) assumes that if multinational enterprises use International Transfer Pricing to minimise taxes, then multinationals with the greatest volume of intercompany international transfers have the most opportunities and the greatest incentive to shift income through International Transfer Pricing policies. The analysis in a later chapter will examine whether companies with greater volumes of intercompany transactions will be subject to greater attention by host country tax authorities than those with low volumes.

International Transfer Pricing Tax Auditing. The sixth question asked whether or not the respondent firms had been the subject of an International Transfer Pricing audit since 1998. The data gathered for this variable will be used to examine the relationship between a firm's tax auditing status and its type of industry, country of origin, and the volume, nature and frequency of intercompany transfers. The analysis in a later chapter will also examine the relationship between the prior International Transfer Pricing auditing experiences of respondent firms, their International Transfer Pricing method choices and their status regarding Advance Pricing Agreements.

Advance Pricing Agreements. An Advance Pricing Agreement is a negotiated agreement between tax authorities and the taxpayer. It establishes a transfer pricing methodology to be applied to the allocation of income among associated units of an enterprise in advance of a transaction. One way for a multinational enterprise to reduce exposure to transfer pricing investigations is to establish an advance pricing agreement with tax authorities. The seventh question therefore asked the respondents to indicate their status regarding advance pricing agreements with local tax authorities. The data obtained for this variable will be used to examine the relationship between an advance pricing agreement and International Transfer Pricing auditing experiences.

International Transfer Pricing Methods Used. Section 2 of the Questionnaire dealt with International Transfer Pricing methods used by the respondent firms. This section contained two questions, numbers eight and nine. Question 8 asked for the actual International Transfer Pricing methods used by the respondents from the point of view of managerial preference, whereas Question 9 related to the use of the legally authorised arm's length methods.

Environmental Variables of International Transfer Pricing. Section 3 contained the final question focused on the seventeen environmental variables which could be held to influence the selection of International Transfer Pricing method choices by multinational enterprises. Most of the environmental variables listed in the Questionnaire for the use of respondents to evaluate were identified and culled from the extant literature as reviewed in Chapter 4. A few modifications to some of the variables were made. One variable – 'tax authority transfer

Table 5.1   Environmental Variables Used in the Questionnaire and Their Sources

Variables	Reference
VAR 01 Differences in income tax rates	Tang and Chan (1979), Tang (1982), Al-Eryani et al. (1990), Tang (1993), Borkowski (1997a)
VAR 02 Rates of customs duties	Tang (1981), Tang (1982), Rushinek and Rushinek (1988), Tang (1993)
VAR 03 Tax authority transfer pricing audits	Borkowski (1997a,b; 2001)
VAR 04 Comply with tax law and regulations	Rushinek and Rushinek (1988), Al-Eryani et al. (1990)
VAR 05 Restrictions on repatriation of income	Tang and Chan (1979), Al-Eryani et al. (1990), Tang (1993), Borkowski (1997a), Oyelere et al. (1999)
VAR 06 Competitive position of the subsidiary	Tang and Chan (1979), Tang (1981), Tang (1982), Tang (1993)
VAR 07 Overall profit to multinational group	Tang and Chan (1979), Tang (1982), Yunker (1983), Al-Eryani et al. (1990), Tang (1993)
VAR 08 Corporate profit of the subsidiary	Oyelere et al. (1999)
VAR 09 Import restrictions	Tang and Chan (1979), Tang (1982), Rushinek and Rushinek (1988)
VAR 10 Foreign currency exchange controls	Al-Eryani et al. (1990)
VAR 11 Good relations with host government	Tang (1982), Rushinek and Rushinek (1988)
VAR 12 Price controls of host government	Al-Eryani et al. (1990)
VAR 13 Existence of local partner	Tang and Chan (1979), Tang (1982), Rushinek and Rushinek (1988)
VAR 14 Performance evaluation	Tang and Chan (1979), Tang (1982), Yunker (1983), Rushinek and Rushinek (1988), Oyelere et al. (1999)
VAR 15 Political and social pressures	Al-Eryani et al. (1990)
VAR 16 Royalty restrictions	Tang (1982), Rushinek and Rushinek (1988)
VAR 17 Maintenance of cashflow	Tang (1982), Oyelere et al. (1999)

pricing audits' – which previously had not been used except by Borkowski (1997a,b; 2001), was added to the Questionnaire to test whether or not International Transfer Pricing auditing is an important factor affecting multinational transfer pricing decisions.

The seventeen environmental variables thus used are shown with their origins in Table 5.1.

The development of the Questionnaire consisted of drafting, pretesting and pilot testing it. In its draft form, containing previously identified International Transfer Pricing methods and environmental variables, it was checked by a manager and a Chinese member of staff of a New Zealand Company with long experience in both New Zealand and Chinese markets. Contacts were also made with three tax consultants of the Institute of Chartered Accountants of New Zealand, four staff members of an international firm of consultant accountants located in the United States, United Kingdom and New Zealand. Their comments and suggestions were incorporated into a revised Questionnaire for a pilot test.

As a pilot test in late 2002, the Questionnaire was sent to thirty financial controllers of subsidiaries located in Australia and New Zealand and seventy financial controllers of subsidiaries located in China. Based upon the responses, some modifications to the original Questionnaire were made.

To confirm that the final contents and terminology of the Questionnaire were appropriate for the Chinese context – whether the questions related to a Chinese company's financial controller's experience – it was important to invite a Chinese financial controller to evaluate the newly revised Questionnaire. Contact for this purpose was made with such a person in a multinational company in Beijing. The controller made some constructive additional suggestions to improve the Questionnaire's applicability in the Chinese context. Both the Questionnaire and the letter of request to be used in China were checked by this financial controller in the Chinese language. Although the Chinese version of the Questionnaire was essentially identical to that for use in Australian and New Zealand, some variation of a non-substantive order was necessary to meet cultural, institutional and language differences.

Sample Selection Method. The sampling frame for the research of International Transfer Pricing in Chinese company practice was the list of the foreign-controlled subsidiaries in China as contained in the publication *Foreign Investment Companies Operating in China* (2001) – a directory listing 22,000 multinational companies located in China, together with another directory entitled *The World Top 500 Multi-national Companies Operating in China* (2003). In addition to the sample assembled from these two directories, a further fifty firms were randomly selected from a network of 1,000 multinationals located in Beijing as listed by a consultancy firm in the city for the purpose of their business. The final Chinese sample, therefore, contained 500 companies assembled from these disparate sources.

In recognition of China's entrenched cultural disposition for secrecy and reluctance to communicate information about a firm's activities to outsiders, it was anticipated at the start of the research that eliciting any responses from Chinese respondents would be difficult when compared with the approaches made to Australian and New Zealand firms. Hence it was necessary to despatch an inordinate number of Questionnaires in the hope of receiving enough returns to fulfil the research objectives.

For the survey of Australian and New Zealand practices, a total of 250 Australian and 300 New Zealand subsidiaries of multinational enterprises were randomly drawn from Dun & Bradstreet's *Business Who's Who* (2001, 2002 and 2003). To ensure the accuracy of the addresses of the intended respondents, the data from the directories were carefully checked on the Internet database. The website addresses used were http://www.yellowpages.com.au and http://www.yellowpages.co.nz respectively.

Questionnaire Distribution and Response Rates. The final version of the Questionnaire was sent by post with its explanatory letter, addressed to the financial controllers of 250 subsidiaries operating in Australia, 300 subsidiaries operating in New Zealand, and 500 subsidiaries operating in China. The sample was reduced to 216 Australian firms, 274 New Zealand firms and 435 Chinese firms respectively by the 125 envelopes that were returned unopened as a result of incorrect addresses or changes of personal employment without forwarding addresses.

To secure viable numbers of returns, it was necessary to send two follow-up letters to Australian and New Zealand firms and three to Chinese firms. For illustrative convenience and consistency, the last two follow-ups to Chinese firms are combined into one in the analysis of these survey distribution data as presented in Table 5.2.

The first follow-up was sent three or four weeks after the initial mail out and included a second shorter letter plus another copy of the Questionnaire and a return stamped envelope. The response rates, which resulted from the second follow-up, are shown in Table 5.3.

Table 5.2   Questionnaire Response Rates from the First Mailing

Country	Survey Mailed	Usable Responses	% of Sample	Unusable Responses	% of Sample	Total Response	% of Sample
Australia	216	28	12.96	1	0.46	29	13.43
New Zealand	274	40	14.60	2	0.73	42	15.33
China	435	20	4.60	7	1.61	27	6.21

Table 5.3   Questionnaire Response Rates from the Second Mailing

Country	Survey Mailed	Usable Responses	% of Sample	Unusable Responses	% of Sample	Total Response	% of Sample
Australia	216	22	10.19	1	0.46	23	10.65
New Zealand	274	21	7.67	2	0.73	23	8.39
China	435	17	3.91	5	1.15	22	5.06

Table 5.4   Questionnaire Response Rates from the Third Mailing

Country	Survey Mailed	Usable Responses	% of Sample	Non-Responses	% of Sample	Total Response	% of Sample
Australia	216	10	4.63	27	12.50	37	17.13
New Zealand	274	14	5.11	63	22.99	77	28.10
China	435	10	2.30	28	6.44	38	8.74

The second follow-up was sent three weeks after the first follow-up. It included a replacement Questionnaire and a return stamped envelope, together with a non-response sheet to be completed by the respondents if they did not intend to answer the Questionnaire. The latter asked for an outline of the reasons why the recipients had not completed the Questionnaire. As a result of the second follow-up, additional Questionnaires were received. The response rates from the second follow-up, are shown in Table 5.4.

The overall response rates from the three steps taken are shown in Table 5.5.

The response rates from the Australian and New Zealand respondents were 41.20% and 52.55% respectively. These response rates were reasonably good, considering the highly sensitive nature of the information requested in the survey. The responses from Chinese companies (87 at 20%) were relatively lower than for Australia and New Zealand. The possible reason for this and the justification for using the limited data from the Chinese companies will be considered later.

Altogether, the overall usable response rate of the three countries was 20%. This was not as high as would be desirable but was still acceptable. Company internal pricing is an extremely sensitive and secretive area for all firms, especially for multinational firms, and compounded in the case of China by a range of cultural factors.

The sensitivity of the subject is due to the increase in investigations and litigation by national government agencies – tax authorities and customs houses – and the growing concerns and interests in the subject of other groups inside and outside a firm, namely stockholders,

Table 5.5   Overall Questionnaire Response Rates

Country	Survey Mailed	Usable Responses	% of Sample	Unusable Responses	Non-responses	% of Sample	Total Response	% of Sample
Australia	216	60	27.77	2	27	13.42	89	41.20
New Zealand	274	77	28.10	4	63	24.45	144	52.55
China	435	47	10.81	12	28	9.20	87	20.00

investors, and local partners. Management is not inclined to share information about their pricing policy with an outsider. It could not be expected, therefore, that firms would welcome and freely respond to an outsider's study of such a confidential matter. However, a satisfactory number of managements eventually cooperated because of the importance of International Transfer Pricing, their expectation of feed-back from the research, and the pledge of confidentiality.

124 respondents to the survey declined participation. A majority of these respondents (52) said that there were no international transfers in their firms or that their volume of international transfers was insignificant. Other reasons cited for refusal included company policy (25), confidentiality (16), and time constraints (22). Details of the reasons for non-usable responses in the three research settings are summarised in Table 5.6.

Non-Response Bias. A chi-square test of homogeneity was carried out as a test for non-response bias on the rate of return data of the Australian, New Zealand, and Chinese respondents. Early responses were compared with late responses on certain characteristics of the companies and International Transfer Pricing methods used. Early respondents are those who responded to the first wave of Questionnaire mail outs, while those who responded to the second and third waves of mail outs are proxies for late respondents (Wallace and Mellor, 1988). Companies were tested as to whether or not there were

Table 5.6   Reasons for Refusal to Participate in the Research

Country	Not Applicable*	Standard Policy of Not Completing Questionnaire	The Questionnaire too Sensitive to be Answered	Lack of Time	Wrong Address	Others**
Australia	13	4	3	5	34	3
New Zealand	29	13	5	15	26	6
China	10	8	8	2	65	0
Total	52	25	16	22	125	9

* This item was interpreted as 'there are no international transfers' or 'the volume of international transfers in the company is insignificant'.
** Six due to corporate changes. Three because the respondents were not knowledgeable about transfer pricing systems.

Table 5.7   Chi-Square Test on the Questionnaire Non-Response Rate

	Australia			New Zealand			China		
	Chi-square	Df	Significance	Chi-square	Df	Significance	Chi-square	Df	Significance
Industry	7.586	7	.371	5.686	7	.577	4.293	3	.232
Methods	.361	1	.545	.251	1	.616	1.349	1	.246

significant differences on the basis of the type of industry and International Transfer Pricing methods used (Borkowski, 1990). The results are shown in Table 5.7.

The test result shown in Table 5.7 indicates that there were no significant differences between the two groups. These results diminish the possibility of the presence of significant non-response bias. Hence, the assumption that later participants were similar to non-participants is valid.

The low usable response rate of 10.81% from Chinese companies may be explained as follows. First, in Chinese society, which has a culture of conservatism and secrecy over matters concerning the holding, retention and disclosure of information, people are literally afraid to disclose data to third parties. Western society has grown used to surveys but Chinese people are far from being adjusted to such practices.

Second, Chinese businesses are traditionally secretive about their finances. The topic of International Transfer Pricing is not only extremely sensitive but very secretive. The data on International Transfer Pricing are related to the commercial information of companies. Many Chinese companies may prohibit their employees from disclosing any sensitive information to an outside party.

Third, the first mailing was sent out at the time that year-end financial reports were being prepared. It was near the Chinese New Year day. Some Chinese financial controllers were too busy to reply.

Fourth, and most importantly, the lower response rate of Chinese companies may have been significantly caused by the recent investigations by Chinese tax authorities and customs houses into the International Transfer Pricing practices of multinational enterprises. There has been a national campaign against tax evasion. The State

Administration of Taxation has tightened regulations seeking to prevent foreign investment enterprises from escaping taxes by passing liabilities between related business units. Shortly before this study was undertaken, the Chinese tax authorities and customs offices had been investigating tax avoidance through multinational transfer pricing abuses and alleged dumping violations by intercompany underpricing transfers.

Though the response rate from China is lower than desired, the number of usable responses, however, is still large enough for an analysis of Chinese International Transfer Pricing practices. Moreover, in a wave analysis, early respondents are compared to late respondents. No significant differences are shown between early and late respondents. Late respondents are considered representative of non-respondents.

Direct contact

To obtain other data needed for the research, in-depth personal interviews with officials of four state tax authorities in China were undertaken. They took place in two contrasting city venues – one, a major coastal city, the other a medium-sized inland provincial capital in a different part of China.

The first of these is a popular destination for foreign investment and has a municipal state tax authority with a sound tax auditing system to prevent its tax base being eroded. In the second city foreign investments are much less in evidence. The tax authorities in inland China in general and in this city in particular are relatively ineffective.

These two cities may be held to represent the developed and developing parts of China. Data about tax authority transfer pricing auditing from these two areas may be taken as representing the range of practices for International Transfer Pricing auditing in China.

Gaining Access to City State Tax Bureaux Officials. Under the habitual practices of Chinese culture it is difficult for an outsider to be allowed to interview someone directly who holds any office in government. Furthermore, since the data on International Transfer Pricing auditing issues are related to the commercial information of companies, and tax officers are prohibited by law from disclosing any sensitive information obtained from audited companies to a third party, there is normally a wall of secrecy and inaccessibility between tax officials and laypeople.

Even if China has opened its doors to the outside world, most Chinese people – especially government officers – remain sceptical regarding the intentions of foreigners, including overseas Chinese, who are collecting data from China. Zhu (1997) found that the most typical concern of Chinese respondents is that of disclosure of their views owing to past political purges that people had suffered as a result of revealing their views.

For the above reasons, it would normally be almost impossible to access any tax officers directly in China. This applies literally in the physical sense as well as at the interpersonal level. On one occasion an attempt was made to enter the inland city tax authority's building. The guard on duty denied an entry, and remained adamant in spite of all the explanations put to him. To achieve the goal of obtaining personal interviews, it seemed that the only way was to find an intermediary to facilitate an access to the Chinese tax authorities.

In the inland city, a tax officer of the city tax authority was privately contacted, with an opportunity to explain the nature and specific objectives of the research involved. Once these matters were understood, this officer agreed to a visit to the office with a view to being able to speak with other officers who were working in the field of International Transfer Pricing auditing

An introduction to the chief tax officer of the inland city tax authority followed. This officer supplied a general overview of the Province's International Transfer Pricing auditing policy and practice. Another tax officer who was responsible for auditing International Transfer Pricing cases, provided detailed information about auditing practice and the current concerns the authorities had about it. In response to careful questioning, this officer answered such questions as to how effectively the inland city transfer pricing auditing system worked and how the inland city tax authority administered International Transfer Pricing tax audits. A further tax officer could not be personally contacted but agreed to respond to a written version of the interview questionnaire – a contract that was duly fulfilled.

In the major coastal city, the assistance of the general manager of a hotel was solicited. He happened to know three tax officers at a district tax authority. On being acquainted with the purpose of the research, the manager invited the tax officers to the hotel. Richardson et al. (1965) noted that the use of a tape recorder to record interviews could influence respondents' answers, so to hold these interviews in an unrestrained and open way, it was decided not to use tape recordings in China. It took one and a half hours to finish the interview with these three tax officers.

Another tax officer of the tax authority was also interviewed as a specialist with many years' experience in the International Transfer

Pricing tax auditing field. With an explanation of the purpose of the study and a guarantee that all the data supplied would only be used for research, the interviewee answered all the questions in detail about International Transfer Pricing auditing issues.

Collecting and Assessing the Evidence. The interviews were recorded in note form in Chinese and were later transcribed into literary form to facilitate an analysis of the data. During this portion of the investigation intensive inquiries were conducted into the four following questions.

1. Why are tax audits initiated on multinational enterprises for their related party transactions?
2. How does the tax authority administer an International Transfer Pricing tax audit?
3. What factors constrain the International Transfer Pricing monitoring system in China?
4. How could the Chinese International Transfer Pricing monitoring system be improved?

A common concern about interviews like these when treated as case studies is that they provide little basis for scientific generalisation (Yin, 1992, p. 10). To overcome this flaw and to permit the generalisability of the main findings from these interviews, a survey was initiated, based on part of the findings from these personal interviews together with items from an archival analysis. They were edited into a one page semi-structured Questionnaire and sent to eighty Chinese tax authorities covering most of the provincial and main city jurisdictions in China, supported by a letter of explanation about the research, and with a promise of research findings feed-back.

Twenty-four Questionnaires were returned on the first round. Four weeks later, a follow-up mailing with a replacement Questionnaire and a reminder letter were sent to non-respondents. This resulted in the return of another fourteen Questionnaires. Overall, thirty-eight usable questionnaires were eventually obtained, representing a response rate of 48%.

Early responses were compared with late responses about their concerns over International Transfer Pricing abuses by multinational enterprises through their related party transactions. Results indicated that there were no significant differences between the two groups, suggesting that there was no significant non-response bias.

Summary

The results of this study are presented in this book using three approaches:

1. The results of a Questionnaire mailed to subsidiaries of multi-national enterprises that operate in Australia, New Zealand, and China
2. The findings of multiple-case studies carried out with four Chinese tax authorities
3. Survey results from canvassed Chinese tax authorities.

Since the design of research includes both quantitative and qualitative data analytical approaches, procedures relevant to both types of analysis are used. While the Questionnaire survey data are subjected to rigorous statistical analysis, data gathered from answers in interviews to open-ended questions are edited and organised into case study reports.

Quantitative Analysis. All data have been coded and analysed using computer programmes available in the Statistical Package for the Social Sciences (SPSS). A number of statistical methods were used to analyse the data collected through the Questionnaire survey. The methods used to analyse the collected data are briefly described as follows:

1. Ratios, means and standard deviations were calculated to describe the nature and characteristics of variables.
2. An R-type, varimax-rotated, common factor analysis was performed using programmes available in the SPSS.
3. Given the categorical or ordinal nature of the data collected in this research, non-parametric statistics were used as the main test technique for the analyses. They include a Chi-square test, and three rank-order tests (the Spearman coefficient, the Mann-Whitney U Test and the Kruskal-Wallis test).

Qualitative Analysis. The major source of the qualitative data was the on-site studies with the Chinese tax authorities. They involved in-depth discussion on transfer pricing tax audit issues with different respondents to gain a broad perspective on the issues at stake from different points of view. Maximum care was and is taken to protect the identity of organisations used in these case studies and in other constituent parts of the research.

6
Research Participants

Introduction

As previously indicated, the individual people who together formed the respondent group supplying the data for the research presented in this book, consisted of two sub groups – the financial officers of the subsidiary companies of multinationals located in Australia, New Zealand and China as their host countries, and an array of tax officers employed by a wide range of tax authorities across the many provinces and cities of China. The latter were canvassed partly by personal interview and partly by postal contact. This chapter presents the data about the companies and the tax authorities represented with suitable analyses of the information acquired for its significance for the practice of trade in the Pacific.

Respondent companies

Industrial Classification. Table 6.1 provides the industry classification of the respondent companies in the three national groups, listed in descending order. The classes were initially based on the Australian and New Zealand Standard Industrial Classification (ANZSIC) codes with minor modifications. There were initially ten categories corresponding to the ANZSIC codes, with the respondents fitting into seven of the categories.

As can be seen in Table 6.1, a wide range of industries is represented in all three countries. In New Zealand, the largest industry of respondent firms is wholesale and retail trade (44.2%). In Australia and China, in contrast, manufacturing is the highest proportion of respondent firms – at 41.7% in Australia and 53.2% in China. Between 85.8% and

Table 6.1   Industrial Classification of Respondent Companies

Industry Type	Australia		New Zealand		China	
	No. of Firms	%	No. of Firms	%	No. of Firms	%
Wholesale trade and retail trade	21	35	34	44.2	12	25.5
Manufacturing	25	41.7	20	26	25	53.2
Services	8	13.3	12	15.6	5	10.6
Finance and insurance	1	1.67	7	9.1	0	0
Mining	1	1.67	1	1.3	0	0
Transport and storage	0	0	1	1.3	0	0
Construction	3	5	1	1.3	3	6.4
Agriculture, forestry and fishing	1	1.67	1	1.3	2	4.3
Total	60	100*	77	100*	47	100*

Note: * Percentage totals are subject to rounding.

90% of respondent firms in total in each of the three countries fall into three categories – wholesale and retail trade, manufacturing, and services industries. The remaining five industries – finance and insurance, mining, transport and storage, construction, agriculture, forestry and fishing – altogether account for merely 10.01% of the respondent firms in Australia, 14.3% of those in New Zealand, and 10.7% of those in China.

Size of the Respondent Companies. The sizes of the participating firms are classified according to total sales/total revenue in 2002. It can be seen in Table 6.2 that the distribution of sales of the respondent companies is unevenly divided among the six categories in all three countries. All values are stated in New Zealand dollars. The Australian and Chinese data were converted from the Australian dollar and the Yuan respectively.

New Zealand companies are, on average, smaller than respondent firms in Australia and China. For example, about 93.6% of the New Zealand respondents have total sales of $200 million or less. Of these, 46.8% of the firms reported total sales of under $20 million. In contrast, 83.3% of Australian companies, of which 40% reported total

Table 6.2   Total Sales/Total Revenue of the Respondent Companies in 2002

Total Sales/Total Revenue (All values in NZ$)	Australia		New Zealand		China	
	No. of Firms	%	No. of Firms	%	No. of Firms	%
Less than $20 million	24	40	36	46.8	17	36.2
$20 million to $100 million	21	35	24	31.2	13	27.7
$101 million to $200 million	5	8.3	12	15.6	8	17
$201 million to $500 million	4	6.7	2	2.6	3	6.4
$501 million to $800 million	1	1.7	1	1.3	5	10.6
More than $800 million	5	8.3	2	2.6	1	2.1
Total	60	100*	77	100*	47	100*

Note: *Percentage totals are subject to rounding.

revenues of under $20 million, and 80.9% of Chinese firms, of which 36.2% reported total revenues of under $20 million, are in the same category.

The size of New Zealand firms is measured in terms of total sales, whereas the size of Australian and Chinese companies is measured by total revenue from sales and other sources during 2002. This difference of measurement of company size must be borne in mind with respect to the New Zealand companies.

The Nationality of the Respondent Companies. The home countries of the respondent subsidiary companies are shown in Table 6.3. A wide range of nations are involved in all three countries. In the case of Australia, subsidiaries of United States, Japanese and United Kingdom companies make up the largest group (66.6%). In New Zealand, subsidiaries of United States, Australian and Japanese companies make up the largest group (71.5%), while in China, subsidiaries of Hong Kong, United States, Japanese and Taiwanese companies make up the largest group (61.7%).

These home countries of the respondent companies are the major trading partners of each of the three countries. They are presented in

Table 6.3   Home Countries of Respondent Subsidiary Companies

Country	Australia		New Zealand		China	
	No. of Firms	%	No. of Firms	%	No. of Firms	%
United States	17	28.3	21	27.3	8	17.0
Australia	0	0	20	26.0	0	0
Japan	14	23.3	14	18.2	6	12.8
United Kingdom	9	15.0	6	7.8	2	4.3
Switzerland	1	1.67	4	5.2	0	0
Germany	6	10	3	3.9	1	2.1
Canada	1	1.7	2	2.6	0	0
France	2	3.3	2	2.6	3	6.4
Sweden	1	1.7	2	2.6	1	2.1
Finland	0	0	1	1.3	0	0
Denmark	1	1.7	1	1.3	0	0
Ireland	1	1.7	1	1.3	0	0
Netherlands	4	6.7	0	0	1	2.1
New Zealand	1	1.7	0	0	0	0
Belgium	1	1.7	0	0	0	0
Italy	0	0	0	0	1	2.1
Korea	1	1.7	0	0	3	6.4
Hong Kong	0	0	0	0	10	21.3
Taiwan	0	0	0	0	5	10.6
Virgin Islands	0	0	0	0	1	2.1
Macao	0	0	0	0	1	2.1
Singapore	0	0	0	0	3	6.4
Thailand	0	0	0	0	1	2.1
Total	60	100*	77	100*	47	100*

Note: * Percentage totals are subject to rounding.

detail in Chapter 7. Table 6.4 shows the nationalities of the Chinese respondent firms and the top fifteen sources of foreign direct investment in China. Consistency can be observed between the national distribution of the sources of foreign direct investment in China and the home country of the respondent companies.

In a different perspective, while sources of foreign direct investment in Australia and New Zealand are predominantly from OECD coun-

Table 6.4   Nationality of Respondent Firms and Top Fifteen Sources of Direct Foreign Investments in China

Nationality of Respondent Firms	Percentage	Top 15 Country/Region	Percentage
Hong Kong	21.3	Hong Kong	45.7
United States	17	United States	8.9
Japan	12.8	Japan	8.1
Taiwan	10.6	Taiwan	7.4
Virgin Islands	2.1	Virgin Islands	5.4
Singapore	6.4	Singapore	4.8
Korea	6.4	Korea	3.4
United Kingdom	4.3	United Kingdom	2.4
Germany	2.1	Germany	1.8
France	6.4	France	1.2
Macao	2.1	Macao	1.1
Netherlands	2.1	Netherlands	1
Sweden	2.1	Cayman Islands	0.9
Italy	2.1	Canada	0.8
Thailand	2.1	Malaysia	0.6
		Others	6.6
Total	100*	Total	100*

Source: Ministry of Commerce of the People's Republic of China, 2004a.

Note: Shaded items are the countries not common to the two groups.
  * Percentage totals are subject to rounding.

tries, all the Australian and New Zealand sample firms are owned by parent companies in these industrialised nations, except for one Australian subsidiary controlled by a Korean parent company.

Volume, Nature and Frequency of Intercompany International Transactions. To determine the importance of intercompany international transfers to the respondent companies, each respondent was asked to estimate the levels of the particular subsidiary's intercompany transfers crossing international boundaries, as a percentage of the company's total transfers – total company transfers meaning a company's worldwide transactions with related or unrelated parties, domestic and international.

The results are shown in Table 6.5. On average, the Chinese respondents engaged in a relatively wider range of related party transactions

Table 6.5   Subsidiary Intercompany International Transfers as Percentages of Total Company Transfers in 2002

The Volume of Transfers	Australia		New Zealand		China	
	No. of Firms	%	No. of Firms	%	No. of Firms	%
Less than 5%	10	16.7	22	29.7	9	19.1
6% to 20%	12	20	7	9.5	12	25.5
21% to 50%	8	13.3	7	9.5	13	27.7
51% to 70%	6	10	5	6.8	6	12.8
71% to 85%	5	8.3	7	9.5	4	8.5
More than 85	19	31.7	26	35.1	3	6.4
Total	60	100**	74*	100**	47	100**

Note: * three companies failed to supply information on intercompany transfers.
   ** Percentage totals are subject to rounding.

with overseas associates than Australian and New Zealand counterparts. However, the results also reveal that nearly a third of Australian respondents – nineteen, or 31.7% – and New Zealand respondents – twenty-six, or 35.1% – engaged heavily in intercompany international transfers, while only a small number of Chinese respondents – three, or 6.4% – engaged heavily in intercompany international transfers.

The respondents were further asked to indicate the nature and frequency of their international transfers with their foreign associates. The responses are shown in Table 6.6. It can be seen that there is a similar ranking of response for all three countries. The transfer of

Table 6.6   Frequencies of the Different Types of Intercompany Transfers

Intercompany Transfers	Australia		New Zealand		China	
	Mean	SD	Mean	SD	Mean	SD
Tangible goods	4.28	1.106	3.95	1.34	3.86	1.15
Services	2.94	1.28	3.18	1.39	3.14	1.23
Financing	2.55	1.316	2.37	1.23	2.76	1.39
Intangibles	1.89	1.23	1.98	1.19	2.38	1.32

Note: A number of companies declined to provide information on the percentages of intercompany transfers of intangibles.

tangible goods is the most common business activity for multinational intercompany transfers in the three countries. The transfer of services is the second most common activity. The transfer of financing is the third most common activity. The least common business activity in the three countries is the transfer of intangibles. Additionally, it can be observed that the Chinese firms are relatively more heavily engaged in intercompany international transfers of intangibles and financing than companies in Australia and New Zealand.

Chinese tax authorities

Taxation Administrative Units in the Study. The unit of analysis of these studies was four state tax bureaux. Two of these were in a major coastal city with provincial status and two were in a medium-sized inland city, the capital city of its province. These two city locations are referred to as City A and City B.

In mainland China, the structure of the state consists of twenty-two Provinces, five Autonomous Regions – Xinjiang, Tibet, Ningxia, Guangxi, and the Inner Mongolia Autonomous Region; and four Municipalities – Beijing, Tianjin, Shanghai, and Chongqing. They are all directly under the jurisdiction of the Central Government. Provinces are generally administratively divided into a number of cities and counties, whereas municipalities are divided into districts and counties. The Autonomous Regions generally are the poorer parts of China, the governments of which, as the titles imply, have comparatively greater discretionary powers over policies pursued in their areas than those permitted by the national government for the provinces at large.

Subject to the national State Administration of Taxation, City A's Municipal State Tax Bureau is responsible for tax investigation and collection. It supervises a large number of County State Tax Bureaux and a few District State Tax Bureaux, each of which selects foreign investment enterprises to audit. In 2002, foreign investment enterprises contributed about 21.8% of City A's total tax revenue.

One in particular of these County State Tax Bureaux, subject to the Municipal State Tax Bureau, operates on the basis of a dozen departments, among which its foreign tax department is responsible for transfer pricing audits throughout its area of the city.

In City B, the Inland Provincial State Tax Bureau, guided by goals established by the national State Administration of Taxation, is responsible for tax investigation and collection in the province. In 2002, fifty-one foreign investment enterprises that had business transactions with their associated enterprises were audited in the province. As a result, the transfer prices of thirty-six foreign investment enterprises were adjusted, resulting in an increase of taxable income by RMB 163.18 million. Eight foreign investment enterprises were adjusted by adopting the comparable uncontrolled price, two were adjusted by adopting the resale price method, seventeen were adjusted by adopting cost plus, one was adjusted by adopting the profit split method and eight were adjusted by adopting the deemed profit method.

These adjustments resulted in a total profit for nine foreign investment enterprises for 2002, sufficient to make up the accumulated loss brought forward from the previous year, which, in turn, resulted in an increase of tax revenue by RMB 46.34 million.

As indicated in Chapter 5, to overcome possible shortcomings arising from the data from other sources, and to permit the generalizability of the main findings from the interviews of the four tax authorities, a one page semi-structured Questionnaire was sent to eighty Chinese tax authorities, representing a wide cross-section of the Chinese tax system. They included twenty-six provincial (municipal) tax bureaux and fifty-four city (district) tax bureaux located in the urban areas of China but only one of the six Autonomous Regions was selected for inclusion. Compared with the other areas of China, the Autonomous Regions attract few foreign direct investments, Guangxi Province being the exception. International Transfer Pricing is therefore not considered a prominent issue for tax authorities in these regions. For the most part they have no officers in place specifically to deal with International Transfer Pricing.

Summary

The profiles of the respondent companies are featured and elaborated in this chapter. Data on major characteristics such as industry types, sales/total revenue, nationality, and the volume, nature and frequency of intercompany transactions of the respondent companies are presented. The sample firms represented a large variety of industries. A number of the respondent firms reported having a significant amount of intercompany transfers crossing international boundaries. Therefore, International Transfer Pricing may be an important issue for those companies.

This chapter concludes with a survey of International Transfer pricing and the plans and preparations undertaken to investigate the practice of it in three countries of the Pacific Region. The rest of the book reports the findings of the research. The next chapter forms the foundation for this by presenting the trade involved across the respondent subsidiary companies in Australia, New Zealand and China.

7
Pacific Trade Perspectives

Introduction

The entire international trade of the world consists of the reciprocal export and import of goods and services between countries, where to speak of a particular country's trade balance is to indicate the difference between its exports and imports on the basis of one suitable measure or another. A positive trade balance indicates that exports are larger than imports, whereas a negative trade balance indicates that imports are larger than exports (International Monetary Fund, 2003). International trade includes a large portion of transfers between related business firms, giving rise to the phenomenon of International Transfer Pricing.

Australia's trade and foreign direct investment

Table 7.1 shows the level of Australian exports and imports from 1995 to 2002. Following a long period of successive deficits in overseas merchandise trade from 1995 to 2000, Australia recorded two years of trade surplus between 2000–2001 and 2001–2002. As shown, between 2000 and 2002, increases were recorded for both exports and imports. Exports grew from A\$119,539 million to A\$121,176 million and imports increased from A\$118,317 million to A\$119,681 million. The merchandise trade surplus increased from A\$1,222 million in 2000–2001 to A\$1,495 million in 2001–2002.

Tables 7.2 and 7.3 summarise the composition of Australian exports and imports between 1998 and 2002. During that time there was a continuous increase in exports for food and live animals, crude materials, mineral fuel, lubricants, chemicals and related products, and

Table 7.1   Australian Overseas Merchandise Trade (A$ million)

Year	Exports	Imports	Balance of Merchandise Trade
1995–1996	76,005	77,792	–1,787
1996–1997	78,932	78,998	–66
1997–1998	87,768	90,684	–2,916
1998–1999	85,991	97,611	–11,620
1999–2000	97,286	110,078	–12,792
2000–2001	119,539	118,317	1,222
2001–2002	121,176	119,681	1,495

Source: Australian Bureau of Statistics, 2003, p. 912.

Table 7.2   Principal Australian Export Commodities (A$ million year ending 30 June)

Commodities	1998–1999	1999–2000	2000–2001	2001–2002
Food and live animals	15,453	16,892	20,759	21,707
Crude materials (inedible) except fuels	17,219	18,381	23,543	22,443
Mineral fuel, lubricants, etc	14,162	18,083	25,206	25,120
Chemicals and related products	3,575	4,195	5,154	5,362
Basic manufactures	10,117	12,328	14,028	13,557
Machinery and transportation equipment	10,324	11,619	13,439	14,140
Miscellaneous manufactured articles	3,447	3,826	4,481	4,466
Non-monetary gold (excl. gold ores and concentrates)	6,335	5,031	5,110	–
Total (incl. Others)	85,991	97,286	119,539	121,176

Source: The Far East and Australasia: Regional Survey of the World (2004), p. 71.

Table 7.3 Principal Australian Import Commodities (A$ million year ending 30 June)

Commodities	1998–1999	1999–2000	2000–2001	2001–2002
Food and live animals	3,760	3,954	4,236	4,614
Mineral fuel, lubricants, etc	4,621	7,680	10,547	9,033
Chemicals and related products	11,435	12,497	14,197	14,637
Basic manufactures	12,855	13,654	14,051	14,821
Machinery and transportation equipment	45,418	51,442	53,492	53,672
Miscellaneous manufactured articles	14,463	15,479	16,798	17,421
Total (incl. Others)	97,611	110,078	118,317	119,681

Source: The Far East and Australasia: Regional Survey of the World (2004), p. 71.

machinery and transportation equipment. The same trend exists in the imports of food and live animals, chemicals and related products, basic manufactures, machinery and transportation equipment, and miscellaneous manufactured articles.

Australia is a net exporter of food and live animals, mineral fuel and lubricants, and a net importer of chemicals and related products, basic manufactures, machinery and transportation equipment, and miscellaneous manufactured articles. The substantial increase in the export commodity categories are in mineral fuels and lubricants. As shown in Table 7.2, the exports of mineral fuels and lubricants have increased from A$14,162 million in 1998–1999 to A$25,120 million in 2001–2002. Machinery and transportation equipment remained the most important commodity category among Australian imports between 1998 and 2002. In 2001–2002, imports of machinery and transportation equipment amounted to A$53,672 million and accounted for 44.85% of total imports.

Top Eight Trading Partners. Tables 7.4 and 7.5 respectively show the value of exports and imports with Australia's top eight trading partners (*Australian Bureau of Statistics*, 1999, pp. 739–41), 2000 (pp. 785–87), 2001 (pp. 1028–30), 2002 (pp. 837–39), and 2003 (p. 920). In 2001–2002, about 61.90% of exports and 62.39% of imports were with the

Table 7.4   Top Eight Destination Countries for Australian Exports
(A$ million year ending 30 June)

Country	1995–1996	1996–1997	1997–1998	1998–1999	1999–2000	2000–2001	2001–2002
Japan	16,429	15,377	17,582	16,566	18,822	23,495	22,769
United States	4,619	5,526	7,794	7,984	9,602	11,652	11,992
Korea	6,615	7,134	6,397	6,320	7,615	9,206	9,856
China	3,781	3,584	3,872	3,948	4,966	6,841	7,781
New Zealand	5,609	6,214	5,663	5,838	6,739	6,882	7,637
United Kingdom	2,829	2,357	3,040	4,471	4,158	4,653	5,197
Singapore	3,556	3,410	3,697	3,417	4,855	6,009	4,936
Taiwan	3,452	3,620	4,180	4,203	4,696	5,894	4,843
Top Eight countries	46,890	47,222	52,225	52,747	61,453	74,567	75,011
Other countries	29,115	31,710	35,543	33,244	35,833	45,035	46,165
Totals	76,005	78,932	87,768	85,991	97,286	119,539	121,176

Table 7.5   Top Eight Source Countries for Australian Imports (A$ million
year ending 30 June)

Country	1995–1996	1996–1997	1997–1998	1998–1999	1999–2000	2000–2001	2001–2002
United States	17,545	17,642	19,834	20,893	23,135	22,351	21,497
Japan	10,816	10,241	12,660	13,587	14,110	15,370	15,471
China	4,010	4,203	5,303	6,106	7,515	9,881	11,278
Germany	4,862	4,558	5,207	6,082	5,791	6,172	6,732
United Kingdom	4,882	5,182	5,593	5,545	6,350	6,321	6,219
New Zealand	3,591	3,685	3,723	3,950	4,372	4,565	4,740
Korea	2,293	2,550	3,767	3,894	4,311	4,709	4,721
Indonesia	1,522	1,864	2,868	3,275	2,701	3,330	4,007
Top Eight countries	49521	49,925	58,955	63,332	68,285	72,699	74,665
Other countries	28271	29,073	31,729	34,279	41,793	45,618	45,016
Totals	77,792	78,998	90,684	97,611	110,078	118,317	119,681

top eight trading partners. In past decades, the United States and Japan remained the major trading partners of Australia. However, of recent developments, the most significant is the increase of the proportion of its trade with China. From 1995 to 2002, exports to China increased from A$3,781 million to A$7,781 million and imports from China increased from A$4,010 million to A$11,278 million. The Australian trade deficit with China totalled A$3,497 million in 2001–2002. China has become an important source for Australian imports.

Levels of Foreign Direct Investment. Foreign direct investments in the reporting economy are the flows of direct investment capital into the host economy. Direct investments are generally shown with a positive figure, reflecting an increase in net inward investment by non-residents, with a corresponding net payment inflow into the reporting economy. Direct investment includes equity capital, reinvested earnings, other capital, and financial derivatives associated with various intercompany transactions between affiliated enterprises (International Monetary Fund, 2003).

In Australia, a foreign direct investment relationship is established when a direct investor, who is a resident in another country, holds 10% or more of the ordinary shares or voting stock of an enterprise (i.e. direct investment enterprise) in Australia. Table 7.6 shows foreign direct investment in Australia during 1995–2002. It totalled US$15,682 million in 2002, up from US$12,026 million in 1995.

Table 7.6   Levels of Foreign Direct Investment in Australia (US$ million)

	1995	1996	1997	1998	1999	2000	2001	2002
Direct Investment in Australia	12,026	6,181	7,631	6,046	5,385	12,884	4,667	15,682

Source: International Monetary Fund, 2003, p. 44.

New Zealand's trade and foreign direct investment

As a relatively small country, New Zealand's economy is heavily dependent on overseas trade. Table 7.7 presents the level of exports and imports between 1992 and 2001. From 1992 to 1994, and in 2001, New Zealand's balance of trade surplus of NZ$5363 million compared with a deficit of NZ$6977 million for 1995 to 2000.

Tables 7.8 and 7.9 summarise the composition of New Zealand exports and imports between 2000 and 2002. During that time there was a continuous increase in imports of food and live animals, basic

Table 7.7 New Zealand's Overseas Merchandise Trade (NZ$ million)

Year	Exports (fob)	Imports (cif)	Balance of Merchandise Trade
1992	17,840	15,483	2,356
1993	18,971	17,332	1,638
1994	19,827	18,468	1,358
1995	20,790	21,260	–470
1996	20,545	21,352	–806
1997	21,033	21,323	–290
1998	21,990	22,588	–598
1999	22,600	24,248	–1648
2000	26,027	29,193	–3,165
2001	31,938	31,926	11

Notes: Some totals are subject to rounding.
Fob = free on board (the value of goods at New Zealand ports before export, including re-exports).
Cif = cost of goods, including insurance and freight to New Zealand.
Source: Statistics New Zealand, 2002, p. 533.

Table 7.8 New Zealand's Principal Export Commodities (NZ$ million)

Commodities	2000	2001	2002
Food and live animals	12,298.3	14,961.6	13,903.8
Crude materials (inedible) except fuels	4,195.2	4,166.8	4,093.2
Chemicals and related products	2,583.0	3,023.9	2,100.6
Basic manufactures	4,015.8	4,176.7	3,968.2
Machinery and transportation equipment	3,074.0	3,016.0	3,043.3
Miscellaneous manufactured articles	1,204.2	1,387.9	1,438.7
Total (incl. Others)	29,257.1	32,670.0	31,033.7

Source: The Far East and Australasia: Regional Survey of the World, 2004, p. 734.

manufactures, machinery and transportation equipment, and miscellaneous manufactured articles. The same trend existed in the exports only for miscellaneous manufactured articles.

Table 7.9   New Zealand's Principal Import Commodities (NZ$ million)

Commodities	2000	2001	2002
Food and live animals	1,716.3	1,945.1	2,015.2
Mineral fuel, lubricants, etc	2,976.5	2,884.6	2,819.1
Chemicals and related products	3,512.7	3,815.7	3,633.3
Basic manufactures	3,943.1	4,022.5	4,141.3
Machinery and transportation equipment	11,543.9	11,576.4	12,225.7
Miscellaneous manufactured articles	3,962.9	4,099.2	4,180.6
Total (incl. Others)	28,851.1	29,612.3	30,328.6

Source: The Far East and Australasia: Regional Survey of the World, 2004, p. 734.

Table 7.10   Top Ten Destination Countries for New Zealand's Exports (NZ$ million)

Country	Year Ended June 1997	Year Ended June 1998	Year Ended June 1999	Year Ended June 2000	Year Ended June 2001
Australia	4,276	4,578	4,841	5,503	6,083
United States	2,085	2,596	3,005	3,739	4,644
Japan	3,138	3,030	2,878	3,371	4,277
United Kingdom	1,354	1,327	1,401	1,609	1,552
Korea	978	762	883	1,172	1,405
Germany	560	579	623	731	1,114
China	575	613	619	710	847
Hong Kong	511	633	535	644	842
Taiwan	554	564	529	649	722
Belgium	307	470	485	426	520
Top Ten countries	14,338	15,153	15,799	18,554	22,006
Other countries	6,695	6,837	6,801	7,474	9,932
Totals	**21,033**	**21,990**	**22,600**	**26,027**	**31,938**

Note: Exports are valued fob – free on board at New Zealand ports before export, including re-exports.
Source: Statistics New Zealand, 2002, p. 551.

New Zealand was a net exporter of food and live animals, and crude materials (inedible). Machinery and transportation equipment remained the most important commodity category among New Zealand imports

Table 7.11   Top Ten Source Countries for New Zealand's Imports (NZ$ million)

Country	Year Ended June 1997	Year Ended June 1998	Year Ended June 1999	Year Ended June 2000	Year Ended June 2001
Australia	5,080	5,579	5,367	6,843	7,010
United States	3,623	3,974	4,283	5,127	5,298
Japan	2,846	2,539	3,056	3,474	3,427
China	889	1,107	1,234	1,630	2,149
Germany	944	995	1,088	1,182	1,419
United Kingdom	1,133	1,199	1,066	1,161	1,187
Malaysia	396	554	547	717	966
Korea	414	450	525	687	700
Taiwan	579	499	518	627	683
Italy	498	445	504	581	676
Top Ten countries	**16,402**	**17,340**	**18,188**	**22,030**	**23,516**
Other countries	4,921	5,249	6,061	7,163	8,411
Totals	**21,324**	**22,589**	**24,248**	**29,193**	**31,927**

Note: Imports are valued cif – cost including insurance and freight.
Source: Statistics New Zealand, 2002, p. 551.

between 2000 and 2002. In 2002, imports of machinery and transportation equipment amounted to NZ$12,225.7 million, accounting for 40.31% of total imports.

Top Ten Trading Partners. Tables 7.10 and 7.11 show New Zealand's top ten countries for exports and imports. For the year ending June 2001, New Zealand's top ten trading partners received 68.9% of its merchandise exports and supplied 73.7% of its merchandise imports. The single most important trading partner for merchandise exports and imports was Australia, followed by the United States and Japan. In the year ending June 2001 these three countries took 47.0% of New Zealand's merchandise exports and provided 49.3% of its imports.

There were some changes in the order of New Zealand's top markets over the 1998/1999 year. Australia was still the most important trading partner of New Zealand, but during the year ending June 1999 the United States overtook Japan as New Zealand's second largest export market, taking 13.3% of total exports, compared with 11.8% the year before. Japan is followed by the United Kingdom and Korea in fourth

Table 7.12   Levels of Foreign Direct Investment in New Zealand (US$ million)

	1995	1996	1997	1998	1999	2000	2001	2002
Direct investment in New Zealand	3,659	2,231	2,624	1,191	1,412	3,347	1,911	823

Source: International Monetary Fund, 2003, p. 666.

and fifth places respectively. With its strong economic growth, China jumped from ninth to sixth as New Zealand's trading partner (Statistics New Zealand, 1999, 2000).

Levels of Foreign Direct Investment. Table 7.12 shows foreign direct investment in New Zealand in the period 1995–2002. The amount of foreign direct investment in New Zealand has almost steadily declined since 1995. The sharpest decrease of foreign direct investment was in 2002.

China's trade and foreign direct investment

The rapid expansion of foreign investment enterprises has contributed significantly to the increase of the international trade of China. Table 7.13 depicts the trends in exports and imports with the imports and exports by foreign investment enterprises during the period 1990 to 2002. Over this period, China's imports increased from US$53.35 billion to US$295.22 billion, whilst exports increased from US$62.09 billion to US$325.57 billion.

Among the factors promoting both import and export growth, foreign direct investment has played an important part. Foreign investment enterprises have become the major driver behind the expansion of China's exporting and importing activities. During the period 1990 to 2002, the value of imports by foreign investment enterprises increased from US$12.3 billion to US$160.29 billion and the value of exports by foreign investment enterprises increased from US$7.81 billion to US$169.94 billion respectively.

Consequently, the share of foreign investment enterprises in the total imports of China increased from 23.06% in 1990 to 54.29% in 2002 and of exports from 12.58% in 1990 to 52.20% in 2002. The impact of foreign direct investment on the trade balance of China has been of major importance. As shown in Table 7.13, except for the year 1993, as shaded, when the major cause of a trade deficit was a more than 50% surge in imports by foreign investment enterprises (Chan and Chow, 1998, p. 20), China enjoyed a long period of trade surplus.

Table 7.13 Trends in Total Exports and Imports and the Imports and Exports of Foreign Investment Enterprises in China, 1990–2002 (US$ billion)

Year	Exports (National Total)	Exports by Foreign Investment Enterprises	Percentage	Imports (National Total)	Imports by Foreign Investment Enterprises	Percentage	Balance of Trade
1990	62.09	7.81	12.58	53.35	12.30	23.06	8.74
1991	71.91	12.05	16.75	63.79	16.91	26.51	8.12
1992	84.94	17.36	20.44	80.59	26.39	32.74	4.35
1993	91.74	25.24	27.51	103.96	41.83	40.24	−12.22
1994	121.01	34.71	28.69	115.62	52.94	45.78	5.39
1995	148.77	46.88	31.51	132.08	62.94	47.66	16.69
1996	151.07	61.51	40.71	138.84	75.60	54.45	12.23
1997	182.70	74.90	41.00	142.36	77.72	54.59	40.34
1998	183.75	80.96	44.06	140.17	76.72	54.73	43.58
1999	194.93	88.63	45.47	165.72	85.88	51.83	29.21
2000	249.20	119.44	47.93	225.09	117.27	52.10	24.11
2001	266.16	133.24	50.10	243.61	125.86	51.70	22.55
2002	325.57	169.94	52.20	295.22	160.29	54.29	30.35

Source: Ministry of Commerce of the People's Republic of China, 2004b.

On the side of foreign investment enterprises, over the period 1990 to 1997, the imports of foreign investment enterprises constantly exceeded their exports. Since 1998, however, the situation has been reversed, the exports of foreign investment enterprises having exceeded their imports. In conclusion, foreign direct investment has greatly increased the volume of Chinese overseas trade.

Table 7.14 depicts the gross industrial output value of foreign investment enterprises as a proportion of national gross industrial output value in the period 1990–2002. The gross industrial output value is the total volume of industrial products sold or available for sale in value terms which reflect the total achievements and overall scale of industrial production during a given period. Gross industrial output value is a main economic indicator (National Bureau of Statistics, 2002, p. 485).

Table 7.14   Industrial Output Value of Foreign Investment Enterprises as a Proportion of National Gross Industrial Output Value in China, 1990–2002 (RMB billion)

Year	National Total	Foreign Investment Enterprises	Percentage
1990	1970.10	44.90	2.28
1991	2313.56	122.33	5.29
1992	2914.93	206.56	7.09
1993	4051.37	370.44	9.15
1994	7686.73	864.94	11.26
1995	9196.33	1315.42	14.31
1996	9959.56	1507.75	15.14
1997	5614.97	1042.70	18.57
1998	5819.52	1416.20	24.00
1999	6377.52	1769.60	27.75
2000	7396.49	2314.56	22.51
2001	9475.18	2651.57	28.05
2002	10119.87	3377.11	33.37

Source: Ministry of Commerce of the People's Republic of China, 2004c.

It can be seen that, during the years 1990 to 2002 the gross industrial output value of foreign investment enterprises increased from US$44.90 billion to US$3,377.11 billion. Accordingly, the gross industrial output value of foreign investment enterprises as a proportion of national gross industrial output value has been considerably increased from 2.28% to 33.37%.

Major Trading Partners. Tables 7.15 and 7.16 show China's major trading partners. The United States, Hong Kong and Japan are China's most important export markets. In 2001, they took 54.8% of China's total merchandise exports. Japan is the largest source of imports to China, followed by Taiwan, the United States and Korea.

Tables 7.17 and 7.18 summarise the composition of Chinese exports and imports between 1998 and 2002. During that period there was a steady increase in exports of chemicals and related products, basic manufactures, machinery and transportation equipment, and miscellaneous manufactured articles. The same trend existed for the imports of crude materials, chemicals and related products, basic manufactures, machinery and transportation equipment, and miscellaneous

Table 7.15   China's Principal Trading Partners – Exports (US$ million)

Exports	1999	2000	2001
United States	41,946.9	52,099.2	54,282.7
Hong Kong	36,862.8	44,518.3	46,546.6
Japan	32,410.6	41,654.3	44,957.6
Korea	7,807.6	11,292.4	12,520.7
Germany	7,779.6	9,277.8	9,754.1
Netherlands	5,413.0	6,687.2	7,282.0
United Kingdom	4,880.0	6,310.1	6,780.5
Singapore	4,502.2	5,761.0	5,791.9
Taiwan	3,949.9	5,039.0	5,000.2
Italy	2,929.5	3,802.0	3,992.6
France	2,921.1	3,705.2	3,685.7
Australia	2,704.4	3,428.9	3,570.4
Canada	2,433.0	3,157.8	3,346.1
Malaysia	1,673.8	2,564.9	3,220.3
Indonesia	1,779.1	3,061.8	2,836.5
Russia	1,497.3	2,233.4	2,711.2
Total (incl. Others)	194,930.9	249,202.6	266,154.6

Source: The Far East and Australasia: Regional Survey of the World, 2004.

manufactured articles. China was a net exporter of food and live animals, basic manufactures, and miscellaneous manufactured articles, and a net importer of mineral fuel, chemicals and related products, and machinery and transportation equipment.

A substantial increase in the export commodity categories has taken place for machinery and transportation equipment, and miscellaneous manufactured articles. As shown in Table 7.17, the exports of machinery and transportation equipment increased from US$50,143 million in 1998 to US$126,983 million in 2002. Machinery and transportation equipment remained the most important commodity category among Chinese imports from 1998 to 2002. In 2002, imports of machinery and transportation equipment amounted to US$137,034 million and accounted for 46.42% of total imports.

The Levels of Foreign Direct Investment. In the past decade, the rapid economic growth in China has been accompanied by a large inflow of foreign direct investment. China has long been the largest single recipient of foreign direct investment among the developing

Table 7.16 China's Principal Trading Partners – Imports (US\$ million)

Exports	1999	2000	2001
Japan	33,763.4	41,509.7	42,796.9
Taiwan	19,526.8	25,493.6	27,339.5
United States	19,478.3	22,363.2	26,202.2
Korea	17,226.2	23,207.4	23,389.2
Germany	8,335.4	10,408.7	13,772.1
Hong Kong	6,891.9	9,429.0	9,423.0
Russia	4,222.6	5,769.9	7,959.4
Malaysia	3,605.6	5,480.0	6,205.2
Australia	3,607.2	5,024.0	5,426.4
Singapore	4,061.1	5,059.6	5,142.5
Thailand	2,780.4	4,380.8	4,712.9
France	3,784.8	3,949.8	4,104.8
Canada	2,433.0	3,751.1	4,028.5
Indonesia	3,050.9	4,402.0	3,888.1
Italy	2,679.9	3,078.4	3,789.2
United Kingdom	2,994.8	3,592.5	3,527.1
Finland	18,31.9	2,353.1	2,376.3
Brazil	968.6	1,621.4	2,347.3
Sweden	2,151.8	2,674.7	2,173.2
Oman	635.4	3,261.8	1,609.6
Total (incl. Others)	165,699.1	225,093.7	243,613.5

Source: The Far East and Australasia: Regional Survey of the World, 2004.

countries and the second largest recipient of foreign direct investment in the world during the period 1993 to 2001, behind the United States (Chan and Chow 1997a,b; 1998). With its strong economic growth, the amount of foreign direct investment in China jumped to US\$52.74 billion in 2002. Since then, China has finally overtaken the United States as the world's largest recipient of foreign direct investment. The cumulative total by 2002 was US\$447.9 billion.

As shown in Table 7.19, over the last decade (1990–2002), foreign direct investment has dramatically increased in China. The number of foreign direct investment projects increased from 7,273 in 1990 to 34,171 in 2002. The contractual value of foreign direct investment projects increased from US\$6.596 billion in 1990 to US\$82.768 billion in

Table 7.17   Principal Chinese Export Commodities (US$ million)

Commodities	1998	1999	2000	2002
Food and live animals	10,599.5	10,447.0	12,270.8	14,623
Mineral fuel, lubricants, etc	5,178.7	4,662.4	7,862.3	8,372
Chemicals and related products	10,205.9	10,230.0	11,917.5	15,329
Basic manufactures	33,067.6	33,858.9	43,305.0	52,957
Machinery and transport equipment	50,143.0	58,748.6	82,443.7	126,983
Miscellaneous manufactured articles	69,585.8	72,000.7	85,582.8	101,168
Total (incl. Others)	183,809.1	194,930.9	249,202.6	325,566

Source: The Far East and Australasia: Regional Survey of the World, 2004, p. 203.

Table 7.18   Principal Chinese Import Commodities (US$ million)

Commodities	1998	1999	2000	2002
Food and live animals	3,763.2	3,590.4	4,742.3	5,237
Crude materials (inedible) except fuels	10,536.1	12,526.9	19,685.8	22,737
Mineral fuel, lubricants, etc	6,834.6	8,994.7	20,756.6	19,285
Chemicals and related products	19,907.2	23,693.3	29,768.7	39,040
Basic manufactures	31,616.2	34,876.5	42,493.0	48,492
Machinery and transport equipment	56,774.7	69,404.1	91,866.0	137,034
Miscellaneous manufactured articles	8,348.6	9,632.8	12,699.8	19,801
Total (incl. Others)	140,236.8	165,699.1	225,093.7	295,202

Source: The Far East and Australasia: Regional Survey of the World, 2004, p. 203.

2002. The realised value of all foreign direct investment projects increased from US$3.487 billion in 1990 to US$52.743 billion in 2002.

The Form of Foreign Direct Investment. The Chinese government allows foreign investment enterprises to operate in China in the form of joint ventures or wholly foreign-owned enterprises. Three types of

Table 7.19   Foreign Direct Investment in China, 1990–2002 (US$ billion)

Year	Number of Projects	Contractual Value	Realised Value
1990	7273	6.596	3.487
1991	12978	11.977	4.366
1992	48764	58.124	11.008
1993	83437	111.436	27.515
1994	47549	82.680	33.767
1995	37011	91.282	37.521
1996	24556	73.236	41.726
1997	21001	51.003	45.257
1998	19799	52.102	45.463
1999	16918	41.223	40.319
2000	22347	62.380	40.715
2001	26140	69.195	46.878
2002	34171	82.768	52.743

Source: Ministry of Commerce of the People's Republic of China, 2004d.

Table 7.20   Forms of Foreign Direct Investment until December 2002 (US$ billion)

Firms	Number of Projects	Percentage	Contractual Value	Percentage	Realized Value	Percentage
EJV	225883	53.25	327.55	39.56	192.20	42.91
CJV	52965	12.49	163.32	19.72	82.78	18.48
WFOE	145165	34.22	332.54	40.16	165.62	36.97
CJD	183	0.04	4.65	0.56	7.36	1.64
Total	424196	100.00	828.06	100.00	447.97	100.00

Note: EJV = Equity Joint Venture. CJV = Cooperative Joint Venture. WFOE = Wholly Foreign-Owned Enterprise. CJD = Cooperative Joint Development.

Source: Ministry of Commerce of the People's Republic of China, 2004e.

joint ventures are in operation, namely, Equity Joint Venture, Cooperative Joint Venture and Cooperative Joint Development. As shown in Table 7.20, Equity Joint Venture (42.91%) has been the most popular form of foreign direct investment.

The Sources of Foreign Direct Investment. Table 7.21 shows the extent of foreign direct investment in China from the top fifteen countries or regions at the end of 2002. The largest source of foreign direct investment is Hong Kong, accounting for 45.73% of accumulated foreign direct investment during 1979–2002, followed by the United

Table 7.21   Foreign Direct Investment from the Top Fifteen Countries/ Regions Until December 2002 (US$ billion)

Country/ Regions	Number of Projects	Percentage	Contractual Value	Percentage	Realised Value	Percentage
Hong Kong	210876	49.71	373.80600	45.14	204.87523	45.73
United States	37280	8.79	76.28190	9.21	39.88943	8.90
Japan	25147	5.93	49.53212	5.98	36.33986	8.11
Taiwan	55691	13.13	61.47086	7.42	33.11028	7.39
Virgin Islands	6659	1.57	49.34803	5.96	24.38765	5.44
Singapore	10727	2.53	40.14955	4.85	21.47270	4.79
Korea	22208	5.24	27.47593	3.32	15.19896	3.39
United Kingdom	3418	0.81	19.63261	2.37	10.69550	2.39
Germany	3053	0.72	14.32209	1.73	7.99367	1.78
France	2033	0.48	7.19215	0.87	5.54335	1.24
Macao	7827	1.85	10.79181	1.3	4.77322	1.07
Netherlands	1065	0.25	8.97448	1.08	4.33815	0.97
Cayman Islands	706	0.17	9.48071	1.14	3.80333	0.85
Canada	6040	1.42	10.37740	1.25	3.35789	0.75
Malaysia	2538	0.60	6.20053	0.75	2.83544	0.63
Others	28928	6.82	63.02364	7.61	29.35131	6.55
Total	424196	100.00	828.05981	100.00	447.96597	100.00

Source: Ministry of Commerce of the People's Republic of China, 2004f.

States (8.90%), Japan (8.11%), Taiwan (7.39%), Virgin Islands (5.44%), Singapore (4.79%), and Korea (3.39%). These seven countries/regions together make up 83.75% of the total.

Summary

In the significantly globalised economy of the present age it may be seen that multinational enterprises are a dominant feature of it and account for a substantial portion of world trade. In conducting their business interchanges, they are faced with environmental factors which variably affect the transfers of assets for business purposes and may inflict high transaction costs on the intercompany transfers of goods and services. In response to market imperfections in the host countries, multinational enterprises may create their own internal markets through the exercise of International Transfer Pricing strategies to overcome such transaction costs. Host countries are then obliged to adopt countermeasures to ensure that multinational enterprises do not thereby escape their just tax liabilities.

This chapter has reviewed and analysed the archival data relating to overseas merchandise trading and foreign direct investment of each of the three research countries. This information has a significant bearing on the International Transfer Pricing practices of Australian, New Zealand and Chinese subsidiaries of multinational enterprises.

The next chapter presents the regulations and guidelines operating in each of the three countries, within which the trading presented in this chapter has had to be conducted, and within which existing and new foreign subsidiaries must come to terms as a working environment for future trading.

8
National Legislation

Introduction

National governmental controls of International Transfer Pricing practices adopted by multinational companies are greatly influenced by the provisions developed and promulgated by the OECD and the United States of America. An overview of both of these latter sets of legislation has been presented in Chapter 3.

Whilst there are differences between the regulations which these two bodies have respectively enacted, the main characteristics of both are similar in their intent to prevent the use of International Transfer Pricing for avoiding taxation liabilities in host countries.

Host countries have therefore been keen to reflect the main tenets of these two sets of regulations as in turn they develop their own national provisions for dealing with the problem in their own countries. These vary in the detail, reflecting the particular conditions and attitudes of the host country concerned, as may be seen in the following presentation of the regulatory provisions which currently apply in Australia, New Zealand and China.

Australian practice

Transfer pricing legislation in Australia follows United States legislation, such as the Section 482 regulations and the Section 6662 transfer pricing penalty regulations of the United States Internal Revenue Code. In addition, it fully endorses the OECD definition of acceptable transfer pricing methodologies. The central purpose underlying Australian transfer pricing legislation is to ensure that the Australian tax base is not eroded by international profit-shifting arrangements.

The Australian Taxation Office has established a comprehensive structure for dealing with related party transfer pricing issues. The Australian statutory rules on transfer pricing are contained in Section 136 of Division 13, in Part III of the *Income Tax Assessment Act* 1936 (ITAA).

The Australian Taxation Office has also issued various taxation rulings concerning transfer pricing. They include Rulings

- TR 92/11
- TR 94/14 (Transfer Pricing)
- TR 95/23 (Advance Pricing Agreement)
- TR 97/20 (Methodologies)
- TR 98/11 (Documentation)
- TR 98/16 (Penalties)
- TR 99/1 (Services)
- TR 99/8 (Australian Taxation Office Adjustments)
- TR 2000/16
- TR 2001/11
- TR 2002/5
- TR 2002/2
- TR 2004/1

These rulings provide guidance with respect to acceptable methodologies, documentation requirements, potential penalties for taxpayers who do not comply with transfer pricing requirements in their international dealings with related parties, relief from double taxation, and advance pricing agreements. The main features of the Australian transfer pricing regime are presented as follows (Campos 1996; Coopers and Lybrand, 1997; Harrison and Glyn-Jones, 1999, p. 14; Clews and Howe, 2001).

Relationship Tests. The test level of common ownership required is not specified by the Australian Taxation Office. This is a significant difference between the Australian and the New Zealand transfer pricing legislation. The New Zealand legislation specifies that the relationship test of associated parties is the existence of ownership of 50% or more. In contrast, the Australian relationship test is based on determining whether the consideration in any transaction between two parties is of arm's length in nature. Therefore, dealings between seemingly unrelated parties in the view of the New Zealand Inland Revenue Department may be caught out by Australian rules. As such, Australian taxpayers are under a burden to confirm that the involved price is of arm's length in nature.

Acceptable Methodologies. The Australian Taxation Office permits the use of the traditional transaction based methods, such as, on the one hand, the comparable uncontrolled price method, the resale price method, and the cost plus method, and on the other hand, the profit based methods, such as the profit split method and the transactional net margin method. These are consistent with the OECD Guidelines on transfer pricing methodologies. However, the Australian regulations do not prescribe any hierarchy or order of preference for applying the various methods. The Australian Taxation Office expects taxpayers to use the method that is 'most appropriate' or 'best suited' to their facts and circumstances. That is, where there is an insufficiency of data, or the existing methods cannot be used, the Australian Taxation Office allows taxpayers to use 'novel' or 'hybrid' methods, provided that these methods can produce a suitable comparable result. Hybrid methods are those methodologies that may be necessary in cases in which the application of more than one method is needed to increase the reliability of the taxpayer's results.

In the survey, the respondent companies were asked to select one or more method(s) used in calculating and adjusting the value of transactions with their related parties outside their local operations for tax purposes. The responses of the sixty Australian companies are shown in Table 8.1.

Table 8.1   Legally Oriented International Transfer Pricing Methods Used by Australian Respondent Companies

	Australia	
Pricing Methods	**No. of Firms**	**%**
Cost plus method	33	46.5
Comparable uncontrolled price	12	16.9
Resale price	10	14.1
Profit split	3	4.2
Comparable profit method (CPM)	1	1.4
The transactional net margin method (TNMM)	12	16.9
Total	71*	100.00

Note: * Some firms used more than one International Transfer Pricing method.
CPM and TNMM may be used interchangeably in practice.

Nineteen companies use more than one International Transfer Pricing method. The three most frequently used International Transfer Pricing methods are cost plus method, comparable uncontrolled price, and the transactional net margin method, which together account for 80.3% of the respondent companies. Ten companies use the resale price method. Three companies use profit split method and one company uses comparable profit method.

Burden of Proof. The Australian Taxation Office imposes the burden of proof upon the taxpayers. The taxpayers are required to demonstrate that their pricing practices equate with the norm of the arm's length pricing. To reduce the risks of disputes with the Australian Commissioner, multinational firms must prepare and retain sufficient documentation as evidence that their transactions with affiliates satisfy the arm's length standards.

Contemporaneous Documentation. The Australian tax regime requires taxpayers to prepare and maintain documentation to demonstrate that the amounts charged in related party transactions are consistent with the arm's length standard. In addition to the ordinary documentation requirements, such as regular books and records and contractual agreements, the Australian Taxation Office also requires taxpayers to create and retain contemporaneous documentation which details pricing methodologies adopted and indicates why a particular method is most appropriate to determine an arm's length price. The contemporaneous documentation requirements are a substantial administrative and operational burden for multinationals in relation to the justification and documentation of international transactions.

The Australian Taxation Office has placed great emphasis upon the value of contemporaneous documentation in demonstrating that two related companies are, in fact, dealing at arm's length. The documentation can be used to justify the use of a method to price cross-border transfers and thus prevent the Australian Commissioner from using his or her power to deem an amount to be arm's length in nature. For a multinational subsidiary operating in Australia, if it wishes to avoid disputes with the Australian Taxation Office on intercompany charges, and if it wishes to avoid double taxation of income, contemporaneous documentation is imperative.

Penalties. Both the Australian and the New Zealand transfer pricing rules emphasise that their tax authorities need to be able to collect a fair share of tax with respect to international transfers. Consequently, the two tax jurisdictions restrict the application of their transfer pricing penalty regimes to transactions that have the effect of depleting their tax bases.

In comparing the two transfer pricing penalty regimes, however, it appears that Australia has adopted the more rigorous approach. In Australia, a non-deductible penalty of 25% of the tax shortfall plus deductible interest will be payable where there is no dominant tax avoidance purpose. In the situation where profit shifting involves a dominant tax avoidance purpose, the relevant penalty will be 50% of the tax shortfall. If certain culpable behaviour has occurred, this penalty may be as high as 90%. If, however, the taxpayer has a reasonably arguable position, as, for example, when the taxpayer's transfer pricing policy is well documented, then the penalty will be reduced to 10% of the tax shortfall.

Advance Pricing Agreements. An advance pricing agreement is a binding legal agreement between the taxpayer and the tax authority. The advance pricing agreement programme provides an important mechanism for taxpayers to obtain certainty that their transfer pricing policies and procedures meet the requirements of the arm's length standard. In June 1995, the Australian Taxation Office released a taxation ruling (TR 95/23) containing guidelines on the advance pricing agreement process. Taxation Ruling 95/23 sets out the factors that will be considered by the Australian Taxation Office in deciding whether to accept an application for an advance pricing agreement, including whether the taxpayer is seeking a bilateral advance pricing agreement and whether the other country involved is a tax treaty partner.

There is a formal application process for an advance pricing agreement in Australia. To initiate the process, a taxpayer must apply to the Australian Taxation Office for a pre-lodgement meeting to discuss the requirements of the proposed advance pricing agreement. Where an advance pricing agreement is considered appropriate, the taxpayer will then be required to lodge a formal application providing details of the following.

- The proposed methodologies
- The documentation supporting the chosen methodologies
- The terms and conditions which govern the advance pricing agreement
- The duration of the advance pricing agreement (Rolfe, 1997).

New Zealand practice

The current New Zealand transfer pricing rules are contained in Sections GD 13, FB 2 and GC 1 of the *Income Tax Act* 1994. The rules are intended to prevent the erosion of the New Zealand tax base by the blatant shifting of income out of the country without a tax liability. The main transfer pricing rule – Section GD 13 – generally only applies to cross-border associated transactions between separate entities which have the potential effect of depleting the New Zealand tax base. Section FB 2 stipulates the use of an arm's length basis to apportion income within a single legal entity such as an overseas head office and its New Zealand branch. In some circumstances, arrangements may occur where the parties are not technically associated. To ensure that the regime is effective, a specific anti-avoidance provision is incorporated in Section GC 1 to deal with certain non-arm's length transactions which are entered into by a taxpayer subject to GD 13, but have the purpose or effect of avoiding the application of GD 13 (Harrison and Glyn-Jones, 1999).

The New Zealand transfer pricing regime applies to income derived in the income year 1996/1997 and all subsequent years. The regime focuses on cross-border transactions between associated parties which may result in a loss of New Zealand tax revenue. The scope of the current regime under Section GD 13 includes the following.

- the supply or acquisition of goods, services, money, other intangible property, or anything else
- the supplier and acquirer who are associated persons – essentially, any two companies with 50% or more common ownership
- arrangements which are cross-border in character
- arrangements on terms other than that of arm's length
- arrangements with the potential to deplete the New Zealand tax base.

Arrangements which do not fall within the transfer pricing rule in Section GD 13 may be subject to the anti-avoidance provisions in Section GC 1 or the head office/branch structure provisions for a single legal entity in Section FB 2.

The main features of the New Zealand regime are presented as follows (Harrison and Glyn-Jones, 1999; Clews and Howe, 2001).

Associated Persons. Section GD 13 applies only to transactions between associated persons. Associated persons is a term defined as companies with common ownership of 50% or more. Common examples of associated persons include the following.

- New Zealand parent companies and their overseas subsidiaries
- Foreign shareholders – both individuals and companies – of New Zealand companies, where the shareholders own more than 50% of the shares

- New Zealand companies and overseas sister subsidiaries
- New Zealand resident settlers of foreign trusts.

The Arm's Length Principle and Acceptable Methods. The basic principle underlying the regime is that the arm's length standard should be adopted as being the overriding benchmark for determining transfer prices between related parties. That is, the transfer price adopted by the related parties must be compared with the price adopted by independent parties operating on the open market. Following the methods contained in the OECD Guidelines, the New Zealand's Guidelines, Section GD 13(7), prescribe five different methods as an acceptable range for transfer pricing, from which the taxpayer can make his choice for calculating the arm's length price. These pricing methodologies can be categorised as either transaction based or profit based methods, where the transaction based methods consist of the comparable uncontrolled price method, the resale price method, and the cost plus method, whilst the profit methods consist of the profit split method and the comparable profit method.

The legislation does not impose a hierarchy of preference for transfer pricing methods. However, in the selection of a pricing method, a taxpayer must select a certain method that may provide the most reliable measure of an arm's length amount. This provides a multinational with opportunities for selecting methods more appropriate for their circumstances. In practice, the availability of comparable data often determines which method can be used. Given the small size of the New Zealand market, reliable comparables are difficult to locate in the New Zealand market itself. The Inland Revenue, therefore, allows overseas comparables in foreign markets, such as the United States and Australia, to be used in the taxpayer's transfer pricing analysis.

In the survey, the responses of the seventy-seven New Zealand companies are shown in Table 8.2.

Eleven companies use more than one International Transfer Pricing method. As shown in Table 8.2, the two most frequently used International Transfer Pricing methods used by the New Zealand companies are cost plus method and comparable uncontrolled price, which together account for 65.1% of the respondent companies. Resale price method, profit split method, and comparable profit method, are each used by nine firms. One company uses the transactional net margin method. Two companies are using other methods – agreed price, and contract manufacturer approach – not specified by the Inland Revenue Department.

Table 8.2 Legally Oriented International Transfer Pricing Methods Used by New Zealand Respondent Companies

	New Zealand	
Pricing Methods	**No. of Firms**	**%**
Cost plus method	42	48.8
Comparable uncontrolled price	14	16.3
Resale price	9	10.5
Profit split	9	10.5
Comparable profit method (CPM)	9	10.5
The transactional net margin method (TNMM)	1	1.2
Others	2*	2.3
Total	86**	100***

Note: * Other pricing methods included 'agreed price', and 'contract manufacturer approach'.
** Some firms used more than one International Transfer Pricing method.
*** Percentage totals subject to rounding.
CPM and TNMM may be used interchangeably in practice.

Burden of Proof. Section GD 13 (9) prescribes that the onus is on the taxpayer to determine an arm's length amount. In this regard, the regime is consistent with the principles contained in the 1995 OECD Guidelines and transfer pricing rules of other tax jurisdictions. However, unlike the regulations of its major trading partners, which explicitly require taxpayers to prepare and maintain transfer pricing documentation to support the method and calculations used to set transfer prices, the Inland Revenue Department puts the onus on the Commissioner to show that the transaction price used by the taxpayer is not of an arm's length consideration. Thus, the burden of proof lies with the Commissioner. If the Commissioner chooses to dispute that the price determined by the taxpayer is at arm's length, the Commissioner must be able to prove that either

- another price provides a more reliable measure of an arm's length amount, or
- that the taxpayer is not co-operating with the Commissioner in the administration of the regime.

Documentation and Penalties. Section GD 13 requires taxpayers to determine their transfer prices in accordance with the arm's length principle. As a practical matter, it would be necessary for taxpayers to prepare and retain sufficient documentation to show

- how their transfer prices have been determined, and
- why these prices are considered to be consistent with the arm's length principle.

Documentation requirements include a functional analysis of the parties, which describes the duties performed, assets used and risks assumed by the business in its transactions with related parties, and the justification for selecting the pricing methodologies actually chosen.

The transfer pricing regime does not have any special penalty provisions. Rather, it is subject to the general penalty provisions applicable to income tax issues. With regard to a taxpayer's transfer pricing arrangements, the taxpayer is likely to be required to demonstrate that the most reliable method has been selected and applied in an appropriate manner. A taxpayer who fails to document transfer pricing arrangements appropriately may incur a minimum penalty of 20% under Section 141C of the Tax Administration Act 1994 for not exercising 'reasonable care'.

In addition, depending on the size and sophistication of a taxpayer, the absence of documentation in the determination of an arm's length amount makes the taxpayer vulnerable to the 40% penalty under Section 141C, on the basis that the taxpayer has been 'grossly careless'. Since these penalties are non-deductible for income tax to the taxpayer, they represent a significant potential cost. To avoid such a penalty, the taxpayer must maintain a sufficient level of supporting documentation to meet the requirements of the transfer pricing regime (Coopers and Lybrand, 1997; Rich and Harrison, 1997; Clews and Howe, 2001).

Advance Pricing Agreements. The New Zealand regime has issued binding advance pricing agreements dealing with the application of the arm's length standard to intercompany transfer prices. An advance pricing agreement is issued as either a private binding ruling by the Commissioner under Section 91E of the Tax Administration Act 1994, or under the Mutual Agreement article of the applicable double taxation agreement (Coopers and Lybrand, 1997; *New Zealand Transfer Pricing Guidelines*, 2000).

Some Specific Transfer Pricing Issues. The arm's length principle underpins the New Zealand transfer pricing rules. Theoretically, the price of an associated party transaction can be demonstrated as arm's length by means of one or more of the prescribed methods in Section GD 13(7).

In practice, however, the establishment of an arm's length price is not a simple matter. The use of the pricing methods is subject to the availability of comparable information. Owing to the lack of third party comparable data in the New Zealand marketplace, however, difficulties may arise for a taxpayer in trying to develop an arm's length price or to demonstrate to the Inland Revenue that his pricing policy is arm's length. Furthermore, in the instance that the goods and services transferred within the members of a multinational group are unique, arm's length prices may not exist. This is particularly the case with the transfer of intangible property, the provision and receipt of intercompany services and cost contribution arrangements.

The Inland Revenue Department acknowledges the difficulties in determining an arm's length price for intercompany services and intangibles, and has adopted pragmatic and flexible ways for dealing with these issues. For example, it allows the establishment of an optional safe harbour for intercompany services to help to reduce a taxpayer's compliance costs. However, to date, it appears that the practical difficulties in the treatment of intangible property, intercompany services and cost contribution arrangements have not yet been resolved (*New Zealand Transfer Pricing Guidelines*, 2000; Hoare and Hainsworth, 2000).

Chinese practice

China is a latecomer to the International Transfer Pricing arena. In 1979 China started a policy of economic intercourse with the rest of the world. In the early years of this policy, International Transfer Pricing was not a significant concern to the Chinese government because its energies were mainly focused on attracting foreign investment and also because China lacked an institutional framework to deal with the issues involved in the country.

Since then, however, China's enormous market potential and cheap labour costs, along with a series of preferential tax policies for foreign investors, have combined to encourage large numbers of foreign investment enterprises to embark on investment opportunities in China. The wide range of related party transactions typically engaged in by foreign investment enterprises with overseas affiliated companies, along with the fact that more than half of the foreign investment enterprises reported an operating loss in the 1980s, have in turn combined to imply that the potential for transfer pricing manipulations in China has been immense.

As a result, since the late 1980s the Chinese government has noted the phenomenon and has taken steps to combat tax avoidance through the use of transfer pricing abuses by foreign investment enterprises in China. In November 1990, the State Administration of Taxation issued a set of provisional rules regarding the administration of taxation for transactions between foreign investment enterprises and their associated enterprises. These rules set forth general guidelines on the transfer prices of these transactions and provided the basis for subsequent legislation.

The Chinese transfer pricing legislation was first introduced in 1991 by the National People's Congress under the Income Tax Law for foreign investment enterprises. The transfer pricing legislation – Article 13 of the Income Tax Law of the People's Republic of China for Enterprises with Foreign Investment and Foreign Enterprises (Tax Law) – adopts the arm's length principle, which stipulates that the prices charged or paid in business dealings between the establishments of foreign investment enterprises within China and their associated enterprises should be the same as the prices charged or paid in comparable uncontrolled transactions between independent, unrelated enterprises. Under Article 13 of the Tax Law, if the transactions are not carried out at arm's length and thus result in a reduction of taxable income, the tax authorities have the right to make reasonable adjustments (Chan and Chow, 1997a; Huang and Yu, 1997).

Article 13 of the Tax Law is further supplemented by Articles 52 to 58 of the Detailed Implementing Rules of the Tax Law (DRR). This Tax Law has been in force since 1 July 1991, and the Implementing Rules (DRR) since 30 June 1991 (Huang and Yu, 1997).

On 23 April 1998, the State Administration of Taxation issued comprehensive transfer pricing regulations entitled *Tax Administrative Rules and Procedures for Transactions between Related Parties* (State Administration of Taxation Circular No. 59). This Circular contains fifty-two articles aimed at setting criteria for selecting tax examination targets, standardising transfer pricing examination procedures, and strengthening internal co-ordination among the local tax bureaux and the State Administration of Taxation (Guo, 2000). These regulations were reflected in the Tax Administration Law (2001) and its Detailed Implementation Rules (2002).

The regulations explicitly indicate that, in addition to providing an attractive investment environment for foreign investors, the Chinese government also intends to secure its fair share of tax revenue from multinational enterprises undertaking business in the country (Guo, 2000).

Unlike other countries' transfer pricing regulations which focus on corporate income tax, the Chinese transfer pricing regulations might be applicable not only to income tax, but also to other taxes, such as value-added tax (VAT), consumption tax, and business tax. Additionally, as a result of China's tax sharing system, not only cross-border transactions but also domestic transactions conducted between associated enterprises are targets for transfer pricing examination – transaction it appears that the Chinese transfer pricing audits have focused mainly on cross-border transactions (Rolfe, 1997; Guo, 2000).

Associated Enterprises. As with transfer pricing rules in other jurisdictions, the Chinese transfer pricing rules only apply to transactions that are conducted between or among related parties or controlled parties. A foreign enterprise and another company, enterprise or organisation will be considered as associated in the following circumstances.

- Where an enterprise directly or indirectly owns 25% or more of another enterprise
- Where two enterprises are directly or indirectly owned by a third enterprise with 25% or more capital interest
- Where an enterprise borrows more than 50% of its loans from another enterprise, or where an enterprise guarantees 10% or more of the loans of another enterprise
- Where one of the managing directors is, or half or more of the board of directors or the executive managers of an enterprise are, appointed by another enterprise
- Where an enterprise's production can only be operated with the provision of proprietary technology owned by another enterprise
- Where the provision of raw materials, parts, and semi-finished goods used by an enterprise in production are supplied or controlled by another enterprise
- Where the sales of the commodities of an enterprise are controlled by another enterprise
- Where the production, trading activities and profits of an enterprise are effectively controlled by another enterprise having mutual benefits, such as the existence of family relationships.

Transfer Pricing Methods Used. As with the approaches to transfer pricing by both the OECD and the United States, the Chinese current transfer pricing regulations endorse and support the arm's length principle as the best approach to address transfer pricing issues. According to the rules, tangible assets must be priced on a transaction basis, using one of three methodologies as follows.

1. The comparable uncontrolled price method as with the price of the same or similar business activities between unrelated enterprises. When applying the comparable uncontrolled price method, transactions between related parties and unrelated parties should be comparable in areas of consideration, for example, as
   - transaction terms – such as the date and place that transactions are conducted, delivery terms and procedures, volumes, and warranties
   - transaction levels – whether the transactions are conducted with manufacturers, distributors, retailers, or exporters
   - product similarity – types of product, brand name, specifications, performance, shape, structure and packaging; and similarity in environment – social, political, and economic environments.

2. The resale price method – the profit level obtainable from resale to unrelated third parties.
3. The cost plus method – the cost plus reasonable expenses and a profit margin. Defined as costs and expenses plus reasonable profits, the cost plus mark-up method is the transfer pricing method most popular with the Chinese tax authorities.

Owing to the lack of reliable public data in China, the tax authorities probably also consider other methods for price transactions as being appropriate. They are profit based methodologies, such as the comparable profit method, profit split method, transactional net margin method, and deemed profit method. It should be noted that the circumstances under which these methods could be applied were not addressed in the regulations.

As for transactions involving intercompany provisions of services, loans and the transfer of other assets, no particular methods are stipulated in determining their arm's length results. Arm's length prices under such circumstances are broadly referred to as any payments or receipts that a third party would agree to for the same kind of transaction (Guo, 2000).

The transfer pricing methods used by the forty-seven Chinese companies, as reported in the survey, are shown in Table 8.3.

Twelve companies use more than one International Transfer Pricing method. As with their Australian and New Zealand counterparts, the

Table 8.3 Legally Oriented International Transfer Pricing Methods Used by Chinese Respondent Companies

	China	
Pricing Methods	**No. of Firms**	**%**
Cost plus method	21	29.2
Comparable uncontrolled price	17	23.6
Resale price	7	9.7
Profit split	6	8.3
Comparable profit method (CPM)	6	8.3
The transactional net margin method (TNMM)	3	4.2
Deemed profit method (DPM)	10	13.9
Others	2*	2.8
Total	72**	100

Note: * Other methods included 'global formulary apportionment' and 'going-rate pricing'.
** Some firms used more than one International Transfer Pricing method.
CPM, TNMM, and DPM may be used interchangeably in practice.

two most frequently used International Transfer Pricing methods by the Chinese firms are cost plus method and comparable uncontrolled price, which together account for 52.8% of the respondent companies. Ten companies use deemed profit method and seven companies use resale price method. Profit split method and comparable profit method are each used by six firms. Three companies are using the transactional net margin method. Two companies use other methods not specified by the State Administration of Taxation.

Burden of Proof. In China, the burden of proof regarding the arm's length price in related party transactions rests with the tax authorities. But the tax authorities are not required to prove that the taxpayer intended to avoid Chinese tax. When the tax authorities suspect that a foreign investment enterprise's income has been reduced as a result of non-arm's length pricing, the tax authorities will require the foreign investment enterprise to provide relevant information regarding transfer pricing (Rolfe, 1997; Guo, 2000).

Documentation. Unlike the practice in the United States and Australia and many other industrial countries, the current Chinese transfer pricing regulations do not require contemporaneous documentation. However, in a transfer pricing audit, the Chinese tax authorities have the right to require that the taxpayer provides information to support its transfer pricing (Article 18 of State Administration of Taxation Circular No. 59,

April 1998). The taxpayer assumes the burden of proof and provides the documentation to support his intercompany pricing policies (Article 24 of State Administration of Taxation Circular No. 59, April 1998). The information that would then be requested includes the following.

- Detailed third party transaction information for such variables as tangible property transactions, intangible property transactions, loans, provision of services, and rent
- Components of price determination, such as transaction volumes, locations, form of product, trade marks, and terms of payment
- Other relevant information associated with the determination of prices and charges.

The following information might also be required for intercompany tangible property transactions.

- Functions performed by all related parties
- Whether the sales of goods and selling prices are affected by seasonal variations
- Any intangible property involved
- The pricing methods used.

The Chinese transfer pricing legislation adopts the arm's length principle and introduces similar methods commonly used in OECD countries for determining appropriate transfer prices. It acknowledges the need for taxpayer documentation of all related party relationships and the arm's length character of its transfer pricing. These signify the Chinese government's attempt to structure its transfer pricing rules in line with that of the OECD nations in order to harmonise its approach with international practice for its participation in world trade.

Advance Pricing Agreements. Advance pricing agreements are common in OECD countries and have been informally adopted in China in practice. As indicated in Circular 59, advance pricing agreements are acceptable avenues of negotiation with the tax authorities. Until recently, Circular 59 had not prescribed the detailed procedures for an advance pricing agreement application and the kind of information that would be required for it but these are now in place in China.

The foreign investment enterprise must provide relevant information and fill out the application form for using the advanced pricing method. After a review of the information and documents, the tax authority may sign an advance pricing agreement with the enterprise and then supervise its implementation.

Under the current Chinese transfer pricing regulations, taxpayers can negotiate advance pricing agreements with provincial tax authorities, and no approval from the State Administration of Taxation is required. The facts that provincial tax authorities are most likely familiar with the taxpayer's operations, and are also responsible for tax collection and audit, can accelerate the negotiation process, and facilitate the implementation of the advance pricing agreement (Guo, 2000).

Summary

This chapter has reviewed transfer pricing regulations and guidelines in Australia, New Zealand and China. These three Pacific countries follow OECD Guidelines. They have unanimously adopted the arm's length standard as the most principled approach to deal with the transfer pricing issue, and adopt a combination of residency and source principles to collect taxes.

As such, their rules and guidelines on transfer pricing are similar to each other in many ways. However, in certain respects there are differences between the three nations. If a multinational enterprise, in conducting its business between two national tax jurisdictions, overlooks such differentials, it may suffer double taxation or incur other tax problems. Tax Commissioners also need to observe the regulatory differences between countries when they carry out tax audits on cross-border transactions.

9
Contemporary Pacific Method Choices

Introduction

This chapter presents crucial findings of the different methods for International Transfer Pricing which are currently in use by the respondent companies in Australia, New Zealand and China. These respondent companies are subsidiaries located in these three countries as their host countries but they are owned by their parent companies which might have home countries anywhere in the world, as indicated in Chapter 6.

There is always an issue for multinational companies, both domestically and internationally, over the prices they should fix for transferring on the one hand assets between their various divisions in their home countries, and on the other hand the prices they should fix for transferring assets between their subsidiaries which are often located in many foreign host countries.

The levels of pricing and the control of those levels are matters of constant concern and importance. For example, it might be desirable to transfer goods at cost price, but in that case it might be at a variable cost, the full cost or some other variation of cost, like standard cost. In contrast, the transfer price could be set at market price, or some other form of negotiated market price.

Specifically at the international level, additional considerations cloud the transfer pricing issue. Since intercompany transfers can be a significant portion of the transfers between a multinational corporation and its various subsidiaries, the transfer prices a multinational corporation chooses to adopt may have as their rationale not only the minimisation of taxation liabilities in the host country for the overall benefit of the corporation, but also the attainment of other financial or commercial objectives.

Classification of adopted methods

At first sight it might be supposed that commercial interests would dominate the attitudes of all trading companies over the issue and practice of International Transfer Pricing, irrespective of their type of business and the particular host countries in which they are located. However, given the putative similarity of the cultures of Australia and New Zealand and the very different culture of China, it might be supposed that host country business environments by contrast might determine any variation.

In this chapter, therefore, the methods actually employed are systematically compared between the three economies involved to clarify the reality. The explanations for any variations on the basis of these expectations that may be discovered are reported and explored in a later chapter in the course of examining policy determinants in the three countries.

The order of preferred usage of each of eleven possible methods in the case of each of the three countries is presented and the results analysed. The eleven methods derive from the full range of possible methods listed in Table 9.1, as indicated by the respondents in their replies.

The eleven methods can be classified as either cost based methods, market based methods or negotiation based methods, according to the following definitions.

Cost Based Methods. Cost based methods are those derived mainly through cost information as opposed to using market price information of the goods transferred. Examples include variable manufacturing costs and full costs. Full costs typically include all manufacturing costs as well as costs from some or all of the other business functions such as research and development, marketing, distribution and customer service. The costs can be either actual costs or standard costs.

Cost based methods have the advantage that they are simple to use, being based on readily available data. They are easy to justify to tax authorities and are easily routinised – features which make cost basis a commonly used method. However, a cost basis may not encourage the units which transfer assets to control their costs as actively as they might, thereby imposing their inefficiency on the company to which the transfer of assets is made.

For example, if the transfer price markup is to be 10% of cost where the total cost is 100 then the subsidiary will pay 110. If subsequently the total cost rises to 120 the subsidiary would have to pay 132. A subsidiary which, for whatever reason, is tied to dependency on continued transactions with the transferring company, is at the mercy of the latter's capability and/or willingness to manage its costs. In other words, there is no incentive for the transferring firm to reduce expenditures. Inefficiencies are passed from one company to the next. This is then an inequitable method for the transfer of goods between related companies.

Market Based Methods. The second group of methods actually used by the respondent companies presented in this chapter is market based methods, which are based on the arm's length principle. This principle establishes the transfer price of goods at the price that would have been obtained between independent enterprises in comparable transactions and comparable circumstances.

A market based transfer pricing system is generally regarded as the most authentic method in transfer pricing. By using market prices, the firms concerned are acting almost as though they were independent companies. It is easier to defend a company's transfer pricing policy and practice on this basis to foreign governments and tax authorities for its reliability as opposed to various forms of arbitrary pricing, which inevitably raise the suspicions and possible investigations of host country authorities.

However, a market based system is not always possible. An arm's length market price can be established only if identical goods and services are traded among unrelated entities. One subsidiary may be the only outlet for the sale of goods of a multinational group, there being no buyers outside the multinational company itself. In such a situation, negotiated market/cost pricing between the selling and buying companies might be more appropriate.

Negotiation Based Methods. The third category in classifying the methods is that of negotiation based methods. In some cases, the subsidiaries of a multinational group are free to negotiate transfer prices between themselves, including negotiation based on costs, negotiation based on market price, and unrestricted negotiations. Available information about costs and market prices may enter into and be used in these negotiations (Evans, Taylor and Rolfe, 1999).

However, negotiation based methods may be justifiably assimilated into the market based methods category – for a two category analysis only, consisting of Cost Based Methods and Market Based Methods.

With regard to negotiation based methods, there is no consistent treatment in previous studies. Al-Eryani et al. (1990) and Tang (1993) treated negotiated pricing as a cost based method but others have counted negotiated and market methods together as market based methods (Chan and Chow, 2001).

In Table 9.1, negotiation pricing approaches such as negotiation based on costs, negotiation based on market price, and unrestricted negotiations, are included in the market based method group.

Australian Companies. Table 9.1 portrays the number and percentage of the respondent Australian companies which are using cost

Table 9.1   International Transfer Pricing Methods Used by the Respondent Companies

Pricing Method	Australia		New Zealand		China	
	No. of Firms	%	No. of Firms	%	No. of Firms	%
Cost Based Methods						
Full plus fixed profit	19	32.2	21	28.4	3	6.8
Full actual cost	6	10.2	9	12.2	7	15.9
Full standard cost	5	8.5	6	8.1	1	2.3
Variable plus fixed contribution	4	6.8	4	5.4	3	6.8
Variable actual cost	2	3.4	2	2.7	0	0
Variable standard cost	0	0	0	0	1	2.3
Subtotal for cost based methods	36	61.0	42	56.8	15	34.1
Market Based Methods						
Negotiation based on market price	13	22	7	9.5	7	15.9
Adjusted market price	4	6.8	7	9.5	6	13.6
Negotiation based on costs	3	5.1	9	12.2	8	18.2
Full market price	3	5.1	6	8.1	8	18.2
Unrestricted negotiations	0	0	3	4.1	0	0
Subtotal for market based methods	23	39	32	43.2	29	65.9
Total – all methods	59	100*	74	100*	44	100*

Note: * Percentage totals subject to rounding.

versus market based methods for International Transfer Pricing. It shows that 61% of the Australian firms use cost based methods and 39% use market based methods for the combined groups. It appears that the Australian firms tend to use cost oriented transfer prices. As for the use of individual transfer pricing methods, 'full plus fixed profit' (19 or 32.2%) is most widely used by respondent companies. Following in descending order of frequency of use are 'negotiation based on market prices' (13 or 22%), 'full actual cost' (6 or 10.2%), 'full standard cost' (5 or 8.5%), 'variable plus fixed contribution' (4 or 6.8%), 'adjusted market price' (4 or 6.8%), 'full market price' (3 or 5.1%), 'negotiation based on costs' (3 or 5.1%), and 'variable actual cost' (2 or 3.4%). 'Variable standard cost' and 'unrestricted negotiations' are not used by the respondents in the sample.

New Zealand Companies. Table 9.1 shows that 56.8% of the New Zealand respondent firms use cost based methods and 43.2% use market based methods for the combined groups. In company with their Australian counterparts, the New Zealand firms tend to use cost oriented transfer prices. As for the use of individual transfer pricing methods, 'full plus fixed profit' (21 or 28.4%) is most widely used by respondent companies. Following in descending order of frequency are 'negotiation based on costs' (9 or 12.2%), 'full actual cost' (9 or 12.2%), 'adjusted market price' (7 or 9.5%), 'negotiation based on market price' (7 or 9.5%), 'full standard cost' (6 or 8.1%), 'full market price' (6 or 8.1%), 'variable plus fixed contribution' (4 or 5.4%), 'unrestricted negotiations' (3 or 4.1%), and 'variable actual cost' (2 or 2.7%). 'Variable standard cost' is used by the New Zealand respondents in the sample.

Chinese Companies. Table 9.1 shows that 34.1% of the Chinese firms use cost based methods and 65.9% use market based methods for the combined groups. Compared with their Australian and New Zealand counterparts, Chinese companies tend to use market oriented methods. As for the use of the individual pricing methods, 'full market price' (8 or 18.2%) and 'negotiation based on costs' (8 or 18.2%) are most commonly used by respondent companies. Following in descending order of frequency are 'full actual cost' (7 or 15.9%), 'negotiation based on market price' (7 or 15.9%), 'adjusted market price' (6 or 13.6%), 'full plus fixed profit' (3 or 6.8%), 'variable plus fixed contribution' (3 or 6.8%), 'full standard cost' (1 or 2.3%), and 'variable standard cost' (1 or 2.3%). 'Variable actual cost' and 'unrestricted negotiations' are not used by the Chinese respondents in the sample.

Comparison of adopted methods

Australian and New Zealand Companies. In comparing the International Transfer Pricing methods used by companies respectively in Australia and New Zealand it was expected that there would be no differences between them. Table 9.2 contrasts transfer pricing methods used by Australian and New Zealand firms. The descriptive statistics provide evidence that there are no significant differences in the International Transfer Pricing methods used by multinational companies in the two countries. 'Full plus fixed profit' is the most common pricing method used by multinationals in both countries. 'Variable standard cost' is used in neither Australia nor in New Zealand. The numbers in parenthesis are ordinal numbers.

A chi-square test was used to compare the transfer pricing methods used by the respondent companies. The results depicted in Table 9.3 show that there is no statistically significant difference in the responses in respect of the International Transfer Pricing methods used in the two national groups, although the sample size needs to be taken into account.

Table 9.2   International Transfer Pricing Methods Used by Australian and New Zealand Respondent Companies

	Australia		New Zealand	
Pricing Method	No. of Firms	%	No. of Firms	%
Full plus fixed profit	19 (1)	32.2	21 (1)	28.4
Negotiation based on market price	13 (2)	22	7 (4/5)	9.5
Full actual cost	6 (3)	10.2	9 (2/3)	12.2
Full standard cost	5 (4)	8.5	6 (6/7)	8.1
Variable plus fixed contribution	4 (5)	6.8	4 (8)	5.4
Adjusted market price	4 (5)	6.8	7 (4/5)	9.5
Negotiation based on costs	3 (6)	5.1	9 (2/3)	12.2
Full market price	3 (6)	5.1	6 (6/7)	8.1
Variable actual cost	2 (7)	3.4	2 (10)	2.7
Unrestricted negotiations	0 (8/9)	0	3 (9)	4.1
Variable standard cost	0 (8/9)	0	0 (11)	0
Total – all methods	59	100*	74	100*

Note: * Percentage totals are subject to rounding.

Table 9.3   Chi-Square Test on Methods Used by Australian and New Zealand Respondent Companies

	International Transfer Pricing Methods
Chi-Squared value	8.830
Degree of freedom	9
Significance. (2-tailed)	.453
N	133

Table 9.4   Comparison of Classified Methods Used by Australian and New Zealand Respondent Companies

Pricing Method	Australia		New Zealand	
	No. of Firms	%	No. of Firms	%
Cost Based Methods	36	61	42	56.8
Market Based Methods	7	11.9	13	17.6
Negotiation Based Methods	16	27.1	19	25.7
Total – all methods	59	100*	74	100*

Note: * Percentage totals are subject to rounding.

In Table 9.4, the eleven individual pricing methods are classified into three method groups – cost based, market based and negotiation based methods – with a view to discovering any variation on such a basis. However, the descriptive statistics provide evidence that at the aggregated levels, the International Transfer Pricing methods used by multinationals when subject to such a classification are not significantly different in the two countries.

Pearson's chi-square test was used to test whether differences among companies of the two national groups in their choices of International Transfer Pricing methods on the basis of the foregoing classification were significant at the aggregated levels. The results in Table 9.5 show that there is no statistically significant difference in responses in respect of International Transfer Pricing methods used at aggregated levels in the two national groups.

The eleven individual pricing methods were further classified into only two different groups – cost based and market based methods. The descriptive statistics shown in Table 9.6 provide support that at the cost based versus market based level of analysis the International

Table 9.5   Chi-Square Test of Classified Methods Used by Australian and New Zealand Respondent Companies

	Cost Based Methods vs Market Based Methods vs Negotiation Based Methods
Chi-Squared value	.838
Degree of freedom	2
Significance. (2-tailed)	.658
N	133

Table 9.6   Comparison of Cost Based and Market Based Methods Used by Australian and New Zealand Respondent Companies

	Australia		New Zealand	
Pricing Method	No. of Firms	%	No. of Firms	%
Cost Based Methods	36	61	42	56.8
Market Based Methods	23	39	32	43.2
Total – all methods	59	100	74	100

Table 9.7   Chi-Square Test of Cost Based and Market Based Methods Used by Australian and New Zealand Respondent Companies

	Cost Based vs Market Based
Chi-Squared value	.101
Degree of freedom	1
Significance. (2-tailed)	.750
N	133

Transfer Pricing methods used by multinationals show a similar pattern in the two countries.

Pearson's chi-square test was used to test whether differences among companies of the two nationals groups in choosing International Transfer Pricing methods were significant at cost based versus market based levels. The results in Table 9.7 show that there is no statistically significant difference in responses in respect of International Transfer Pricing methods used in the two national groups on this basis.

The results in Tables 9.2 to 9.7 provide evidence that there are no statistically significant differences across the two national groups

Table 9.8   International Transfer Pricing Methods Used by Australian and Chinese Respondent Companies

Pricing Method	Australia		China	
	No. of Firms	%	No. of Firms	%
Full plus fixed profit	19 (1)	32.2	3 (6/7)	6.8
Negotiation based on market price	13 (2)	22	7 (3/4)	15.9
Full actual cost	6 (3)	10.2	7 (3/4)	15.9
Full standard cost	5 (4)	8.5	1 (8/9)	2.3
Variable plus fixed contribution	4 (5/6)	6.8	3 (6/7)	6.8
Adjusted market price	4 (5/6)	6.8	6 (5)	13.6
Negotiation based on costs	3 (7/8)	5.1	8 (1/2)	18.2
Full market price	3 (7/8)	5.1	8 (1/2)	18.2
Variable actual cost	2 (9)	3.4	0 (10)	0
Variable standard cost	0 (10)	0	1 (8/9)	2.3
Total	59	100*	44	100*

Note: * Percentage totals are subject to rounding.

regarding International Transfer Pricing methods used at both individual and aggregated levels. Therefore, the expectation of similarities arising from the assumption of common cultural factors over the adoption of particular International Transfer Pricing methods used by multinationals in Australia and New Zealand has some validity.

Australian and Chinese Companies. Table 9.8 contrasts transfer pricing methods used by Australian and Chinese firms. The descriptive statistics provide evidence that there are differences in International Transfer Pricing methods used by multinationals in the two countries according to their country of origin. The numbers in parenthesis are ordinal numbers.

A chi-square test was used to compare the transfer pricing methods used by the respondent companies. The results depicted in Table 9.9 show that there are statistically significant differences in responses with respect to individual International Transfer Pricing methods used in the two national groups, although sample size needs to be taken into account.

In Table 9.10 the eleven individual pricing methods are classified into three method groups – cost based, market based and negotiation based. The descriptive statistics provide evidence that at the aggregated

Table 9.9   Chi-Square Test on Methods Used by Australian and Chinese Respondent Companies

	International Transfer Pricing Methods
Chi-Squared value	22.562***
Degree of freedom	9
Significance. (2-tailed)	.007
N	103

Note: *** Significant at the .01 level.

Table 9.10   Comparison of Classified Methods Used by Australian and Chinese Respondent Companies

	Australia		China	
Pricing Method	**No. of Firms**	**%**	**No. of Firms**	**%**
Cost Based Methods	36	61	15	34.1
Market Based Methods	7	11.9	14	31.8
Negotiation Based Methods	16	27.1	15	34.1
Total – all methods	59	100	44	100

levels, International Transfer Pricing methods used by multinationals are different in the two countries on this basis.

Pearson's chi-square test was used to test whether differences among companies of the two nationals groups in choosing International Transfer Pricing methods were significant at the aggregated levels. The results in Table 9.11 show that there are statistically

Table 9.11   Chi-Square Test of Classified Methods Used by Australian and Chinese Respondent Companies

	Cost Based Methods vs Market Based Methods vs Negotiation Based Methods
Chi-Squared value	9.019**
Degree of freedom	2
Significance. (2-tailed)	.011
N	103

Note: ** Significant at the .05 level.

Table 9.12   Comparison of Cost Based and Market Based Methods Used by Australian and Chinese Respondent Companies

Pricing Method	Australia		China	
	No. of Firms	%	No. of Firms	%
Cost Based Methods	36	61	15	34.1
Market Based Methods	23	39	29	65.9
Total – all methods	59	100	44	100

significant differences in responses with respect to International Transfer Pricing methods used at aggregated levels in the two national groups on the foregoing basis.

The eleven individual pricing methods were further classified into only two groups – cost based and market based methods. The descriptive statistics shown in Table 9.12 provide support that at the cost based versus market based level of analysis, International Transfer Pricing methods used by multinationals in Australia and China are different in the two countries.

Pearson's chi-square test was used to test whether differences among companies of the two national groups in choosing International Transfer Pricing methods were significant at the cost based versus market based level of analysis. The results in Table 9.13 show that there are statistically significant differences in response with respect to the International Transfer Pricing methods used in the two national groups.

The results in Tables 9.8 to 9.13 provide evidence that there are statistically significant differences across the two country groups with regard to the International Transfer Pricing methods used by companies at both

Table 9.13   Chi-Square Test of Cost Based and Market Based Methods Used by Australian and Chinese Respondent Countries

	Cost Based vs Market Based
Chi-Squared value	6.272**
Degree of freedom	1
Significance. (2-tailed)	.012
N	103

Note: ** Significant at the .05 level.

Table 9.14 International Transfer Pricing Methods Used by New Zealand and Chinese Respondent Companies

	New Zealand		China	
Pricing Method	No. of Firms	%	No. of Firms	%
Full plus fixed profit	21 (1)	28.4	3 (6/7)	6.8
Full actual cost	9 (2/3)	12.2	7 (3/4)	15.9
Negotiation based on costs	9 (2/3)	12.2	8 (1/2)	18.2
Adjusted market price	7 (4/5)	9.5	6 (5)	13.6
Negotiation based on market price	7 (4/5)	9.5	7 (3/4)	15.9
Full standard cost	6 (6/7)	8.1	1 (8/9)	2.3
Full market price	6 (6/7)	8.1	8 (1/2)	18.2
Variable plus fixed contribution	4 (8)	5.4	3 (6/7)	6.8
Unrestricted negotiations	3 (9)	4.1	0 (10/11)	0
Variable actual cost	2 (10)	2.7	0 (10/11)	0
Variable standard cost	0 (11)	0	1 (8/9)	2.3
Total – all methods	74	100*	44	100*

Note: * Percentage totals are subject to rounding.

individual and aggregated levels. Therefore, an expectation that the cultural contrasts between Australia and China might be subordinate to the imperatives of shared commercial interests, resulting in no differences in International Transfer Pricing methods used by multinationals in Australia and China, can be discarded.

New Zealand and Chinese Companies. Table 9.14 contrasts transfer pricing methods used by New Zealand and Chinese firms. The descriptive statistics provide evidence that there are differences in the Inter-

Table 9.15 Chi-Square Test on Methods Used by New Zealand and Chinese Respondent Companies

	International Transfer Pricing Methods
Chi-Squared value	17.382*
Degree of freedom	10
Significance. (2-tailed)	.066
N	118

Note: * Significant at the .1 level.

national Transfer Pricing methods used by multinationals in the two countries. Numbers in parenthesis are ordinal numbers.

A chi-square test was used to compare the transfer pricing methods used by the respondent companies. The results depicted in Table 9.15 show that there are statistically significant differences in responses with respect to individual International Transfer Pricing methods used in the two national groups.

In Table 9.16 the eleven individual pricing methods are classified into three method groups – cost based, market based and negotiation based. The descriptive statistics provide evidence that at the aggregated levels International Transfer Pricing methods used by multinationals are different in the two countries.

Pearson's chi-square test was used to test whether differences among companies of the two national groups in choosing International Transfer Pricing methods were significant at the aggregated levels. The results in Table 9.17 show that there are statistically significant differences in

Table 9.16   Comparison of Classified Methods Used by New Zealand and Chinese Respondent Companies

Pricing Method	New Zealand		China	
	No. of Firms	%	No. of Firms	%
Cost Based Methods	42	56.8	15	34.1
Market Based Methods	13	17.6	14	31.8
Negotiation Based Methods	19	25.7	15	34.1
Total – all methods	74	100	44	100

Table 9.17   Chi-Square Test on Classified Methods Used by New Zealand and Chinese Respondent Companies

	Cost Based Methods vs Market Based Methods vs Negotiation Based Methods
Chi-Squared value	6.062**
Degree of freedom	2
Significance. (2-tailed)	.048
N	118

Note: ** Significant at the .05 level.

Table 9.18   Comparison of Cost Based and Market Based Methods Used by New Zealand and Chinese Respondent Companies

Pricing Method	New Zealand		China	
	No. of Firms	%	No. of Firms	%
Cost Based Methods	42	56.8	15	34.1
Market Based Methods	32	43.2	29	65.9
Total – all methods	74	100	44	100

responses in respect of International Transfer Pricing methods used at aggregated levels in the two national groups on this basis.

The eleven individual pricing methods were further classified into only two groups – cost based and market based methods. The descriptive statistics provide support that at the cost based versus market based level of analysis International Transfer Pricing methods used by multinationals show significant differences between the two countries, as shown in Table 9.18.

Pearson's chi-square test was used to test whether differences among companies of the two nationals groups in choosing International Transfer Pricing methods were significant at the cost based versus market based level of analysis. The results in Table 9.19 show that there are statistically significant differences in the responses of companies with respect to the International Transfer Pricing methods used in the two national groups.

The results in Tables 9.14 to 9.19 provide evidence that there are statistically significant differences across the two country groups with regard to the International Transfer Pricing methods used at both individual and aggregated levels. Therefore, an expectation on prima facie

Table 9.19   Chi-Square Test of Cost Based and Market Based Methods Used by New Zealand and Chinese Respondent Companies

	Cost Based vs Market Based
Chi-Squared value	4.805**
Degree of freedom	1
Significance. (2-tailed)	.028
N	118

Note: ** Significant at the .05 level.

Table 9.20   Summary of Statistical Results Regarding the Methods Used by Australian, New Zealand and Chinese Respondent Companies

	Raw	Cost Based vs Market Based vs Negotiation Based	Cost Based vs Market Based
Australia and New Zealand			
Australia and China	***	**	**
New Zealand and China	*	**	**

Note: * Significant at the .1 level.
** Significant at the .05 level.
*** Significant at the .01 level.

grounds of differences in International Transfer Pricing methods used by multinationals in New Zealand and China is justified.

Summary

This chapter conducted a cross-national comparison of International Transfer Pricing methods used by Australian, New Zealand and Chinese respondent companies. Table 9.20 summarises the statistical test results. The survey results reveal statistically significant differences between the transfer pricing methods used by Australian and New Zealand companies on the one hand, and Chinese companies on the other. The next chapter examines policy determinants for the choice of multinational transfer pricing methods in the three countries.

10
Policy Determinants

Introduction

Given the wide range of turbulent conditions prevailing in the global trading market, it is only to be expected that the factors which actually govern the policies adopted by companies over International Transfer Pricing would vary. A single, invariably efficacious method in International Transfer Pricing patently does not exist. If it did so, the governmental interests of host countries could marshal their defences with greater effectiveness and the whole issue of International Transfer Pricing would be less of a controversial subject and major concern.

In the studies undertaken for this book, therefore, it was expected that variety would prevail but that some trends might be discoverable. Hypothetically and in particular there was the possibility that the determinants of International Transfer Pricing might reveal major variation according to the country of origin and the type and size of company involved.

In the event, to discover the realities in practice, seventeen environmental variables were selected in designing an instrument for data collection. A 5-point scale was used by respondent companies to rate the importance of each of these possible determinants of the methods adopted in International Transfer Pricing.

In this chapter, Tables 10.2, 10.7 and 10.11 respectively show the relative importance attached by the sample companies in each country to all these variables. The rankings of the importance were made according to the mean scores of the variables. The mean for each variable was based on a 5-point scale of 1 for extremely important; 2 for very important; 3 for important; 4 for slightly important, and 5 for not important. In using the recode function in the Statistical Package for the Social Sciences (SPSS), the original Likert-like code was reversed. That is, on the 5-point scale, a 1 is recoded as a 5, a 2 is recorded as a 4, a 3 as a 3, a 4 as a 2, and a 5 as a 1. Thus, the higher the numbers are, the greater their importance. The standard deviation of responses is also presented in the tables, indicating the extent of agreement in the rating of individual variables among the respondents.

Section III of the Questionnaire contained the list of the seventeen environmental variables that were variously expected to determine the selection of International Transfer Pricing method choices by multinational enterprises. Most of these environmental variables in the Questionnaire were identified and culled from reviews of extant literature. A few modifications to the wording of some of the variables were made. One variable, 'tax authority transfer pricing audits', which previously had not been used except by Borkowski (1997a,b; 2001), was included in the Questionnaire to test whether or not auditing is an important factor affecting International Transfer Pricing decisions. Table 10.1 lists the seventeen variables

Table 10.1   Environmental Variables

Variables

VAR 01 Differences in income tax rates

VAR 02 Rates of customs duties

VAR 03 Tax authority transfer pricing audits

VAR 04 Comply with tax law and regulations

VAR 05 Restrictions on repatriation of income

VAR 06 Competitive position of the subsidiary

VAR 07 Overall profit to multinational group

VAR 08 Corporate profit of the subsidiary

VAR 09 Import restrictions

VAR 10 Foreign currency exchange controls

VAR 11 Good relations with host government

VAR 12 Price controls of host government

VAR 13 Existence of local partner

VAR 14 Performance evaluation

VAR 15 Political and social pressure

VAR 16 Royalty restrictions

VAR 17 Maintenance of cash flow

that were expected to be cited as determinants of International Transfer Pricing decisions, as introduced in Chapter 5 (Table 5.1).

Australian perspective

For the Australian part of the research, a total of 250 subsidiaries of multinational enterprises were randomly drawn from Dun & Bradstreet's Business Directories Who's Who (2001, 2002 and 2003). To ensure the accuracy of the addresses of the intended respondents, the data from the directories were carefully checked on the Internet database. The website address used was http://www.yellowpages.com.au. A total of sixty completely usable returns were obtained, revealing information which is presented and analysed in the following tables.

'Comply with tax law and regulations' was perceived by the Australian respondent firms as the most important variable in transfer pricing decisions. The low standard deviation for this variable indicates

Table 10.2 Environmental Variables Ranked for Their Importance by Respondent Firms in Australia (n = 60)

Environmental Variables	Mean	Rank	Standard Deviation
VAR 04 Comply with tax law and regulations	4.05	1	1.166
VAR 06 Competitive position of the subsidiary	3.28	2	1.335
VAR 08 Corporate profit of the subsidiary	3.14	3	1.206
VAR 07 Overall profit to multinational group	2.86	4	1.317
VAR 03 Tax authority transfer pricing audits	2.79	5	1.321
VAR 17 Maintenance of cash flows	2.55	6	1.404
VAR 01 Differences in income tax rates	2.43	7	1.464
VAR 14 Performance evaluation	2.41	8	1.298
VAR 11 Good relations with host government	2.26	9	1.292
VAR 02 Rates of customs duties	2.12	10/11	1.312
VAR 10 Foreign currency exchange controls	2.12	10/11	1.326
VAR 05 Restrictions on repatriation of income	1.97	12/13	1.169
VAR 09 Import restrictions	1.97	12/13	1.199
VAR 12 Price controls of host government	1.95	14	1.30
VAR 13 Existence of local partner	1.84	15	1.203
VAR 16 Royalty restrictions	1.71	16/17	.973
VAR 15 Political and social pressure	1.71	16/17	.975

that there was relatively great agreement among respondents on the importance of legal considerations. Other variables considered to be very important included 'competitive position of the subsidiary' and 'corporate profit of the subsidiary'.

Eight variables were considered moderately important by the respondent firms. They were 'overall profit to multinational group', 'tax authority transfer pricing audits', 'maintenance of cash flows', 'differences in income tax rates', 'performance evaluation', 'good relations with host government', 'rates of customs duties', and 'foreign currency exchange controls'.

Variables which were considered of only slight importance included 'restrictions on repatriation of income', 'import restrictions', 'price controls of host government', 'existence of local partner', 'royalty restrictions' and 'political and social pressure'.

To overcome the potential problem of multicollinearity and to identify a relatively small number of underlying dimensions or behavioural traits, an R-type, principal components factor analysis that is orthogonally rotated, based on the Varimax procedures, was performed on the data. Since factor analysis is concerned with relations among observations, it commonly starts with a matrix of correlations as its input (Tang, 1982).

The correlations matrix of environmental variables in Table 10.3 shows that some variables are highly correlated. For instance, Variable 14 (performance evaluation) and Variable 17 (maintenance of cash flows) have a correlation coefficient of .73. Variable 1 (differences in income tax rates) and Variable 2 (rates of customs duties) have a correlation coefficient of .69, while Variable 11 (good relations with host government) and Variable 15 (political and social pressure) have a correlation coefficient of .68. The high correlation of the variables provided justification for performing a factor analysis.

The matrix shown in Table 10.4 is the product of a varimax rotation. Three factors (or dimensions) were extracted and labelled as follows:

- Factor 1: Legal considerations and corporate competitive position
- Factor 2: Government restrictions
- Factor 3: Tax and customs duties.

In Table 10.4 the communality column shows the degree to which the factor accounts for or explains each of the variables. For a given variable, the three factors summarise between 39.2% (VAR 06) and 82.7% (VAR 02) of the variation.

Table 10.3   Correlations Matrix of Environmental Variables – Australian Companies

Variable	1	2	3	4	5	6	7	8	9	10	11	12	13	14	15	16	17
VAR 01																	
VAR 02	.69																
VAR 03	.28	.27															
VAR 04	.33	.32	.57														
VAR 05	.28	.44	.34	.44													
VAR 06	.02	.28	.30	.28	.23												
VAR 07	.32	.24	.45	.35	.40	.30											
VAR 08	.28	.43	.44	.40	.13	.52	.44										
VAR 09	.13	.34	.16	.31	.46	.23	.35	.38									
VAR 10	.34	.51	.16	.29	.46	.29	.35	.44	.76								
VAR 11	.15	.22	.62	.53	.42	.45	.43	.36	.33	.39							
VAR 12	.18	.24	.42	.41	.42	.27	.43	.35	.30	.36	.61						
VAR 13	.26	.37	.19	.31	.62	.25	.34	.25	.41	.53	.35	.45					
VAR 14	.19	.34	.35	.44	.36	.45	.43	.53	.46	.52	.42	.31	.47				
VAR 15	.18	.23	.52	.37	.50	.40	.43	.38	.47	.49	.68	.47	.47	.67			
VAR 16	.25	.18	.21	.30	.50	.13	.38	.13	.46	.37	.37	.37	.47	.40	.47		
VAR 17	.25	.33	.41	.47	.46	.37	.56	.54	.49	.60	.52	.35	.48	.73	.57	.53	

Note: Shaded items identify the highly correlated variables.

Table 10.4 Factor Analysis of Environmental Variables – Australian Companies

Variables	Factor 1	Factor 2	Factor 3	h^2 (communality)
VAR 01 Differences in income tax rates	.122	.132	.847*	.749
VAR 02 Rates of customs duties	.168	.263	.854*	.827
VAR 03 Tax authority transfer pricing audits	.813*	.009	.154	.684
VAR 04 Comply with tax law and regulations	.627*	.207	.256	.502
VAR 05 Restrictions on repatriation of income	.236	.687*	.183	.561
VAR 06 Competitive position of the subsidiary	.610*	.123	.072	.392
VAR 07 Overall profit to multinational group	.542*	.347	.182	.448
VAR 08 Corporate profit of the subsidiary	.631*	.112	.413	.582
VAR 09 Import restrictions	.145	.751*	.154	.609
VAR 10 Foreign currency exchange controls	.168	.730*	.373	.700
VAR 11 Good relations with host government	.772*	.331	−.068	.710
VAR 12 Price controls of host government	.554*	.375	.014	.448
VAR 13 Existence of local partner	.168	.730*	.176	.592
VAR 14 Performance evaluation	.525*	.524	.137	.569
VAR 15 Political and social pressure	.608*	.564	−.061	.691
VAR 16 Royalty restrictions	.175	.724*	−.027	.556
VAR 17 Maintenance of cash flows	.526	.591*	.158	.650
Sum of squares (Eigenvalue)	7.244	1.589	1.426	
Percentage of trace (Variance)	42.6	9.3	8.4	60.3

Note: * Indicates highest factor loading for variables.

Table 10.5   Summary of Three Dimensions of Variables – Factor Analysis for Australian Companies

Dimensions and Variables	Rotated Factor Loadings	Communality	Eigenvalue	Variance Summarised (Eignvalue/no. of Variable)
Factor 1 Legal considerations and corporate competitive position			7.244	.426
VAR 03 Tax authority transfer pricing audits	.813	.684		
VAR 11 Good relations with host government	.772	.710		
VAR 08 Corporate profit of the subsidiary	.631	.582		
VAR 04 Comply with tax law and regulations	.627	.502		
VAR 06 Competitive position of the subsidiary	.610	.392		
VAR 15 Political and social pressure	.608	.691		
VAR 12 Price controls of host government	.554	.448		
VAR 07 Overall profit to multinational group	.542	.448		
VAR 14 Performance evaluation	.525	.569		

Table 10.5   Summary of Three Dimensions of Variables – Factor Analysis for Australian Companies – *continued*

Dimensions and Variables	Rotated Factor Loadings	Communality	Eigenvalue	Variance Summarised (Eignvalue/no. of Variable)
Factor 2 Government restrictions			1.589	.093
VAR 09 Import restrictions	.751	.609		
VAR 10 Foreign currency exchange controls	.730	.700		
VAR 13 Existence of local partner	.730	.592		
VAR 16 Royalty restrictions	.724	.556		
VAR 05 Restrictions on repatriation of income	.687	.561		
VAR 17 Maintenance of cash flows	.591	.650		
Factor 3 Tax and customs duties			1.426	.084
VAR 02 Rates of customs duties	.854	.827		
VAR 01 Differences in income tax rates	.847	.749		
Total				.603

In Table 10.5 the eigenvalue of each factor is the sum of the squares of the factor's unrotated loadings and is normally used to compute the fraction of total variance in the variable explained by the factor (Tang, 1982, p. 185). The percentage of total variance summarised by each factor is equal to its eigenvalue divided by seventeen (the number of variables). For example, Factor 1 summarises 42.6% of the total variance, Factor 2 summarises 9.3% of the total variance, and Factor 3 summarises 8.4% of the total variance. Together, the three factors summarise 60.3% of the total variance in the seventeen variables.

Cronbach's coefficient alphas for reliability were estimated for each of the factors to ascertain the extent to which variables making up each factor share a common core and the extent to which items in the Questionnaire were related to each other. Cronbach's alpha is based on the average inter-item correlation. Table 10.6 shows the high reliability held for items which composed Factor 1, while the rest of the two factors were satisfactory or better. A consideration of the dimensionality of each of the factors follows.

Factor 1 is the most dominant factor. Within this most significant factor, 'tax authority transfer pricing audits' is the most important variable, followed in descending order by 'good relations with host government', 'corporate profit of the subsidiary', 'comply with tax law and regulations', 'competitive position of the subsidiary', 'political and social pressure', 'price controls of host government', 'overall profit to multinational group', and 'performance evaluation'. This means that the respondents who placed a great deal of importance on 'tax

Table 10.6   Cronbach's Alpha Reliability – Australian Companies

Factor	Variables	Cronbach's Alpha
Factor 1: Legal considerations and corporate competitive position	VAR 03, VAR 11, VAR 08, VAR 04, VAR 06, VAR 15, VAR 12, VAR 07, VAR 14, VAR 13,	.8734
Factor 2: Government restrictions	VAR 09, VAR 10, VAR 16, VAR 05, VAR 17	.8576
Factor 3: Tax and customs duties	VAR 02, VAR 01	.8099

authority transfer pricing audits' also tended to regard other variables that loaded highly on Factor 1 as important.

Factor 2 has very high loadings on 'import restrictions', 'foreign currency exchange controls' 'existence of local partner' and 'royalty restrictions'. These variables together form another important dimension of environmental variables.

Factor 3 has high loadings on 'rates of customs duties' and 'differences in income tax rates'.

New Zealand perspective

A total of 300 New Zealand subsidiaries of multinational enterprises were randomly drawn from Dun & Bradstreet's Business Directories Wh'o Whom (2001, 2002 and 2003). To ensure the accuracy of the respondents' addresses, the data from the directories were carefully

Table 10.7 Environmental Variables Ranked for Their Importance by Respondent Firms in New Zealand (n = 77)

Environmental Variables	Mean	Rank	Standard Deviation
VAR 04 Comply with tax law and regulations	3.96	1	1.069
VAR 08 Corporate profit of the subsidiary	3.38	2	1.089
VAR 06 Competitive position of the subsidiary	3.31	3	1.369
VAR 07 Overall profit to multinational group	3.05	4	1.157
VAR 03 Tax authority transfer pricing audits	2.82	5	1.254
VAR 17 Maintenance of cash flows	2.71	6	1.422
VAR 14 Performance evaluation	2.51	7	1.242
VAR 01 Differences in income tax rates	2.47	8	1.363
VAR 05 Restrictions on repatriation of income	2.43	9	1.261
VAR 11 Good relations with host government	2.18	10	1.262
VAR 10 Foreign currency exchange controls	2.09	11	1.248
VAR 13 Existence of local partner	2.07	12	1.258
VAR 02 Rates of customs duties	2.00	13/14	1.147
VAR 09 Import restrictions	2.00	13/14	1.192
VAR 15 Political and social pressure	1.96	15	1.094
VAR 12 Price controls of host government	1.95	16	1.210
VAR 16 Royalty restrictions	1.82	17	1.109

checked on the Internet, using the website address http://www.yellow-pages.co.nz. Of the total number of Questionnaires despatched, a final return of seventy-seven completely usable responses was achieved. Table 10.7 and subsequent tables record the assessment of differential importance that these companies attached to the seventeen environmental variables as determinants of their decisions regarding International Transfer Pricing, together with analytical treatments of the results.

It can be seen that 'comply with tax law and regulations' was perceived by the New Zealand respondent firms as the most important variable in transfer pricing decisions. Other variables considered very important included 'corporate profit of the subsidiary', 'competitive position of the subsidiary' and 'overall profit to multinational group'.

Eight variables were considered to be moderately important by the respondent firms. They were 'tax authority transfer pricing audits', 'maintenance of cash flows', 'performance evaluation', 'differences in income tax rates', 'restrictions on repatriation of income', 'good relations with host government', 'foreign currency exchange controls', and 'existence of local partner'.

Variables which were considered only slightly important included 'import restrictions', 'rates of customs duties', 'import restrictions', 'political and social pressure', 'price controls of host government', and 'royalty restrictions'.

An R-type, principal components factor analysis that is orthogonally rotated based on the Varimax procedure was performed on these data. The correlations matrix of environmental variables in Table 10.8 shows that some variables are highly correlated. For instance, Variable 11 (good relations with host government) and Variable 12 (price controls of host government) have a correlation coefficient of .77. Variable 10 (foreign currency exchange controls) and Variable 12 (price controls of host government) have a correlation coefficient of .73, while Variable 09 (import restrictions) and Variable 10 (foreign currency exchange controls) have a correlation coefficient of .71. The high correlation of the variables provided justification for performing a factor analysis.

Three factors (or dimensions) and their reliability scores (Chronbach's alpha), as shown in Table 10.9, were extracted and labelled as follows:

- Factor 1: Government restrictions (Chronbach's alpha = .9236).
- Factor 2: Tax and legal considerations (Chronbach's alpha = .7287).
- Factor 3: Corporate competitive position (Chronbach's alpha = .6624).

Table 10.8   Correlations Matrix of Environmental Variables – New Zealand Companies

Variable	1	2	3	4	5	6	7	8	9	10	11	12	13	14	15	16	17
VAR 01																	
VAR 02	.60																
VAR 03	.43	.44															
VAR 04	.29	.29	.32														
VAR 05	.56	.58	.52	.27													
VAR 06	.15	.34	.24	.14	.33												
VAR 07	.30	.40	.40	.30	.46	.45											
VAR 08	.07	.33	.23	.18	.23	.31	.45										
VAR 09	.28	.60	.21	.20	.52	.52	.54	.35									
VAR 10	.29	.61	.26	.20	.49	.38	.56	.33	.71								
VAR 11	.27	.51	.33	.29	.34	.49	.49	.33	.64	.62							
VAR 12	.37	.58	.28	.31	.48	.40	.50	.30	.70	.73	.77						
VAR 13	.33	.54	.20	.10	.34	.41	.44	.21	.63	.62	.54	.51					
VAR 14	.22	.50	.36	.22	.41	.50	.36	.45	.53	.53	.48	.57	.49				
VAR 15	.38	.57	.38	.24	.53	.36	.46	.30	.50	.65	.59	.60	.53	.63			
VAR 16	.32	.46	.37	.14	.65	.34	.49	.30	.52	.57	.49	.59	.48	.48	.65		
VAR 17	.29	.47	.30	.17	.56	.40	.53	.32	.42	.51	.43	.41	.42	.40	.47	.58	

Note: Shaded items indicate highly correlated variables.

Table 10.9   Factor Analysis of Environmental Variables – New Zealand Companies

Variables	Factor 1	Factor 2	Factor 3	h^2 (communality)
VAR 01 Differences in income tax rates	.278	.779*	–.191	.721
VAR 02 Rates of customs duties	.601*	.548	.075	.668
VAR 03 Tax authority transfer pricing audits	.087	.729*	.312	.636
VAR 04 Comply with tax law and regulations	–.025	.525*	.393	.430
VAR 05 Restrictions on repatriation of income	.447	.697*	.088	.694
VAR 06 Competitive position of the subsidiary	.495	.014	.497*	.492
VAR 07 Overall profit to multinational group	.451	.312	.530*	.581
VAR 08 Corporate profit of the subsidiary	.194	.071	.788*	.663
VAR 09 Import restrictions	.808*	.112	.235	.720
VAR 10 Foreign currency exchange controls	.820*	.182	.179	.738
VAR 11 Good relations with host government	.718*	.148	.311	.633
VAR 12 Price controls of host government	.777*	.089	.034	.697
VAR 13 Existence of local partner	.791*	.089	.034	.635
VAR 14 Performance evaluation	.582*	.177	.443	.566
VAR 15 Political and social pressure	.685*	.363	.159	.625
VAR 16 Royalty restrictions	.641*	.370	.156	.572
VAR 17 Maintenance of cash flows	.499*	.348	.293	.456
Sum of squares (Eigenvalue)	7.956	1.475	1.097	
Percentage of trace (Variance)	46.8	8.7	6.5	62.0

Note: * Indicates highest factor loading for variables.

From Table 10.9 it may be seen that Factor 1 summarises 46.8% of the total variance, Factor 2 summarises 8.7% of the total variance, and Factor 3 summarises 6.5% of the total variance. Together, therefore, the

Table 10.10 Summary of Three Dimensions of Variables – Factor Analysis for New Zealand Companies

Dimensions and Variables	Rotated Factor Loadings	Communality	Eigenvalue	Variance Summarised (Eignvalue/no. of Variable)
Factor 1 Government restrictions			7.956	.468
VAR 10 Foreign currency exchange controls	.820	.738		
VAR 09 Import restrictions	.808	.720		
VAR 13 Existence of local partner	.791	.635		
VAR 12 Price controls of host government	.777	.697		
VAR 11 Good relations with host government	.718	.633		
VAR 15 Political and social pressure	.685	.625		
VAR 16 Royalty restrictions	.641	.572		
VAR 02 Rates of customs duties	.601	.668		
VAR 14 Performance evaluation	.582	.566		
VAR 17 Maintenance of cash flows	.499	.456		

Table 10.10   Summary of Three Dimensions of Variables – Factor Analysis for New Zealand Companies – *continued*

Dimensions and Variables	Rotated Factor Loadings	Communality	Eigenvalue	Variance Summarised (Eignvalue/no. of Variable)
Factor 2 Tax and legal considerations			1.475	.087
VAR 01 Differences in income tax rates	.779	.721		
VAR 03 Tax authority transfer pricing audits	.729	.636		
VAR 05 Restrictions on repatriation of income	.697	.694		
VAR 04 Comply with tax law and regulations	.525	.430		
Factor 3 Corporate competitive position			1.097	.065
VAR 08 Corporate profit of the subsidiary	.788	.663		
VAR 07 Overall profit to multinational group	.530	.581		
VAR 06 Competitive position of the subsidiary	.497	.492		
Total				.620

three factors summarise 62.0% of the total variance in the seventeen variables.

The data in Table 10.10 indicate that Factor 1 is the most dominant factor. Within this most significant factor, 'foreign currency exchange controls' is the most important variable, followed in descending order by 'import restrictions', 'existence of local partner', 'price controls of host government', and 'good relations with host government'. This means that the respondents who placed a great deal of importance on 'foreign currency exchange controls' also tended to regard other variables that loaded highly on Factor 1 as important.

Factor 2 has very high loadings on 'differences in income tax rates' and 'tax authority transfer pricing audits'. These two variables together form another important dimension of environmental variables.

Factor 3 has a high loading on 'corporate profit of the subsidiary', but relatively low loadings on the other variables such as 'overall profit to multinational group' and 'competitive position of the subsidiary'.

Chinese perspective

The sampling frame to research the determinants of International Transfer Pricing in Chinese practice was the list of the foreign-controlled subsidiaries in China as contained in the publication *Foreign Investment Companies Operating in China* (2001) – a directory listing 22,000 multinational companies located in China, together with another directory entitled *The World Top 500 Multinational Companies Operating in China* (2003). In addition to the sample assembled from these two directories, a further fifty firms were randomly selected from a network of 1,000 multinationals located in Beijing as listed by a consultancy firm in the city for the purposes of their business. The final Chinese sample contained 500 companies extracted from the disparate sources. That is, 450 firms were randomly drawn from the two directories and another fifty firms were randomly drawn from the network of the 1,000 multinationals on the Beijing consultancy firm's list.

In recognition of the entrenched cultural disposition in China for secrecy and reluctance to communicate information about a firm's activities to outsiders, it was anticipated at the start of the research that eliciting any responses from Chinese respondents would be difficult when compared with the approaches made to Australian and New Zealand firms.

Hence it was necessary to despatch an inordinate numbers of Questionnaires in the hope of receiving enough returns to fulfil the research

Table 10.11   Environmental Variables Ranked for Their Importance by Respondent Firms in China (n = 47)

Environmental Variables	Mean	Rank	Standard Deviation
VAR 07 Overall profit to multinational group	4.07	1	.827
VAR 08 Corporate profit of the subsidiary	4.04	2	.842
VAR 04 Comply with tax law and regulations	3.96	3	1.134
VAR 06 Competitive position of the subsidiary	3.91	4	.905
VAR 02 Rates of customs duties	3.74	5	.999
VAR 17 Maintenance of cash flows	3.65	6	.971
VAR 11 Good relations with host government	3.59	7	1.045
VAR 14 Performance evaluation	3.50	8	.863
VAR 01 Differences in income tax rates	3.37	9	1.162
VAR 05 Restrictions on repatriation of income	3.26	10	1.084
VAR 13 Existence of local partner	3.24	11	1.119
VAR 10 Foreign currency exchange controls	3.04	12	1.228
VAR 03 Tax authority transfer pricing audits	3.00	13	1.229
VAR 09 Import restrictions	2.96	14	1.246
VAR 16 Royalty restrictions	2.78	15	1.134
VAR 15 Political and social pressure	2.74	16	1.273
VAR 12 Price controls of host government	2.65	17	1.320

objectives. In the event forty-seven usable returns were obtained, producing the data as presented in Table 10.11 and the following tables containing analyses of the data.

In China, 'overall profit to multinational group' and 'corporate profit of the subsidiary' were perceived as the most important variables in transfer pricing decisions. Other variables considered very important included 'comply with tax law and regulations', 'competitive position of the subsidiary', 'rates of customs duties', 'maintenance of cash flows', 'good relations with host government', and 'performance evaluation'.

Eight variables were considered moderately important by the respondent firms. They were 'differences in income tax rates', 'restrictions on repatriation of income', 'existence of local partner', 'foreign currency exchange controls', and 'tax authority transfer pricing audits'. Variables which were considered slightly important included 'import

Table 10.12   Correlations Matrix of Environmental Variables – Chinese Companies

Variable	1	2	3	4	5	6	7	8	9	10	11	12	13	14	15	16	17
VAR 01																	
VAR 02	.33																
VAR 03	.31	.22															
VAR 04	.38	.26	.53														
VAR 05	.33	.17	.38	.32													
VAR 06	.21	.29	.22	.19	.33												
VAR 07	.14	.18	.42	.26	.18	.55											
VAR 08	.28	.44	.17	.33	.23	.62	.41										
VAR 09	.24	.46	.38	.22	.62	.31	.22	.40									
VAR 10	.30	.32	.27	.19	.51	.15	.00	.08	.71								
VAR 11	.44	.38	.35	.53	.51	.52	.26	.48	.38	.26							
VAR 12	.35	.23	.34	.15	.69	.19	.16	.33	.73	.56	.43						
VAR 13	.04	.06	.07	.04	.44	.49	.13	.32	.45	.30	.39	.45					
VAR 14	.10	.13	.36	.43	.33	.67	.45	.37	.31	.15	.48	.23	.54				
VAR 15	.17	.26	.44	.27	.63	.34	.31	.05	.60	.55	.39	.54	.38	.36			
VAR 16	.27	.42	.51	.25	.57	.28	.37	.24	.75	.65	.32	.69	.48	.34	.65		
VAR 17	.27	.27	.22	.57	.53	.44	.20	.26	.39	.35	.60	.25	.41	.56	.48	.33	

Note: Shaded items indicate highly correlated variables.

Table 10.13   Factor Analysis of Environmental Variables – Chinese Companies

Variables	Factor 1	Factor 2	Factor 3	h^2 (communality)
VAR 01 Differences in income tax rates	.201	.071	.671*	.495
VAR 02 Rates of customs duties	.268	.191	.472*	.331
VAR 03 Tax authority transfer pricing audits	.292	.153	.657*	.540
VAR 04 Comply with tax law and regulations	.051	.328	.755*	.681
VAR 05 Restrictions on repatriation of income	.731*	.263	.206	.645
VAR 06 Competitive position of the subsidiary	.138	.872*	.050	.781
VAR 07 Overall profit to multinational group	.032	.586*	.261	.413
VAR 08 Corporate profit of the subsidiary	.084	.657*	.251	.501
VAR 09 Import restrictions	.839*	.208	.178	.779
VAR 10 Foreign currency exchange controls	.810*	−.063	.190	.695
VAR 11 Good relations with host government	.287	.586*	.434	.614
VAR 12 Price controls of host government	.820*	.125	.144	.708
VAR 13 Existence of local partner	.545	.591*	−.433	.834
VAR 14 Performance evaluation	.184	.813*	.079	.702
VAR 15 Political and social pressure	.726*	.235	.173	.613
VAR 16 Royalty restrictions	.815*	.193	.219	.749
VAR 17 Maintenance of cash flows	.338	.544*	.295	.498
Sum of squares (Eigenvalue)	6.811	2.123	1.644	
Percentage of trace (Variance)	40.1	12.5	9.7	62.3

Note: * Indicates highest factor loading for variables.

restrictions', 'royalty restrictions', 'political and social pressure', and 'price controls of host government'.

An R-type, principal components factor analysis that is orthogonally rotated based on the Varimax procedure was performed. The correlations matrix of environmental variables in Table 10.12 shows that some variables are highly correlated. For instance, Variable 9 (import restrictions) and Variable 12 (price controls of host government) have a correlation coefficient of .73. Variable 5 (restrictions on repatriation of income) and Variable 16 (royalty restrictions) have a correlation coefficient of .69 with Variable 12 (price controls of host government). The high correlation of the variables provided justification for performing a factor analysis.

Three factors (or dimensions) and their reliability scores (Chronbach's alpha) were extracted and labelled as follows:

- Factor 1: Government restrictions (Chronbach's alpha = .9094).
- Factor 2: Corporate competitive position (Chronbach's alpha = .8396).
- Factor 3: Tax and legal considerations (Chronbach's alpha = .6749).

Table 10.13 shows that Factor 1 summarises 40.1% of the total variance, Factor 2 summarises 12.5% of the total variance, and Factor 3 summarises 9.7% of the total variance. Together, the three factors summarise 62.3% of the total variance in the seventeen variables.

Factor 1 is the most dominant factor. Table 10.14 shows that within this most significant factor, 'import restriction' is the most important variable, followed in descending order by 'price controls of host government', 'royalty restrictions', 'foreign currency exchange controls', 'restrictions on repatriation of income', and 'political and social pressure'. This means that the respondents who placed a great deal of importance on 'import restriction' also tended to regard other variables that loaded highly on Factor 1 as important.

Factor 2 has very high loadings on 'competitive position of the subsidiary', and 'performance evaluation'. These variables together form another important dimension of environmental variables.

Factor 3 has high loadings on 'comply with tax law and regulations', 'differences in income tax rates', and 'tax authority transfer pricing audits'.

Summary

This Chapter reports the importance that companies in three Pacific countries attach to each of a range of business environmental variables

Table 10.14   Summary of Three Dimensions of Variables – Chinese Companies

Dimensions and Variables	Rotated Factor Loadings	Communality	Eigenvalue	Variance Summarised (Eignvalue/no. of Variable)
Factor 1 Government restrictions			6.811	.401
VAR 09 Import restrictions	.839	.779		
VAR 12 Price controls of host government	.820	.708		
VAR 16 Royalty restrictions	.815	.749		
VAR 10 Foreign currency exchange controls	.810	.695		
VAR 05 Restrictions on repatriation of income	.731	.645		
VAR 15 Political and social pressure	.726	.613		

Table 10.14   Summary of Three Dimensions of Variables – Chinese Companies – *continued*

Dimensions and Variables	Rotated Factor Loadings	Communality	Eigenvalue	Variance Summarised (Eignvalue/no. of Variable)
Factor 2 Corporate competitive position			2.123	.125
VAR 06 Competitive position of the subsidiary	.872	.781		
VAR 14 Performance evaluation	.813	.702		
VAR 08 Corporate profit of the subsidiary	.657	.501		
VAR 13 Existence of local partner	.591	.834		
VAR 07 Overall profit to multinational group	.586	.413		
VAR 11 Good relations with host government	.586	.614		
VAR 17 Maintenance of cash flows	.544	.498		
Factor 3 Tax and legal considerations			1.644	.097
VAR 04 Comply with tax law and regulations	.755	.681		
VAR 01 Differences in income tax rates	.671	.495		
VAR 03 Tax authority transfer pricing audits	.657	.540		
VAR 02 Rates of customs duties	.472	.331		
Total				.623

when they are making decisions about International Transfer Pricing. 'Comply with tax law and regulations' received the highest rating by both the New Zealand and Australian respondent companies, whereas 'overall profit to multinational group' was rated as the single most crucial variable by the respondent companies in China. Other important variables in all the three countries included 'corporate profit of the subsidiary' and 'competitive position of the subsidiary'.

In addition to the four key individual variables identified, three dimensions (factors) of environmental variables were also extracted from the samples in each country by factor analysis.

11
International Comparisons

Introduction

In Chapter 9 a comparison of the International Transfer Pricing methods actually used by the respondent companies showed that those for whom China was the host country adopted different methods from those whose host countries were Australia and New Zealand. Chapter 10 examined a variety of environmental factors and their relative importance in each of the three countries. The sharp cultural differences between Australia and New Zealand on the one hand and China on the other might suggest that the respective business environments involved played an important determining influence and might be the origin for explanations of the differences.

To discover any such determining influences from this source, the companies in the study were asked to assess the relative importance of each of a range of environmental factors which could affect their International Transfer Pricing decisions. This chapter, therefore, contains the responses from the multinational subsidiary companies operating in the three host countries Australia, New Zealand and China, together with the results of statistical tests that were applied to the results to establish if any significantly different valuations were placed on the environmental variables according to the host country.

Environmental variables – comparison of ratings

The ranking of the importance of each of a range of environmental variables by the respondent companies in Australia, New Zealand and China is given in Table 11.1. The ranking of importance is according to the mean scores of the variables. The standard deviation indicates the

Table 11.1   Comparison of Ratings and Rankings of the Importance of Environmental Variables for International Transfer Pricing by Australian, New Zealand and Chinese Companies

Environmental Variables	Australia			New Zealand			China		
	Mean	Rank	SD	Mean	Rank	SD	Mean	Rank	SD
VAR 04 Comply with tax law and regulations	4.05	1	1.166	3.96	1	1.069	3.96	3	1.134
VAR 06 Competitive position of the subsidiary	3.28	2	1.335	3.31	3	1.369	3.91	4	.905
VAR 08 Corporate profit of the subsidiary	3.14	3	1.206	3.38	2	1.089	4.04	2	.842
VAR 07 Overall profit to multinational group	2.86	4	1.317	3.05	4	1.157	4.07	1	.827
VAR 03 Tax authority transfer pricing audits	2.79	5	1.321	2.82	5	1.254	3.00	13	1.229
VAR 17 Maintenance of cash flows	2.55	6	1.404	2.71	6	1.422	3.65	6	.971
VAR 01 Differences in income tax rates	2.43	7	1.464	2.47	8	1.363	3.37	9	1.162
VAR 14 Performance evaluation	2.41	8	1.298	2.51	7	1.242	3.50	8	.863
VAR 11 Good relations with host government	2.26	9	1.292	2.18	10	1.262	3.59	7	1.045
VAR 10 Foreign currency exchange controls	2.12	10/11	1.326	2.09	11	1.248	3.04	12	1.228
VAR 02 Rates of customs duties	2.12	10/11	1.312	2.00	13/14	1.147	3.74	5	.999
VAR 05 Restrictions on repatriation of income	1.97	12/13	1.169	2.43	9	1.261	3.26	10	1.084
VAR 09 Import restrictions	1.97	12/13	1.199	2.00	13/14	1.192	2.96	14	1.246
VAR 12 Price controls of host government	1.95	14	1.300	1.95	16	1.210	2.65	17	1.320
VAR 13 Existence of local partner	1.84	15	1.203	2.07	12	1.258	3.24	11	1.119
VAR 15 Political and social pressure	1.71	16/17	.975	1.96	15	1.094	2.74	16	1.273
VAR 16 Royalty restrictions	1.71	16/17	.973	1.82	17	1.109	2.78	15	1.134

extent of agreement in the rating of individual variables among the respondents. It can be seen that the Chinese companies place more emphasis than the Australian and New Zealand firms on nearly all of the seventeen environmental variables.

One possible interpretation of this result is that different measurement scales might have been used by the three national groups (China vis-à-vis Australia and New Zealand) in responding to the Questionnaire. The Questionnaire used in China was presented in the Chinese language. Although the content version of the Chinese Questionnaire was identical to that of the Australian and New Zealand Questionnaires, some modification was necessary, owing to cultural, institutional and language differences.

However, there is no substantive evidence to support this interpretation. A more likely explanation for it is that Chinese multinationals engage in a relatively wider range of intercompany transactions and business operations in China, where they are subject to more economic, political and social risks arising from the peculiar Chinese business environment (Chan and Chow, 1998). Hence, the incentives and motives driving transfer pricing manoeuvres are stronger for Chinese firms than for Australian and New Zealand companies.

To investigate possible differences in the ranking of the environmental variables, a Kruskal-Wallis test was used for analysis. The results of the test are presented in Table 11.2. There are statistically significant differences in the ranking of these variables by members of the three national groups, the environmental measure being significant at the .01 level.

To investigate further possible differences in the ranking of individual environmental variables, a Kruskal-Wallis test was employed to

Table 11.2   Kruskal-Wallis Test Applied to the Ratings of the Importance of Environmental Variables for International Transfer Pricing by Australian, New Zealand and Chinese Companies (n = 177)

	Australia	New Zealand	China
Mean Rank	71.47	76.87	130.00
N	55	76	46
Chi-Squared value	40.172***		
Degree of freedom	2		
Significance. (2-tailed)	.000		

Note: *** Significant at the .01 level.

Table 11.3   Kruskal-Wallis Test Applied to the Ratings of the Importance of the Individual Items of Environmental Variables for International Transfer Pricing by Australian, New Zealand and Chinese Companies

	Mean Rank			Test Statistics	
Environmental Variables	Australia	New Zealand	China	Chi-Squared Value	Significance (p)
VAR 04 Comply with tax law and regulations	95.63	89.02	90.36	.621	.733
VAR 06 Competitive position of the subsidiary	84.28	86.94	107.93	6.73	.035**
VAR 08 Corporate profit of the subsidiary	76.71	86.08	117.26	17.95	.000***
VAR 07 Overall profit to multinational group	75.69	81.95	125.46	28.87	.000***
VAR 03 Tax authority transfer pricing audits	88.44	89.81	96.23	.67	.714
VAR 17 Maintenance of cash flows	78.21	84.20	118.51	18.40	.000***
VAR 01 Differences in income tax rates	81.16	83.13	116.59	15.54	.000***
VAR 14 Performance evaluation	77.99	81.73	122.92	24.54	.000***
VAR 11 Good relations with host government	78.85	75.91	129.28	36.23	.000***
VAR 10 Foreign currency exchange controls	81.54	81.25	119.24	19.34	.000***
VAR 02 Rates of customs duties	77.32	73.68	137.25	51.50	.000***
VAR 05 Restrictions on repatriation of income	69.58	88.47	122.25	27.93	.000***
VAR 09 Import restrictions	80.00	81.77	120.33	21.16	.000***
VAR 12 Price controls of host government	84.38	82.71	111.09	10.85	.004***
VAR 13 Existence of local partner	71.63	80.87	125.52	34.40	.000***
VAR 15 Political and social pressure	73.41	84.82	116.58	20.71	.000***
VAR 16 Royalty restrictions	81.40	77.73	123.80	27.65	.000***

Note: ** Significant at the .05 level. *** Significant at the .01 level.

Table 11.4   Comparison of Ratings of the Importance of Environmental Variables for International Transfer Pricing by Australian and New Zealand Companies

Environmental Variables	Australia			New Zealand		
	Mean	Rank	SD	Mean	Rank	SD
VAR 04 Comply with tax law and regulations	4.05	1	1.166	3.96	1	1.069
VAR 06 Competitive position of the subsidiary	3.28	2	1.335	3.31	3	1.369
VAR 08 Corporate profit of the subsidiary	3.14	3	1.206	3.38	2	1.089
VAR 07 Overall profit to multinational group	2.86	4	1.317	3.05	4	1.157
VAR 03 Tax authority transfer pricing audits	2.79	5	1.321	2.82	5	1.254
VAR 17 Maintenance of cash flows	2.55	6	1.404	2.71	6	1.422
VAR 01 Differences in income tax rates	2.43	7	1.464	2.47	8	1.363
VAR 14 Performance evaluation	2.41	8	1.298	2.51	7	1.242
VAR 11 Good relations with host government	2.26	9	1.292	2.18	10	1.262
VAR 10 Foreign currency exchange controls	2.12	10/11	1.326	2.09	11	1.248
VAR 02 Rates of customs duties	2.12	10/11	1.312	2.00	13/14	1.147
VAR 05 Restrictions on repatriation of income	1.97	12/13	1.169	2.43	9	1.261
VAR 09 Import restrictions	1.97	12/13	1.199	2.00	13/14	1.192
VAR 12 Price controls of host government	1.95	14	1.300	1.95	16	1.210
VAR 13 Existence of local partner	1.84	15	1.203	2.07	12	1.258
VAR 15 Political and social pressure	1.71	16/17	.9750	1.96	15	1.094
VAR 16 Royalty restrictions	1.71	16/17	.9730	1.82	17	1.109

Note: The shaded item contributes most to the differences between the two national groups.

test each individual variable. The results of the test are presented in Table 11.3. Differences are found in the case of fifteen environmental variables, fourteen being significant at the .01 level, while that of 'competitive position of the subsidiary' is significant at the .05 level. No differences are recorded in the case of the ranking of two environmental variables, 'comply with tax law and regulations' and 'tax authority transfer pricing audits'.

Australia and New Zealand. The rankings of the importance of environmental variables by the respondent firms in Australia and New Zealand are given in Table 11.4. The rankings of the importance of the variables are according to the mean scores of the variables. The standard deviation indicates the extent of agreement in the rating of individual variables among the respondents.

To investigate possible differences in the ranking of environmental variables, a Mann-Whitney U Test was used for analysis. The results of the test are presented in Table 11.5. There are no statistically significant differences in the ranking of these variables by members of the two national groups, the scores for the environmental variables being not significant at even the .1 level.

To investigate further possible differences in the ranking of the individual environmental variables, a Mann-Whitney U test was employed to test each individual variable. The results of the test are presented in Table 11.6. The scores of sixteen environmental variables are not even significant at the .1 level. Only one environmental variable, 'restrictions on repatriation of income' is shown with any significant difference.

Australia and China. The rankings of the importance of environmental variables for International Transfer Pricing by the respondents of Australia and China are given in Table 11.7. The rankings are according to the mean scores of the variables. The standard deviation

Table 11.5   Mann-Whitney U Test Applied to the Ranking of the Importance of Environmental Variables for International Transfer Pricing by Australian and New Zealand Companies

	Australia	New Zealand
Mean Rank	63.56	67.76
N	55	76
z-value		–.626
Significance. (p)		.532

Table 11.6 Mann-Whitney U Test Applied to the Ratings of the Importance of the Individual Items of Environmental Variables for International Transfer Pricing by Australian and New Zealand Companies

Environmental Variables	Mean Rank		Test Statistics	
	Australia	New Zealand	Z-value	Significance (p)
VAR 04 Comply with tax law and regulations	71.53	66.18	−.832	.405
VAR 06 Competitive position of the subsidiary	66.94	68.80	−.282	.778
VAR 08 Corporate profit of the subsidiary	63.68	71.25	−1.163	.245
VAR 07 Overall profit to multinational group	64.71	70.48	−.876	.381
VAR 03 Tax authority transfer pricing audits	67.41	68.44	−.156	.876
VAR 17 Maintenance of cash flows	65.49	69.89	−.668	.504
VAR 01 Differences in income tax rates	67.05	68.71	−.254	.800
VAR 14 Performance evaluation	66.22	69.34	−.476	.634
VAR 11 Good relations with host government	68.69	66.59	−.324	.746
VAR 10 Foreign currency exchange controls	68.00	68.00	.000	1.000
VAR 02 Rates of customs duties	69.14	67.14	−.313	.755
VAR 05 Restrictions on repatriation of income	59.92	74.08	−.2189	.029**
VAR 09 Import restrictions	67.14	68.65	−.239	.811
VAR 12 Price controls of host government	68.32	66.88	−.231	.818
VAR 13 Existence of local partner	62.38	69.53	−1.157	.247
VAR 15 Political and social pressure	61.52	70.06	−1.368	.171
VAR 16 Royalty restrictions	66.64	69.03	−.393	.684

Note: ** Significant at the .05 level.

Table 11.7   Comparison of Ratings of the Importance of Environmental Variables for International Transfer Pricing by Australian and Chinese Companies

Environmental Variables	Australia			China		
	Mean	Rank	SD	Mean	Rank	SD
VAR 04 Comply with tax law and regulations	4.05	1	1.166	3.96	3	1.134
VAR 06 Competitive position of the subsidiary	3.28	2	1.335	3.91	4	.905
VAR 08 Corporate profit of the subsidiary	3.14	3	1.206	4.04	2	.842
VAR 07 Overall profit to multinational group	2.86	4	1.317	4.07	1	.827
VAR 03 Tax authority transfer pricing audits	2.79	5	1.321	3.00	13	1.229
VAR 17 Maintenance of cash flows	2.55	6	1.404	3.65	6	.971
VAR 01 Differences in income tax rates	2.43	7	1.464	3.37	9	1.162
VAR 14 Performance evaluation	2.41	8	1.298	3.50	8	.863
VAR 11 Good relations with host government	2.26	9	1.292	3.59	7	1.045
VAR 10 Foreign currency exchange controls	2.12	10/11	1.326	3.04	12	1.228
VAR 02 Rates of customs duties	2.12	10/11	1.312	3.74	5	.999
VAR 05 Restrictions on repatriation of income	1.97	12/13	1.169	3.26	10	1.084
VAR 09 Import restrictions	1.97	12/13	1.199	2.96	14	1.246
VAR 12 Price controls of host government	1.95	14	1.300	2.65	17	1.320
VAR 13 Existence of local partner	1.84	15	1.203	3.24	11	1.119
VAR 15 Political and social pressure	1.71	16/17	.975	2.74	16	1.273
VAR 16 Royalty restrictions	1.71	16/17	.973	2.78	15	1.134

Note: The shaded items contribute most to the differences between the two national groups.

Table 11.8   Mann-Whitney U Test Applied to the Ranking of the Importance of Environmental Variables for International Transfer Pricing by Australian and Chinese Companies

	Australia	China
Mean Rank	35.91	69.04
N	55	46
z-value		−5.663
Significance. (p)		.000***

Note: *** Significant at the .01 level.

indicates the extent of agreement in the rating of individual variables among the respondents.

To investigate possible differences in the ranking of the environmental variables, a Mann-Whitney U Test was used for analysis. The results of the test are presented in Table 11.8. There are statistically significant differences in the ranking of these factors by members of the two national groups, the scores of the environmental variables being significant at the .01 level.

To investigate further possible differences in the ranking of individual environmental variables, a Mann-Whitney U Test was employed to test each individual variable. The results of the test are presented in Table 11.9. There are significant differences in the case of fifteen environmental variables. There are no significant differences in the case of the other two environmental variables, 'comply with tax law and regulations' and 'tax authority transfer pricing audits'.

New Zealand and China. The rankings of importance of the environmental variables by the respondent firms in New Zealand and China are given in Table 11.10. The rankings are according to the mean scores of the variables. The standard deviation indicates the extent of agreement in the rating of individual variables among the respondents.

To investigate possible differences in the ranking of the environmental variables, a Mann-Whitney U Test was used for analysis. The results of the test are presented in Table 11.11. There are statistically significant differences in the ranking of these factors by members of these two national groups, the scores for the environmental variables being significant at the .01 level.

To investigate further possible differences in the ranking of the individual environmental variables, a Mann-Whitney U Test was employed to test each individual variable. The results of the test are presented in

Table 11.9 Mann-Whitney U Test Applied to the Ratings of the Importance of the Individual Items of Environmental Variables for International Transfer Pricing by Australian and Chinese Companies

Environmental Variables	Mean Rank		Test Statistics	
	Australia	China	Z-value	Significance (p)
VAR 04 Comply with tax law and regulations	54.09	51.60	−.443	.658
VAR 06 Competitive position of the subsidiary	46.81	60.64	−2.407	.016**
VAR 08 Corporate profit of the subsidiary	42.53	65.08	−3.926	.000***
VAR 07 Overall profit to multinational group	40.48	67.65	−4.702	.000***
VAR 03 Tax authority transfer pricing audits	50.53	54.99	−7.68	.442
VAR 17 Maintenance of cash flows	42.22	65.47	−4.015	.000***
VAR 01 Differences in income tax rates	43.60	63.72	−3.453	.001***
VAR 14 Performance evaluation	41.27	66.66	−4.390	.000***
VAR 11 Good relations with host government	39.66	68.68	−4.982	.000***
VAR 10 Foreign currency exchange controls	43.04	64.42	−3.692	.000***
VAR 02 Rates of customs duties	37.68	71.18	−5.763	.000***
VAR 05 Restrictions on repatriation of income	39.16	69.33	−5.206	.000***
VAR 09 Import restrictions	42.36	65.28	−3.979	.000***
VAR 12 Price controls of host government	45.56	61.25	−2.749	.006***
VAR 13 Existence of local partner	37.74	68.25	−5.371	.000***
VAR 15 Political and social pressure	39.89	64.28	−4.356	.000***
VAR 16 Royalty restrictions	40.59	67.51	−4.725	.000***

Note: ** Significant at the .05 level.
*** Significant at the .01 level.

Table 11.10   Comparison of Ratings of the Importance of Environmental Variables for International Transfer Pricing by New Zealand and Chinese Companies

Environmental Variables	New Zealand			China		
	Mean	Rank	SD	Mean	Rank	SD
VAR 04 Comply with tax law and regulations	3.96	1	1.069	3.96	3	1.134
VAR 08 Corporate profit of the subsidiary	3.38	2	1.089	4.04	2	.842
VAR 06 Competitive position of the subsidiary	3.31	3	1.369	3.91	4	.905
VAR 07 Overall profit to multinational group	3.05	4	1.157	4.07	1	.827
VAR 03 Tax authority transfer pricing audits	2.82	5	1.254	3.00	13	1.229
VAR 17 Maintenance of cash flows	2.71	6	1.422	3.65	6	.971
VAR 14 Performance evaluation	2.51	7	1.242	3.50	8	.863
VAR 01 Differences in income tax rates	2.47	8	1.363	3.37	9	1.162
VAR 05 Restrictions on repatriation of income	2.43	9	1.261	3.26	10	1.084
VAR 11 Good relations with host government	2.18	10	1.262	3.59	7	1.045
VAR 10 Foreign currency exchange controls	2.09	11	1.248	3.04	12	1.228
VAR 13 Existence of local partner	2.07	12	1.258	3.24	11	1.119
VAR 02 Rates of customs duties	2.00	13/14	1.147	3.74	5	.999
VAR 09 Import restrictions	2.00	13/14	1.192	2.96	14	1.246
VAR 15 Political and social pressure	1.96	15	1.094	2.74	16	1.273
VAR 12 Price controls of host government	1.95	16	1.210	2.65	17	1.320
VAR 16 Royalty restrictions	1.82	17	1.109	2.78	15	1.134

Note: the shaded items contribute most to the differences between the two national groups.

Table 11.11 Mann-Whitney U Test Applied to the Ranking of the Importance of Environmental Variables for International Transfer Pricing by New Zealand and Chinese Companies

	New Zealand	China
Mean Rank	47.61	84.46
N	76	46
z-value		−5.580
Significance. (p)		.000***

Note: *** Significant at the .01 level.

Table 11.12. There are significant differences in the case of fifteen environmental variables. There are no significant differences in the case of the remaining two environmental variables, 'comply with tax law and regulations' and 'tax authority transfer pricing audits'.

Environmental variables – comparison of rankings

Australia and New Zealand. Tests on the aggregate rank order of environmental variables for the three countries were also conducted. To determine whether the rank orders of each pairing of the national groups on all seventeen variables were correlated, the Spearman's rank correlation coefficient test was applied. This test was based on the rank order data presented in Table 11.1.

In the case of Australia and New Zealand, the results of the test are presented in Table 11.13. The Spearman rank correlation coefficient is .947 and the test is significant at the .01 level. The result shows that there is a substantial correlation between the rankings of the variables by the respective groups of Australian and New Zealand companies. In other words, the Australian and New Zealand respondents share a high level of agreement on the relative importance of the seventeen variables. However, differences in the rank orderings of the two national groups on some variables still exist. It can be seen in Table 11.4 that the variable 'restrictions on repatriation of income' is ranked twelfth/ thirteenth by the Australian firms but ninth by the New Zealand companies. This variable contributed most of the difference between the two national groups.

Australia and China. To determine whether the rank orders of these two national groups on all seventeen variables were correlated, the Spearman's rank correlation coefficient test was conducted. This test

Table 11.12   Mann-Whitney U Test Applied to the Ratings of the Importance of the Individual Items of Environmental Variables for International Transfer Pricing by New Zealand and Chinese Companies

Environmental Variables	Mean Rank		Test Statistics	
	New Zealand	China	Z-value	Significance (p)
VAR 04 Comply with tax law and regulations	61.84	62.26	−.066	.947
VAR 08 Corporate profit of the subsidiary	53.82	75.68	−3.450	.001***
VAR 06 Competitive position of the subsidiary	57.14	71.29	−2.219	.026**
VAR 07 Overall profit to multinational group	50.47	81.30	−4.824	.000***
VAR 03 Tax authority transfer pricing audits	60.36	64.74	−.677	.498
VAR 17 Maintenance of cash flows	53.31	76.54	−3.591	.000***
VAR 14 Performance evaluation	51.39	79.76	−4.425	.000***
VAR 01 Differences in income tax rates	53.42	76.37	−3.542	.000***
VAR 05 Restrictions on repatriation of income	53.38	76.42	−3.566	.000***
VAR 11 Good relations with host government	47.82	84.10	−5.626	.000***
VAR 10 Foreign currency exchange controls	52.25	78.32	−4.048	.000***
VAR 13 Existence of local partner	49.84	80.77	−4.836	.000***
VAR 02 Rates of customs duties	45.53	89.57	−6.808	.000***
VAR 09 Import restrictions	52.12	78.54	−4.119	.000***
VAR 15 Political and social pressure	53.76	75.79	−3.448	.001***
VAR 12 Price controls of host government	54.34	73.34	−3.035	.002***
VAR 16 Royalty restrictions	51.37	79.79	−4.488	.000***

Note: ** Significant at the .05 level.
*** Significant at the .01 level.

Table 11.13   Rank Order Test on the Levels of Importance Attached by Australian and New Zealand Companies for International Transfer Pricing

	Australia vs New Zealand
Spearman's rho	.947***
Significance (2-tailed)	.000
N	17

Note: *** Significant at the .01 level.

Table 11.14   Rank Order Test on the Levels of Importance Attached by Australian and Chinese Companies for International Transfer Pricing

	Australia vs China
Spearman's rho	.805***
Significance (2-tailed)	.000
N	17

Note: *** Significant at the .01 level.

was based on the rank order data presented in Table 11.1. The results of the test are presented in Table 11.14. The Spearman rank correlation coefficient is .805, the test being significant at the .01 level. The result shows that there is a substantial correlation between the rankings of the variables by the two groups. In other words, the Australian and Chinese respondents shared considerable agreement on the relative importance of the seventeen variables. However, differences in the rank orders of the two national groups on some variables still exist. It can be seen in Table 11.7 that the variable 'rates of custom duties' is ranked tenth/eleventh by the Australian companies but fifth by the Chinese firms. In contrast, the variable 'tax authority transfer pricing audits' is ranked fifth by the Australian companies but thirteenth by the Chinese corporations. These two variables contributed most of the difference between the two national groups.

New Zealand and China. To determine whether the rank orders of these two national groups on all seventeen variables were correlated, the Spearman's rank correlation coefficient test was conducted. This test was based on the rank order data presented in Table 11.1. The results of the test are presented in Table 11.15. The Spearman rank correlation coefficient is .791, the test being significant at the .01 level. The result shows that there is substantial correlation

Table 11.15 Rank Order Test on the Levels of Importance Attached by New Zealand and Chinese Companies for International Transfer Pricing

	New Zealand vs China
Spearman's rho	.791***
Significance (2-tailed)	.000
N	17

Note: *** Significant at the .01 level.

between the rankings of the variables by the two groups. In other words, the New Zealand and Chinese respondents shared some agreement on the relative importance of the seventeen variables. Obviously, differences in the rank orderings of the two national groups on some variables still exist. It can be seen in Table 11.10 that the variable 'rates of customs duties' is ranked thirteen/fourteen by the New Zealand companies but fifth by the Chinese firms. In contrast, the variable 'tax authority transfer pricing audits' is ranked fifth by the New Zealand companies but thirteenth by the Chinese corporations. These two variables contributed most to the difference between the two national groups.

In conclusion, it is plain that the highest correlation exists between the rankings of variables by the Australian and New Zealand respondents. This means that there is substantial agreement between these two groups on the relative importance of each of the variables. The second highest correlation was recorded between the rankings of variables by Australian and Chinese respondents. The rankings of New Zealand and Chinese respondents had the lowest correlation coefficient.

The results are consistent with previous studies (Tang, 1979; 1981; Oyelere et al., 1999). Despite national differences, there is a high degree of consistency in the perception of companies located in contrasting host countries of the risks and opportunities inherent in the overall business environment with regard to their International Transfer Pricing decisions.

Summary

In this chapter statistically significant differences are indicated between the three sets of companies regarding the degree of emphasis they respectively place on environmental factors affecting their International Transfer Pricing policies. When the three sets are paired with

Table 11.16   Summary of Results of the Relative Importance of Environmental Variables Attached by National Groups for International Transfer Pricing

	Australia vs New Zealand	Australia vs China	New Zealand vs China
VAR 01 Differences in income tax rates		***	***
VAR 02 Rates of customs duties		***	***
VAR 03 Tax authority transfer pricing audits			
VAR 04 Comply with tax law and regulations			
VAR 05 Restrictions on repatriation of income	**	***	***
VAR 06 Competitive position of the subsidiary		**	**
VAR 07 Overall profit to multinational group		***	***
VAR 08 Corporate profit of the subsidiary		***	***
VAR 09 Import restrictions		***	***
VAR 10 Foreign currency exchange controls		***	***
VAR 11 Good relations with host government		***	***
VAR 12 Price controls of host government		***	***
VAR 13 Existence of local partner		***	***
VAR 14 Performance evaluation		***	***
VAR 15 Political and social pressure		***	***
VAR 16 Royalty restrictions		***	***
VAR 17 Maintenance of cash flow		***	***

** Significant at the .05 level.
*** Significant at the .01 level.

Table 11.17   Summary of Results of the Rank Orders of the Environmental Variables Rated for Their Importance by National Groups for International Transfer Pricing

	Spearman Correlation Coefficient
Australia vs New Zealand	.947***
Australia vs China	.805***
New Zealand vs China	.791***

Note: *** Significant at the .01 level.

each other, high correlation exists between the rankings of the variables in the case of each of the three pairings of national groups. The statistical test results are summarised in Tables 11.16 and 11.17.

12
Cross-National Analysis

Introduction

The previous chapter has identified four important variables affecting International Transfer Pricing policies in the three countries – 'comply with tax law and regulations', 'competitive position of the subsidiary', 'overall profit to multinational group', and 'corporate profit of the subsidiary'. Three variables that contributed most to the differentiation between each pair of national groups are also identified. These environmental variables are 'rates of customs duties', 'tax authority transfer pricing audits', and 'restrictions on repatriation of income'. This chapter provides a brief discussion and analysis of these seven key individual environmental variables as they affect International Transfer Pricing policies in Australia, New Zealand and China.

Crucial policy determinants

Comply with Tax Law and Regulations. Tables 12.1 and 12.2 indicate the importance of the Variable 04 – 'Comply with Tax Law and Regulations' – as it affects International Transfer Pricing policies of respondent firms operating in Australia, New Zealand and China. Respondents of the three national groups consistently consider the variable as highly important. Seventy-eight respondents consider this variable to be extremely important. The mean rating 4.05 of the variable given by the Australian respondents is slightly higher than that of their New Zealand and Chinese counterparts, whose mean ratings are both 3.96. The variable is ranked first by both the Australian and New Zealand respondents and third by the Chinese respondents.

Table 12.1 Comparison of the Ratings of Variable 04 'Comply with Tax Law and Regulations' for International Transfer Pricing by Australia, New Zealand and China

Rank	Extremely Important		Very Important		Important		Slightly Important		Not Important	
	N	%	N	%	N	%	N	%	N	%
Australia	26	44.1	21	35.6	5	8.5	3	5.1	4	6.8
New Zealand	31	40.3	20	26.0	21	27.3	2	2.6	3	3.9
China	21	45.7	9	19.6	9	19.6	7	15.2	0	0

Table 12.2 Statistical Data for the Comparison of the Ratings of Variable 04 'Comply with Tax Law and Regulations' for International Transfer Pricing by Australia, New Zealand and China

VAR 04 'Comply with Tax Law and Regulations'	N	Rank	Mean	Standard Deviation
Australia	59	1	4.05	1.166
New Zealand	77	1	3.96	1.069
China	46	3	3.96	1.134

Burns (1980) showed that both legal and tax variables are important factors to consider when selecting pricing strategies. Al-Eryani et al. (1990) suggested that market based methods are used more intensively by companies that are concerned about satisfying legal requirements. Chan and Chow (1998) discovered that United States multinational enterprises operating in developing countries perceive compliance with tax and customs regulations as the most important variable in International Transfer Pricing decisions.

The finding of this survey is an echo of previous studies. 'Comply with tax law and regulations' is considered to be highly important to respondent firms in Australia, New Zealand and China when they are formulating their pricing policies

Competitive Position of the Subsidiary. Tables 12.3 and 12.4 indicate the importance of Variable 06 – 'Competitive Position of the Subsidiary' – as it affects International Transfer Pricing policies of respondent firms operating in Australia, New Zealand and China. 'Competitive position of the subsidiary' is given fairly high ratings by the three groups. The mean rating 3.91 given by the Chinese

Table 12.3 Comparison of the Ratings of Variable 06 'Competitive Position of the Subsidiary' for International Transfer Pricing by Australia, New Zealand and China

Rank	Extremely Important		Very Important		Important		Slightly Important		Not Important	
	N	%	N	%	N	%	N	%	N	%
Australia	11	19.0	18	31.0	15	25.9	4	6.9	10	17.2
New Zealand	15	19.5	28	36.4	14	18.2	6	7.8	14	18.2
China	13	27.7	21	44.7	9	19.1	4	8.5	0	0

Table 12.4 Statistical Data for the Comparison of the Ratings of Variable 06 'Competitive Position of the Subsidiary' for International Transfer Pricing by Australia, New Zealand and China

VAR 06 'Competitive Position of the subsidiary'	N	Rank	Mean	Standard Deviation
Australia	58	2	3.28	1.335
New Zealand	77	3	3.31	1.369
China	47	4	3.91	.905

respondents is moderately higher than that of Australia at 3.28 and New Zealand at 3.31. The variable is ranked fourth by the Chinese respondents but second and third by Australian and New Zealand respondents respectively.

Australia and China are vast countries where lucrative opportunities exist but in tough marketing conditions. As a small economy, New Zealand has a comparatively low level of market competition. Until 1984 New Zealand was something of a command economy, but since then, the New Zealand government has freed price, wages and interest rates, floated the exchange rate, progressively removed tariffs and subsidies, deregulated the financial system, reduced income tax rates and encouraged overseas investment in the country. These New Zealand developments are observed as being more radical than those carried out in any other industrialised country (Lamminmaki and Drury, 2001, p. 330). The pervasive liberalisation and deregulation of the New Zealand economy pursued over the past decade dramatically increased the competitive pressure on New Zealand firms. Hence, competitive position is regarded as an important variable by the New Zealand respondents, as well as by their Australian and Chinese counterparts.

Foreign direct investment is attracted to China in part because of China's enormous domestic market. Because of their unfamiliarity with local market conditions, multinational enterprises engaging in business in China are at a disadvantage compared with local firms. To compete successfully with local firms in China, multinational enterprises must be able to exploit certain specific advantages not possessed by their local competitors. A multinational group may use the International Transfer Pricing mechanism to enhance its subsidiary's competitive position in the Chinese market to redress the balance. For example, a foreign manufacturing firm may charge its related Chinese distributor a below market price as part of a market penetration strategy.

Overall Profit to Multinational Group. Tables 12.5 and 12.6 indicate the importance of Variable 07 – 'Overall Profit to Multinational Group' – as it affects International Transfer Pricing policies of respondent firms operating in Australia, New Zealand and China. The Chinese respondents consider this variable to be very important. The mean

Table 12.5 Comparison of the Ratings of Variable 07 'Overall Profit to Multinational Group' for International Transfer Pricing by Australia, New Zealand and China

Rank	Extremely Important		Very Important		Important		Slightly Important		Not Important	
	N	%	N	%	N	%	N	%	N	%
Australia	7	12.1	13	22.4	15	25.9	11	19.0	12	20.7
New Zealand	7	9.1	21	27.3	29	37.7	9	11.7	11	14.3
China	15	32.6	21	45.7	8	17	2	4.3	0	0

Table 12.6 Statistical Data for the Comparison of the Ratings of Variable 07 'Overall Profit to Multinational Group' for International Transfer Pricing by Australia, New Zealand and China

VAR 07 'Overall Profit to Multinational Group'	N	Rank	Mean	Standard Deviation
Australia	58	4	2.86	1.317
New Zealand	77	4	3.05	1.157
China	47	1	4.07	.827

rating 4.07 given by the Chinese respondents is much higher than that of Australia at 2.86 and New Zealand at 3.05. The variable is ranked first by the Chinese respondents and fourth by both Australian and New Zealand respondents.

Twenty-nine companies consider this variable to be extremely important. It is understandable why so many subsidiaries pay great attention to the overall profit of their multinational group. The maximisation of global profit is the major objective of a multinational group. Multinationals have often been denounced for shifting income between different geographic regions to minimise global taxes. In China, foreign subsidiaries are heavily dependent on their overseas parent companies for supplies of materials and components. Subsidiary production and operational decisions are often controlled by their parent companies. Corporate policies in general and transfer pricing policies in particular are frequently set or directly affected by headquarters of the parent companies, located overseas. For this reason, these companies may be more concerned with group overall profitability than the corporate profit of subsidiaries.

Corporate Profit of the Subsidiary. Tables 12.7 and 12.8 indicate the importance of Variable 08 – 'Corporate Profit of the Subsidiary' – as it affects International Transfer Pricing policies of respondent firms operating in Australia, New Zealand and China. Corporate profit of the subsidiary is given very high ratings by the three groups. The mean rating 4.04 given by the Chinese respondents is higher than that of Australia at 3.14 and New Zealand at 3.38. The variable is ranked third by the Australian respondents and second by both New Zealand and Chinese respondents.

It is plain to see that 'corporate profit of the subsidiary' is consistently given very high ratings by the three national groups. The

Table 12.7   Comparison of the Ratings of Variable 08 'Corporate Profit of the Subsidiary' for International Transfer Pricing by Australia, New Zealand and China

Rank	Extremely Important		Very Important		Important		Slightly Important		Not Important	
	N	%	N	%	N	%	N	%	N	%
Australia	8	13.8	15	25.9	19	32.8	9	15.5	7	12.1
New Zealand	12	15.6	22	28.6	33	42.9	3	3.9	7	9.1
China	15	32.6	20	43.5	9	19.6	2	4.3	0	0

Table 12.8   Statistical Data for the Comparison of the Ratings of Variable 08 'Corporate Profit of the Subsidiary' for International Transfer Pricing by Australia, New Zealand and China

VAR 08 'Corporate Profit of the Subsidiary'	N	Rank	Mean	Standard Deviation
Australia	58	3	3.14	1.206
New Zealand	77	2	3.38	1.089
China	47	2	4.04	.842

objective of the maximisation of global profit of a multinational group may conflict with that of the corporate profit of the subsidiary and the performance evaluation of subsidiary managers. The arbitrarily shifting of profits from a foreign subsidiary through International Transfer Pricing, while enhancing overall corporate profitability may affect the measured profitability of that subsidiary and, in turn, distort the performance of the subsidiary managers. In designing transfer pricing, local managers are likely to seek to balance the interests of the overall profit of the multinational group with that of the corporate profit of the subsidiary. To address the issue, some multinational enterprises either incur the fixed cost of maintaining 'two sets of books', or mandate a centralised system of control, evaluation, and reward that can work around tax distorted transfer prices.

Policy differentiation

Rates of Customs Duties. Tables 12.9 and 12.10 indicate the importance of Variable 02 – 'Rates of Customs Duties' – as it affects the International Transfer Pricing policies of respondent firms operating in

Table 12.9   Comparison of the Ratings of Variable 02 'Rates of Customs Duties' for International Transfer Pricing by Australia, New Zealand and China

Rank	Extremely Important		Very Important		Important		Slightly Important		Not Important	
	N	%	N	%	N	%	N	%	N	%
Australia	5	8.6	4	6.9	11	19.0	11	19.0	27	45.0
New Zealand	3	3.9	5	6.5	17	22.1	16	20.8	36	46.8
China	10	21.7	21	45.7	9	19.6	5	10.9	1	2.2

Table 12.10   Statistical Data for the Comparison of the Ratings of Variable 02 'Rates of Customs Duties' for International Transfer Pricing by Australia, New Zealand and China

VAR 02 'Rates of Customs Duties'	N	Rank	Mean	Standard Deviation
Australia	58	10/11	2.12	1.312
New Zealand	77	13/14	2.00	1.147
China	46	5	3.74	.999

Australia, New Zealand and China. Compared with Australian and New Zealand companies, the Chinese firms place significantly greater importance on 'rates of customs duties'. The mean rating 3.74 of the variable given by the Chinese respondents is considerably higher than that of Australian companies at 2.12 and New Zealand at 2.00. The variable is ranked fifth by the Chinese respondents but tenth/eleventh and thirteen/fourteen by the Australian and New Zealand respondents respectively.

Partly because the possible savings are small, or partly because costly litigation can result (Caves, 1996, p. 210), the minimisation of customs duties is not considered as important for Australian and New Zealand firms as for Chinese firms. In China, the current tariffs for the exports and imports of foreign investment enterprises are quite preferential, with exports effectively being tariff free. Imports by foreign investment enterprises which are used as investment goods and for producing exports are also tariff free. Only those imports by foreign investment enterprises that are to be used in producing goods to be sold in the domestic market are subject to some import tariffs. Therefore, tariffs applied to export oriented foreign investment enterprises in China are generous, and should generate no particular incentive for multinational enterprises to practice transfer pricing manoeuvres (Chan and Chow, 1998; Sun, 1999).

The high importance of this particular variable, 'rates of customs duties', as rated by the Chinese respondents might be the result of the investigative action of current Chinese customs houses over the International Transfer Pricing practices of multinational enterprises. For example, shortly before this study was undertaken, the Chinese customs offices had been investigating tax avoidance through multinational transfer pricing abuses and for alleged dumping violations as a result of underpricing intercompany transfers. When goods are transferred from a parent company abroad to a subsidiary in a host country, the host government may impose antidumping charges on the multi-national group to protect its home industries against the dumping of excess production by companies of other countries (Belkaoui, 1991).

Tax Authority Transfer Pricing Audits. Tables 12.11 and Table 12.12 indicate the importance of the Variable 03 – 'Tax Authority Transfer Pricing Audits' – as it affects International Transfer Pricing policies of respondent firms operating in Australia, New Zealand and China. Transfer pricing auditing by tax authorities is not a significant concern for the Chinese respondents in formulating their International Transfer Pricing policies. 39.2% of the Chinese respondents considered the variable as only slightly important or not important at all. The mean rating 3.00 of the variable given by the Chinese respondents is slightly higher than that of their Australian and New Zealand counter-parts, whose mean ratings are 2.79 and 2.82 respectively. In contrast, the variable is ranked thirteenth by the Chinese respondents and fifth by both the Australian and New Zealand respondents.

Published literature (Brean, 1979; Plasschaet 1985; Al-Eryani et al., 1990; and Lin et al., 1993) suggests that a great number of developed

Table 12.11   Comparison of the Ratings of Variable 03 'Tax Authority Transfer Pricing Audits' for International Transfer Pricing by Australia, New Zealand and China

Rank	Extremely Important		Very Important		Important		Slightly Important		Not Important	
	N	%	N	%	N	%	N	%	N	%
Australia	7	12.1	10	17.2	19	32.8	8	13.3	14	24.1
New Zealand	7	9.1	16	20.8	27	35.1	10	13.0	17	22.1
China	6	13	11	23.9	11	23.9	13	28.3	5	10.9

Table 12.12   Statistical Data for the Comparison of the Ratings of Variable 03 'Tax Authority Transfer Pricing Audits' for International Transfer Pricing by Australia, New Zealand and China

VAR 03 'Tax Authority Transfer Pricing Audits'	N	Rank	Mean	Standard Deviation
Australia	58	5	2.79	1.321
New Zealand	77	5	2.82	1.254
China	46	13	3.00	1.229

countries have enacted sophisticated tax regulations and own highly qualified professional tax experts to deal with the issue of International Transfer Pricing. On the other hand, though they may have become aware of the losses of tax revenues as a result of International Transfer Pricing manipulations, developing country governments find it difficult to deal with the problem as they lack institutional frameworks and administrative expertise to analyse the complex set of factors at work. The governments of developing countries may find it even difficult to detect it at all, or when they are able to do so they simply do not have the resources to control and monitor it effectively.

The Chinese government has constituted a primary legal framework to deal with the taxation of foreign firms and transfer pricing. The extant law and regulations of China grant the tax authorities power to perform tax auditing and to take legal action against transfer pricing. In practice, however, tax auditing on transfer pricing by Chinese tax authorities is far from being fully implemented. This is due to the shortage of well-trained personnel to conduct tax auditing and pricing surveillance. Hence, the threat of transfer pricing auditing by Chinese tax authorities might not be conceived as imminent and a realistic threat by the Chinese respondent multinationals.

Restrictions on Repatriation of Income. Tables 12.13 and 12.14 indicate the importance of Variable 05 – 'Restrictions on Repatriation of Income' – as it affects International Transfer Pricing policies of respondent firms operating in Australia, New Zealand and China. It is of moderate importance in the three countries. The mean rating 1.97 given by Australian respondents is much lower than that for New Zealand at 2.43 and China at 3.26. The variable is ranked twelfth/thirteenth by the Australian respondents and ninth and tenth by the New Zealand and Chinese respondents respectively.

Table 12.13   Comparison of the Ratings of Variable 05 'Restrictions on Repatriation of Income' for International Transfer Pricing by Australia, New Zealand and China

Rank	Extremely Important		Very Important		Important		Slightly Important		Not Important	
	N	%	N	%	N	%	N	%	N	%
Australia	2	3.4	5	8.6	11	19.0	11	19.0	29	50.0
New Zealand	6	7.8	7	9.1	27	35.1	11	14.3	26	33.8
China	6	13	15	32.6	11	23.9	13	27.7	1	2.1

Table 12.14   Statistical Data for the Comparison of the Ratings of Variable 05 'Restrictions on Repatriation of Income' for International Transfer Pricing by Australia, New Zealand and China

VAR 05 'Restrictions on Repatriation of Income'	N	Rank	Mean	Standard Deviation
Australia	58	12/13	1.97	1.169
New Zealand	77	9	2.43	1.261
China	47	10	3.26	1.084

Australian, New Zealand and Chinese governments do not impose restrictions on foreign subsidiaries against the repatriation of their share of profits to their parent firms abroad. In fact, most of the overseas investing countries in the world such as the United States, the United Kingdom, Japan and Germany adopt a system under which credit is allowed in respect of withholding tax charges levied by host countries.

Withholding tax in Australia, New Zealand and China on the payments of interest, rentals, and royalties to affiliated companies is levied at between 10% and 20%. Given that such withholding tax rates are lower than the home country income tax rate, a host country's withholding tax on the payments can be waived or taken into account as a charge on the home country's income taxes under bilateral tax treaties. Thus, 'restrictions on repatriation of income' is not considered important by all three countries.

It is worth noting, however, that, among China's major investors, Hong Kong adopts a system of source based taxation whereby corporate taxes are charged only on income sourced in Hong Kong. Profits or revenues repatriated by foreign subsidiaries are exempt from Hong Kong taxation. For Hong Kong based foreign investment enterprises, withholding taxes charged by Chinese fiscal authorities become an additional burden on the corporation's tax charge (Chan and Chow, 1997b, p. 1274). Hence, Hong Kong based firms may place greater importance on this variable.

Summary

In the previous chapter, Chapter 11, four important business environmental variables in common that affect International Transfer Pricing policies in the three countries were identified. They are 'comply with tax law and regulations', 'competitive position of the subsidiary', 'overall profit to multinational group', and 'corporate profit of the subsidiary'. Three variables that account for most of the differentiation between the three national groups are also identified. These environmental variables are 'rates of customs duties', 'tax authority transfer pricing audits', and 'restrictions on repatriation of income'.

In this chapter it has been found that among the three environmental variables that contribute most to the differentiation between the national groups, 'tax authority transfer pricing audits' is an important concern in pricing decisions for Australian and New Zealand companies. By comparison, it is regarded as relatively unimportant by the Chinese firms. This is perhaps because the Australian and New Zealand tax authorities are more aggressive than their Chinese counterparts in administering and enforcing their transfer pricing rules. The next chapter, therefore, reports factors that are likely to trigger International Transfer Pricing audits by tax authorities in the three countries.

13
Current Audit Practice

Introduction

In a study of International Transfer Pricing tax audits in China, Chan and Chow (1997b) discovered that a number of corporate attributes might lead to an increased risk of tax audits. The research for this book, therefore, was generally based on the expectation that particular attributes of a company are likely to be associated with International Transfer Pricing audits by the tax authorities.

These corporate attributes were expected to include:

1. the industrial scope of a company
2. the nationality of the multinational enterprise concerned
3. the size of the multinational enterprise
4. the annual volume of intercompany transactions
5. the nature and frequency of intercompany transactions.

It remained open to discover the nature of the relationship between International Transfer Pricing tax audits and multinational companies according to the foregoing variables and the relative valency of each in this regard.

The respondents were asked if they had been the subject of an International Transfer Pricing audit since 1998. The responses are shown in Table 13.1. Overall, forty-five companies (26%) had been subject to International Transfer Pricing tax audits. The table also shows that 33% of Chinese firms had been audited – a higher rate than companies from Australia (28%) and New Zealand (18%).

Table 13.1 Frequencies of International Transfer Pricing Audits Reported by Respondent Companies in Australia, New Zealand and China Since 1998

Australia			New Zealand			China			Overall		
Yes	No	Subtotal	Yes	No	Subtotal	Yes	No	Subtotal	Yes	No	Total
17	43	60	13	58	71*	15	30	45**	45	131	176
28%	72%	100%	18%	82%	100%	33%	67%	100%	26%	74%	100%

Note:* Six New Zealand firms provided no information on International Transfer Pricing audits.
** Two Chinese firms provided no information on International Transfer Pricing audits.

Table 13.2 Likelihood of an International Transfer Pricing Audit According to a Firm's Type of Industry in Australia

Industry Type	Audit		No Audit		Subtotals	
	No. of Firms	%	No. of Firms	%	No. of Firms	%
Wholesale and Retail Trade	7	33.3	14	66.7	21	100
Manufacturing	4	16.0	21	84.0	25	100
Services	2	25.0	6	75.0	8	100
Finance and Insurance	0	0	1	100	1	100
Mining	1	100	0	0	1	100
Construction	2	66.7	1	33.3	3	100
Agriculture, Forestry and Fishing	0	0	1	100	1	100
Total	16	26.7	44	73.3	60	100

Note: Shaded items are combined into one category.

Australian company experience

Audit and Type of Industry. Given the number of responses obtained, to yield reliable test results, companies were regrouped into three industry types, namely wholesale and retail trade, manufacturing, and services. Other industries with small samples were combined into one category as in Table 13.2. As shown in Table 13.3, the data regarding International Transfer Pricing tax auditing and the type of industry of a firm (χ^2 = 3.614, df = 3) indicate that there is no significant difference at even the α = .1 level for this variable in the respondent Australian companies.

Audit and Home Country. Given the number of respondents, to yield reliable test results, companies were regrouped again according to their home countries, which were primarily the United States and Japan. Other home countries with small samples were combined into one category as in Table 13.4. As shown in Table 13.5, the data regarding International Transfer Pricing tax auditing according to the nationality of firms (χ^2 = 8.696 df = 2) are significant at the α = .05 level. This indicates a disproportionate focus of International Transfer Pricing tax audits on the firms with Japan as their home country, although caution must be exercised when making this statement because of the small sample from each country.

Buckley and Hughes (2001) examined prevalent allegations that Japanese multinationals operated transfer pricing policies to the deliberate disadvantage of host countries and therefore were frequently audited by the host countries' tax authorities. They concluded that obtaining a tax advantage was not the primary reason for Japanese transfer pricing practices. Rather, the unique management control systems, corporate structures and business cultures of Japanese companies were suggested as the reasons.

Table 13.3   Chi-Square Test on the Data for the Likelihood of an International Transfer Pricing Audit According to a Firm's Type of Industry in Australia

	Industry
Chi-Square value	3.614
Degrees of freedom	3
Significance. (2-tailed)	.306
N	60

Table 13.4   Audits Reported by Australian Respondent Companies According to Their Home Countries

Industry Type	Audit		No Audit		Subtotals	
	No. of Firms	%	No. of Firms	%	No. of Firms	%
USA	3	17.6	14	82.4	17	100
Japan	8	57.1	6	42.9	14	100
UK	1	11.1	8	88.9	9	100
Switzerland	1	100	0	0	1	100
Germany	0	0	6	100	6	100
Canada	0	0	1	100	1	100
Sweden	0	0	1	100	1	100
France	0	0	2	100	2	100
Denmark	0	0	1	100	1	100
Ireland	0	0	1	100	1	100
Netherlands	2	50.0	2	50.0	4	100
New Zealand	0	0	1	100	1	100
Belgium	1	100	0	0	1	100
Korea	1	100	0	0	1	100
Total	17	28.3	43	71.7	60	100

Note: Shaded items are combined into one category.

Table 13.5   Chi-Square Test on the Audits Reported by Australian Respondent Companies According to Their Home Countries

	Country
Chi-Square value	8.696**
Degrees of freedom	2
Significance. (2-tailed)	.013
N	60

** Significant at the .05 level.

Audit and Total Revenues. As shown in Table 13.6, companies with total revenues of more than $800 million have been subjected to tax audits, whilst no firm with total revenues of less than $20 million has been subjected to tax audits. Table 13.7 indicates that the data regarding International Transfer Pricing tax auditing and company size are significant at the α = .01 level. This indicates a disproportionate focus of International Transfer Pricing tax audits on large firms.

Audit and Volumes of Intercompany Transactions. As shown in Table 13.8, 42.1% of companies with volumes of intercompany transactions of more than 85% have been subjected to tax audits. In contrast, 10% of firms with volumes of intercompany transactions of less than 5% have been subjected to tax audits. Table 13.9 indicates that the data regarding International Transfer Pricing tax auditing and volume of international transactions are significant at the α = .1 level, indicating a disproportionate focus of International Transfer Pricing tax audits on companies with the greater volumes of intercompany transactions. The empirical result suggests that Australian firms with high volumes of intercompany transactions appear to be audited by the Australian Taxation Office more than others.

Audit and Types of Transactions. Tables 13.10 to 13.14 provide descriptive statistics for the relationship between International Transfer Pricing tax audits and certain types of multinational intercompany transactions. Whilst the data for intangible goods are significant at the .1 level, the data regarding International Transfer Pricing tax auditing and the transfer of tangible goods, financing and services respectively are statistically insignificant. Nevertheless, these data are in the direction expected, so they but provide some support for the proposition that there is a positive relationship between International Transfer Pricing tax audits and certain types of multinational intercompany transactions.

Table 13.6 Audits Reported by Australian Respondent Companies According to Their Total Revenues

Industry Type	Audit		No Audit		Subtotals	
	No. of Firms	%	No. of Firms	%	No. of Firms	%
Less than $20 million	0	0	24	100	24	100
$20 million to $100 million	8	38.1	13	61.9	21	100
$101 million to $200 million	2	40	3	60	5	100
$201 million to $500 million	2	50	2	50	4	100
$501 million to $800 million	0	0	1	100	1	100
More than $800 million	5	100	0	0	5	100
Total	17	28.3	43	71.7	60	100

Table 13.7 Correlation Analysis on the Data for Audits Reported by Australian Respondent Companies According to Their Total Revenues

	Size
Spearman's rho	.571***
Significance (1-tailed)	.000
Predicted sign	+
N	60

Note: *** Significant at the .01 level.

Table 13.8   Audits Reported by Australian Respondent Companies According to Their Volumes of Intercompany Transactions

Industry Type	Audit		No Audit		Subtotals	
	No. of Firms	%	No. of Firms	%	No. of Firms	%
Less than 5%	1	10	9	90	10	100
5% to 20%	2	16.7	10	83.3	12	100
21% to 50%	2	25	6	75	8	100
51% to 70%	3	50	3	50	6	100
71% to 85%	0	0	5	100	5	100
More than 85%	8	42.1	11	57.9	19	100
Total	16	26.7	44	73.3	60	100

Table 13.9   Correlation Analysis of the Data on Audits Reported by Australian Respondent Companies According to Their Volumes of Intercompany Transactions

	Volume
Spearman's rho	.190*
Significance (1–tailed)	.072
Predicted sign	+
N	60

Note: * Significant at the .1 level.

Table 13.10   Audits Reported by Australian Respondent Companies According to Their Volumes of Intercompany Transactions of Tangible Goods

Tangible Goods	Audit		No Audit	
Rank	No. of Firms	%	No. of Firms	%
Always	11	28.9	27	71.1
Often	2	18.2	9	81.8
Sometimes	1	20	4	80.0
Rarely	2	66.7	1	33.3
Never	0	0	2	100

Table 13.11   Audits Reported by Australian Respondent Companies According to Their Volumes of Intercompany Transactions of Intangible Goods

Intangibles	Audit		No Audit	
Rank	No. of Firms	%	No. of Firms	%
Always	1	50	1	50
Often	3	50	3	50
Sometimes	2	100	0	0
Rarely	2	18.2	9	81.8
Never	5	20	20	80.0

Table 13.11 indicates that the data regarding International Transfer Pricing tax auditing and the transfer of intangibles are significant at the $\alpha = .1$ level, indicating a disproportionate focus of International

Table 13.12   Audits Reported by Australian Respondent Companies According to Their Volumes of Intercompany Transactions as Financing

Financing Rank	Audit		No Audit	
	No. of Firms	%	No. of Firms	%
Always	1	25	3	75
Often	1	11.1	8	88.9
Sometimes	7	50	7	50
Rarely	2	25.0	6	75.0
Never	3	18.8	13	81.2

Table 13.13   Audits Reported by Australian Respondent Companies According to Their Volumes of Intercompany Transactions as Services

Services Rank	Audit		No Audit	
	No. of Firms	%	No. of Firms	%
Always	3	42.9	4	57.1
Often	5	45.5	6	54.5
Sometimes	3	16.7	15	83.3
Rarely	2	25.0	6	75.0
Never	2	20.0	8	80.0

Table 13.14   Correlation Analysis of the Data on Audits Reported by Australian Respondent Companies According to Their Volumes of Four Types of Intercompany Transactions

	Tangibles	Intangibles	Financing	Services
Spearman's rho	.006	.220*	.098	.161
Significance (1–tailed)	.481	.071	.247	.123
Predicted sign	+	+	+	+
N	60	46	51	54

Note: * Significant at the .1 level.

194

Table 13.15   Likelihood of an International Transfer Pricing Audit According to a Firm's Type of Industry in New Zealand

Industry Type	Audit		No Audit		Subtotals	
	No. of Firms	%	No. of Firms	%	No. of Firms	%
Wholesale and retail trade	5	29.4	12	70.6	17	100
Manufacturing	4	12.5	28	87.5	32	100
Services	3	25	9	75	12	100
Finance and insurance	0	0	6	100	6	100
Mining	1	100	0	0	1	100
Transport and storage	0	0	1	100	1	100
Construction	0	0	1	100	1	100
Agriculture, Forestry and Fishing	0	0	1	100	1	100
Total	13	18.3	58	81.7	71	100

Note: Shaded items are combined into one category.

Table 13.16   Chi-square Test of the Data on the Likelihood of an International Transfer Pricing Audit According to a Firm's Type of Industry in New Zealand

	Industry
Chi-Square Value	2.944
Degrees of Freedom	3
Significance (2-tailed)	.400
N	71

Transfer Pricing tax audits on companies with the greater volume of its intercompany transactions as intangibles.

New Zealand company experience

Audit and Type of Industry. Given the size of the data, to yield reliable test results, companies were regrouped into three industry types, namely wholesale and retail trade, manufacturing, and services. Other industries with small samples were combined into one category as in Table 13.15. As shown in Table 13.16, the data regarding International Transfer Pricing tax auditing and the type of industry of firms ($\chi^2 = 2.944$, df = 3) indicate no significant difference at even the a = .1 level.

Audit and Home Country. Given the size of the data, to yield reliable test results, companies were regrouped according to their home countries, which were primarily the United States, Australia and Japan. Other home countries of the respondent firms with small samples were combined into one category as in Table 13.17. As shown in Table 13.18, the data regarding International Transfer Pricing tax auditing and the home country of the respondent firms ($\chi^2 = 2.174$, df = 3) indicate no significant difference at even the a = .1 level.

Audit and Total Revenues. As shown in Table 13.19, the company with total revenues of more than $800 million and 50% of companies with total revenues of $101 million to $200 million have been subjected to tax audits, whilst only 8.8% of firms with total revenues of less than $20 million have been subjected to tax audits. Table 13.20 shows that the data regarding International Transfer Pricing tax auditing and company size are significant at the $\alpha = .01$ level, indicating a disproportionate focus of International Transfer Pricing tax audits on large firms.

Table 13.17   Audits Reported by New Zealand Respondent Companies According to Their Home Countries

Nationality	Audit		No Audit		Subtotals	
	No. of Firms	%	No. of Firms	%	No. of Firms	%
United States	3	10	18	90	20	100
Australia	4	22	14	78	18	100
Japan	4	29	10	71	14	100
United Kingdom	0	0	6	100	6	100
Switzerland	1	25	3	75	4	100
Germany	0	0	3	100	3	100
Canada	2	100	0	0	2	100
Finland	0	0	1	100	1	100
Sweden	N/A	N/A	N/A			
France	3	0	2	100	2	100
Denmark	0	0	1	100	1	100
Ireland	N/A	N/A	N/A			
Total	13	18	58	82	71	100

Note: Shaded items are combined into one category.

Table 13.18   Chi-Square Test on the Data for Audits Reported by New Zealand Respondent Companies According to Their Home Countries

	Country
Chi-Square Value	2.174
Degrees of Freedom	3
Significance (2-tailed)	.537
N	71

Table 13.19   Audits Reported by New Zealand Respondent Companies According to Their Total Revenues

Total Revenues in New Zealand $	Audit		No Audit		Subtotals	
	No. of Firms	%	No. of Firms	%	No. of Firms	%
Less than $20 million	3	8.8	31	91.2	34	100
$20 million to $100 million	3	14.3	18	85.7	21	100
$101 million to $200 million	6	50	6	50	12	100
$201 million to $500 million	0	0	2	100	2	100
$501 million to $800 million	0	0	1	100	1	100
More than $800 million	1	100	0	0	1	100
Total	13	18.3	58	81.7	71	100

Table 13.20 Correlation Analysis of the Data for Audits Reported by New Zealand Respondent Companies According to Their Total Revenues

	Size
Spearman's rho	.306***
Significance (1-tailed)	.005
Predicted sign	+
N	71

Note: *** Significant at the .01 level.

Table 13.21 Audits Reported by New Zealand Respondent Companies According to Their Volumes of Intercompany Transactions

Volumes of Transactions	Audit		No Audit		Subtotals	
	No. of Firms	%	No. of Firms	%	No. of Firms	%
Less than 5%	3	15	17	85	20	100
5% to 20%	2	33.3	4	66.7	6	100
21% to 50%	1	14.3	6	85.7	7	100
51% to 70%	1	20	4	80	5	100
71% to 85%	2	28.6	5	71.4	7	100
More than 85%	4	16.7	20	83.3	24	100
Total	13	18.8	56	81.2	69	100

Jensen and Meckling (1976) contended that larger firms encountered more government scrutiny than smaller firms. The data gathered for this book discovered that the Australian Taxation Office and the New Zealand Inland Revenue Department tended to audit large-sized multinationals. Large firms in non-competitive environments, whose International Transfer Prices are not readily compared with market prices, can maintain complex transfer pricing systems aimed in part at tax avoidance. Small companies facing more competition, whose transfer prices the tax officers can readily check against market prices, do not have the opportunity to find such manoeuvres to their tax advantage (Caves, 1996). The Australian and New Zealand tax authorities therefore focus their tax audit efforts on large firms that lack arm's length bases for setting transfer prices. Large companies are usually involved in a large number of transactions. Given their finite investigative resources, relative to the potential demand for their use, it pays governments to spend time and effort in the scrutiny of large company activities.

Audit and Volumes of Intercompany Transactions. Table 13.21 provides descriptive statistics for the relationship between International Transfer Pricing tax audits and volumes of intercompany transfers. Table 13.22 indicates that the data regarding International Transfer Pricing tax auditing and volume of international transactions are insignificant, but are in the direction expected.

Audit and Types of Transactions. Tables 13.23 to 13.26 provide descriptive statistics for the relationship between International Transfer Pricing tax audits and certain types of multinational intercompany transactions. Table 13.27 shows that the data regarding International Transfer Pricing tax auditing and the transfer of tangible goods are significant at the $\alpha = .1$ level. This indicates a disproportionate focus of International Transfer Pricing tax audits on companies with the greater volume of their intercompany transfers in tangible goods.

Table 13.22   Correlation Analysis on the Data for Audits Reported by New Zealand Respondent Companies According to Their Volumes of Intercompany Transactions

	Volume
Spearman's rho	.007
Significance (1-tailed)	.478
Predicted sign	+
N	69

Table 13.23   Audits Reported by New Zealand Respondent Companies According to Their Volumes of Intercompany Transactions of Tangible Goods

Tangible Goods	Audit		No Audit	
Rank	No. of Firms	%	No. of Firms	%
Always	9	25	27	75
Often	1	7.7	12	92.3
Sometimes	0	0	5	100
Rarely	1	14.3	6	85.7
Never	1	16.7	5	83.3

Table 13.24   Audits Reported by New Zealand Respondent Companies According to Their Volumes of Intercompany Transactions of Intangible Goods

Intangibles	Audit		No Audit	
Rank	No. of Firms	%	No. of Firms	%
Always	2	66.7	1	33.3
Often	0	0	6	100
Sometimes	0	0	9	100
Rarely	4	30.8	9	69.2
Never	7	22.6	24	77.4

Table 13.25   Audits Reported by New Zealand Respondent Companies According to Their Volumes of Intercompany Transactions as Financing

Financing	Audit		No Audit	
Rank	No. of Firms	%	No. of Firms	%
Always	1	25.0	3	75.0
Often	2	28.6	5	71.4
Sometimes	1	7.1	13	92.9
Rarely	3	17.6	14	82.4
Never	4	19.0	17	81.0

The data regarding International Transfer Pricing tax auditing and transfers of intangibles, financing and services are statistically insignificant. However, except for the transfer of intangibles, the data are in

Table 13.26 Audits Reported by New Zealand Respondent Companies According to Their Volumes of Intercompany Transactions as Services

Services	Audit		No Audit	
Rank	No. of Firms	%	No. of Firms	%
Always	4	25.0	12	75.0
Often	3	21.4	11	78.6
Sometimes	3	18.8	13	81.3
Rarely	1	11.1	8	88.9

Table 13.27 Correlation Analysis of the Data on Audits Reported by New Zealand Respondent Companies According to Their Volumes of Four Types of Intercompany Transactions

	Tangibles	Intangibles	Financing	Services
Spearman's rho	.167*	−.056	.002	.096
Significance (1-tailed)	.088	.333	.493	.220
Predicted Sign	+	+	+	+
N	67	62	63	67

Note: * Significant at the .1 level.

the same direction as expected, so they but provide some support for the proposition that there is a positive relationship between International Transfer Pricing tax audits and certain types of multinational intercompany transactions.

Chinese company experience

Audit and Type of Industry. Given the size of the data, to yield reliable test results, companies were regrouped into three industry types, namely wholesale and retail trade, manufacturing, and services. Other industries with small samples were combined into one category as in Table 13.28. As shown in Table 13.29, the data regarding International Transfer Pricing tax auditing and the industry type of firms (χ^2 = 3.091, df = 3) indicate no significant difference at even the α = .1 level.

Audit and Home Country. Given the size of the data, to yield reliable test results, companies were regrouped into two home country categories, namely Hong Kong and other home countries as in

Table 13.28   Likelihood of an International Transfer Pricing Audit According to a Firm's Type of Industry in China

Industry Type	Audit		No Audit		Subtotals	
	No. of Firms	%	No. of Firms	%	No. of Firms	%
Wholesale and Retail Trade	6	50	6	50	12	100
Manufacturing	5	21.7	18	78.3	23	100
Services	2	40	3	60	5	100
Construction	1	33.3	2	66.7	3	100
Agriculture, forestry and fishing	1	50	1	50	2	100
Total	15	33.3	30	66.7	45	100

Note: Shaded items are combined into one category.

Table 13.29   Chi-Square Test on the Data for the Likelihood of an International Transfer Pricing Audit According to a Firm's Type of Industry in China

	Industry
Chi-Square value	3.091
Degrees of Freedom	3
Significance. (2-tailed)	.378
N	45

Table 13.30   Audits Reported by Chinese Respondent Companies According to Their Home Countries

Country	Audit		No Audit		Subtotals	
	No. of Firms	%	No. of Firms	%	No. of Firms	%
Hong Kong	6	60	4	40	10	100
Taiwan	2	40	3	60	5	100
Macao	1	100	0	0	1	100
Singapore	0	0	3	100	3	100
Korea	0	0	3	100	3	100
Virgin Islands	0	0	1	100	1	100
Thailand	0	0	1	100	1	100
Japan	2	33.3	4	66.7	6	100
United States	4	50	4	50	8	100
France	0	0	2	100	2	100
Italy	0	0	1	100	1	100
Sweden	0	0	1	100	1	100
United Kingdom	0	0	2	100	2	100
Netherlands	0	0	1	100	1	100
Totals	15	33.3	30	66.7	45	100

Note: Shaded items are combined into one category.

Table 13.31   Chi-Square test on the Data for Audits Reported by Chinese Respondent Companies According to Their Home Countries

	Country
Chi-Square value	4.050**
Degrees of Freedom	1
Significance. (2-tailed)	.044
N	45

Note: ** Significant at the .05 level.

Table 13.30. As shown in Table 13.31, but bearing in mind the small sample for each country, the data regarding International Transfer Pricing tax auditing and the home countries of firms are significant at the α = .05 level, indicating a disproportionate focus of International Transfer Pricing tax audits on the Hong Kong based firms. This is an explicable finding. Given Hong Kong's generous tax system and low income tax rate, Hong Kong based firms may have the incentive to try to minimise tax liability by artificially shifting profits from China to Hong Kong though transfer pricing mechanisms. Chinese tax authorities therefore put relatively greater efforts into auditing the transfer pricing practices of Hong Kong based companies.

Audit and Total Revenues. As shown in Table 13.32, 52.9% of companies with total revenues of less than $20 million have been subjected to tax audits, whilst only 25% of firms with total revenues of $501 million to $800 million have been subjected to tax audits. The company with total revenues of more than $800 has not been subject to a tax audit. Table 13.33 shows that the data regarding International Transfer Pricing tax audits and company size are significant at the α = .01 level, indicating a disproportionate focus of International Transfer Pricing tax audits on small firms.

As the audits of large companies require sophisticated techniques, the Chinese tax authorities claim that they lack sufficient staff resources and experience to tackle large multinationals for transfer pricing issues. Conjecturally, the reason for this might have been to encourage large companies to establish themselves in China. But in the future, the Chinese tax authorities intend to pay more attention to the intercompany transactions of large-sized multinationals.

Audit and Volumes of Intercompany Transactions. Table 13.34 provides descriptive statistics for the relationship between International Transfer Pricing tax audits and volumes of intercompany

Table 13.32   Audits Reported by Chinese Respondent Companies According to Their Total Revenues

Total Revenues in New Zealand $	Audit		No Audit		Subtotals	
	No. of Firms	%	No. of Firms	%	No. of Firms	%
Less than $20 million	9	52.9	8	47.1	17	100
$20 million to $100 million	4	30.8	9	69.2	13	100
$101 million to $200 million	1	12.5	7	87.5	8	100
$201 million to $500 million	0	0	2	100	2	100
$501 million to $800 million	1	25	3	75	4	100
More than $800 million	0	0	1	100	1	100
Total	15	33.3	30	66.7	45	100

Table 13.33   Correlation Analysis of the Data on Audits Reported by Chinese Respondent Companies According to Their Total Revenues

	Size
Spearman's rho	−.345***
Significance (1-tailed)	.01
Predicted sign	+
N	45

Note: *** Significant at the .01 level.

Table 13.34 Audits Reported by Chinese Respondent Companies According to Their Volumes of Intercompany Transactions

Volumes of Transactions	Audit		No Audit		Subtotals	
	No. of Firms	%	No. of Firms	%	No. of Firms	%
Less than 5%	1	11.1	8	88.9	9	100
5% to 20%	5	41.7	7	58.3	12	100
21% to 50%	5	38.5	8	61.5	13	100
51% to 70%	3	50	3	50	6	100
71% to 85%	1	50	1	50	2	100
More than 85%	0	0	3	100	3	100
Total	15	33.3	30	66.7	45	100

Table 13.35 Correlation analysis of the Data for Audits Reported by Chinese Respondent Companies According to Their Volumes of Intercompany Transactions

	Volume
Spearman's rho	.118
Significance (1-tailed)	.221
Predicted sign	+
N	45

Table 13.36 Audits Reported by Chinese Respondent Companies According to Their Volumes of Intercompany Transactions of Tangible Goods

Tangible Goods	Audit		No Audit	
Rank	No. of Firms	%	No. of Firms	%
Always	7	41.2	10	58.8
Often	5	45.5	6	54.5
Sometimes	3	27.3	8	72.7
Rarely	0	0	3	100
Never	0	0	2	100

Table 13.37 Audits Reported by Chinese Respondent Companies According to Their Volumes of Intercompany Transactions as Intangibles

Intangibles	Audit		No Audit	
Rank	No. of Firms	%	No. of Firms	%
Always	3	60	2	40
Often	0	0	3	100
Sometimes	4	50	4	50
Rarely	4	30.8	9	69.2
Never	3	23.1	10	76.9

Table 13.38 Audits Reported by Chinese Respondent Companies According to Their Volumes of Intercompany Transactions as Financing

Financing	Audit		No Audit	
Rank	No. of Firms	%	No. of Firms	%
Always	4	80	1	20
Often	4	28.6	7	63.6
Sometimes	1	20	4	80
Rarely	2	18.2	9	81.8
Never	3	30	7	70

transfers. Table 13.35 indicates that the data regarding International Transfer Pricing tax auditing and the volume of international transfers are not statistically significant. However, the data are in the direction expected.

Audit and Types of Transactions. Tables 13.36 to 13.39 provide descriptive statistics for the relationship between International Transfer Pricing tax audits and certain types of multinational intercompany transactions. Table 13.40 shows that the data regarding International Transfer Pricing tax auditing and transactions as tangible goods and financing are respectively significant at the $\alpha = .05$ and $\alpha = .1$ levels, indicating a disproportionate focus of International Transfer Pricing tax audits on companies with the greater volume of their intercompany transactions as tangible goods and financing.

The data regarding International Transfer Pricing tax auditing and transactions involving intangibles and services are insignificant. However, the data are in the direction expected, so they but they still provide some support for the proposition that there is a positive

Table 13.39   Audits Reported by Chinese Respondent Companies According to Their Volumes of Intercompany Transactions as Services

Services	Audit		No Audit	
Rank	No. of Firms	%	No. of Firms	%
Always	3	33.3	6	66.7
Often	3	60	2	40
Sometimes	4	26.7	11	73.3
Rarely	4	36.4	7	63.6
Never	0	0	3	100

Table 13.40   Correlation Analysis of the Data on Audits Reported by Chinese Respondent Companies According to Their Volumes of Four Types of Intercompany Transactions

	Tangibles	Intangibles	Financing	Services
Spearman's rho	.251**	.181	.255*	.120
Significance (1-tailed)	.05	.125	.052	.221
Predicted sign	+	+	+	+
N	44	42	42	43

* Significant at the .1 level
** significant at the .05 level.

Table 13.41   Summary of Statistical Test Results on Reported Audits by Respondent Companies According to a Range of Company Variables in Australia, New Zealand and China

	Australia	New Zealand	China
	Audit vs Non-audit	Audit vs Non-audit	Audit vs Non-audit
Industry			
Nationality	**		**
Size	***	***	***
Volume of intercompany transfers	*		
Tangible goods		*	**
Intangibles	*		
Financing			*
Services			

Note: * Significant at the .1 level. ** Significant at the .05 level. *** Significant at the .01 level.

relationship between International Transfer Pricing tax audits and certain types of multinational intercompany transactions.

Summary

This chapter has examined a number of corporate variables which are associated with at least a potential risk of tax audit. Table 13.41 summarises the results of the statistical tests carried out on the data regarding International Transfer Pricing tax auditing and a range of such variables.

The Australian and Chinese tax authorities tended to focus their International Transfer Pricing tax audits on companies whose home countries are respectively Japan and Hong Kong.

The size of company is correlated with tax audit, the Australian Taxation Office and the New Zealand Inland Revenue Department both tending to audit large-sized multinationals.

In contrast, the Chinese tax authorities focused their tax audit efforts on relatively small-sized firms.

The Australian Taxation Office tended to audit companies with the greater volumes of intercompany transactions.

For Australian companies, the data regarding International Transfer Pricing tax auditing and transactions in intangibles are significant at the $\alpha = .1$ level. For Chinese companies, the data regarding International Transfer Pricing tax auditing and transactions as tangible goods and financing are significant respectively at the $\alpha = .05$ and $\alpha = .1$ levels. For New Zealand companies, the data regarding International Transfer Pricing tax auditing and transactions in tangible goods are significant at the $\alpha = .1$ level.

Except for transactions as intangibles for New Zealand firms, the other data are in the same direction as expected, hence they constitute some support for the proposition that there is a positive relationship between International Transfer Pricing tax audits and certain types of multinational intercompany transactions – according, that is, to whether they constitute transfers of tangible goods, intangibles, financing, or services.

The results of the survey provide evidence that transfer pricing audits are associated with some types of corporate attributes. In interpreting the data, however, it is important to bear in mind that correlation does not automatically imply causation. After all, the initiation of a tax audit on related party transactions ultimately depends on the extent of the perceived tax risks associated with the affected company's transfer pricing practices.

With these survey findings on International Transfer Pricing tax audits in mind, four Chinese tax authorities were approached by personal contact, together with a further eighty Chinese tax authorities by means of a Questionnaire. The next chapter reports the results from these two investigations.

14
Tax Monitoring in China

Introduction

In Chapter 6 it was explained how the qualitative evidence from four
Chinese tax authorities was obtained. The purpose of the case studies
was to have an in-depth and on-site investigation of the Chinese
International Transfer Pricing auditing system and practices and their
effectiveness in restricting multinational transfer pricing manipulation
in China.

Coupled with the presentation of the findings from these case studies, this chapter presents the results of the Questionnaire survey regarding Chinese International Transfer Pricing auditing practices, generated
from thirty-eight respondent Chinese tax authorities. The Questionnaire consisted of five questions, of which four were closed. The survey
allowed the qualitative evidence to be tested and to be generalised for
the population.

Abuses in China

Many foreign investment enterprises are heavily engaged in transactions
with overseas associates. A large number of foreign investment enterprises
have reported accounting losses (Chan and Chow, 1998). From the statistics of tax revenues, it appears that 35% to 40% of foreign investment
enterprises were in a loss-making position from 1988 to 1993. For 1994 and
1995, the percentage increased to between 50% and 60%. The percentage
further increased to between 60% and 70% for 1996 (Cho, 1998, p. 90).

The Chinese government suspects that transfer pricing has caused
serious losses of tax revenue to the country (Chan and Chow, 1997a, b).
These data on losses may be taken as justification for that suspicion.

In the interviews reported in this book, all the four tax authorities approached expressed deep concern that foreign investment enterprises were not actually paying their fair share of taxes in China. The tax officials justified their concern for the alleged transfer pricing abuses by citing the magnitude of accountable losses of taxable income relating to transfer pricing.

Three in four tax authorities considered that the issue of profit shifting through International Transfer Pricing manipulations in their province or city was significant. Their verbatim comments included the following.

'We have noted that many foreign investment enterprises report persistent losses but continue to expand their operations. Except for normal operating losses, a number of foreign investment enterprises may engage in tax avoidance by transferring their profits abroad and reporting losses in China'.

'Foreign investment enterprises highly rely on imported inputs including machinery and equipment, intermediate products and raw materials. Many foreign investment enterprises have reported operating losses. Some of those foreign investment enterprises may be engineering losses by the importing of materials and equipment into China from their overseas associates at a high price and the exporting of goods to their affiliated firms abroad at a low price. The issue of tax avoidance by transfer pricing is becoming all the more pressing as the number and types of cross-border transactions are expected to increase as the volume of multinational enterprises doing business in China continues to grow'.

Many developing economies are so eager to attract foreign investment that they have little interest in International Transfer Pricing controls (Rahman and Scapens, 1986; Lin et al., 1993). China has long adopted a zone policy whereby preferential tax rates and tax incentives are available for foreign investment enterprises that operate in the designated investment incentive cities and regions along the coast of China.

Attributable to the series of preferential tax policies which they have adopted in their jurisdictions, the facts are that foreign direct investments are concentrated in the coastal provinces or cities. 'The different tax treatment for foreign investment enterprises brought some problems. For example, regional discrepancies at multiple levels in existing preferential tax policies hamper foreign investment in the development of inland, remote and poor areas. At the same time, it also triggers harmful competition between local governments by wilfully formulating preferential policies, leading to unnecessary losses for the State'.

Transfer pricing manipulations are not a significant practical concern to the tax authority in the inland city. The tax officers of the inland city tax authority explained the reasons for their lack of attention to transfer pricing issues:

'Compared to the coastal cities in China, International Transfer Pricing manipulation is not a serious concern to our tax authority. In the city, corporate income tax accounts for a relatively small proportion of total tax revenue. On average, corporate income taxes contributed only 16.7% of the total tax revenue in 2002. As an inland city, it is not easy to attract foreign direct investments. The local government often attempts to provide an attractive investment environment for foreign investors and therefore is reluctant for the tax authority to adopt strict transfer pricing scrutiny for fear of inducing a flight of capital. In addition, from the government's viewpoint, the losses of corporate income taxes collected from foreign investment enterprises can be more than compensated by a significant increase in foreign direct investment, for the increased foreign investment should produce significant increases in revenues from other more productive taxes such as value-added taxes, consumption taxes and business taxes'.

Another reason is that 'Most of the foreign investment enterprises operating in the city are newly established and should still be covered by tax holiday and tax rate reduction periods. Income adjustments to related party transactions of these foreign investment enterprises do not significantly affect the collection of tax revenues'.

Although the inland city tax authority has not devoted much attention to transfer pricing issues in the past, it has now started to challenge foreign investment enterprises on the issue of transfer pricing. 'Though the auditing sector was erected in 1992, the government worries that the imposition of tight control practices might impede foreign investment in the city. For many years, our central objective was to attract foreign investments rather than to collect income tax revenues from foreign investment enterprises. Not until very recent years has our tax authority noted the International Transfer Pricing manipulation issue and taken steps to combat tax avoidance by transfer pricing abuses of foreign investment enterprises in the city. At present, there are four tax officers who fully concentrate on International Transfer Pricing tax auditing in our tax authority'.

In the case of China, to shift profits made by a Chinese subsidiary to the home country of its parent company, the parent company can use International Transfer Pricing manipulation in a simple form, such as deliberately overpricing imports sent from the parent company to its Chinese subsidiary, or intentionally undervaluing exports by the subsidiary to its parent firm. An interviewed tax officer describes the situation. 'It is often the case that an overseas parent company controls the purchases and sales of products of a foreign investment enterprise that operates in China. On the one hand, it intentionally inflates the price of equipment, raw materials and spare parts purchased and imported by the Chinese subsidiary. On the other hand, it suppresses the prices of finished products exported from China'.

Besides cross-border transactions of goods or services, tax avoidance through the 'thin capitalisation' of Chinese subsidiaries of multinational enterprises is also involved. 'Foreign investors sometimes do not invest sufficient capital in their Chinese subsidiaries. The capital needed for operations has to be borrowed from parent companies abroad at high interest rates. As a result, the foreign investment enterprises' interest expense is increased.'

Initiating an audit

As a check for compliance with the arm's length pricing principle for related party transactions, the Chinese transfer pricing rules not only provide for the circumstances under which high-risk foreign investment enterprises can be identified but also require the Chinese tax authorities to audit at least 30% of the enterprises on the target list. These circumstances include the following.

1. Production and operational decisions controlled by associated enterprises
2. Large transaction amounts with associated enterprises
3. Long periods of losses – for more than two consecutive years
4. Lower profits or losses for an extended period, but a continuously expanding scale of operations
5. Fluctuating profit patterns, with frequent interchanging of profits and losses
6. Transactions with associated enterprises established in tax havens
7. Lower profitability than enterprises in the same industry

8. Lower profit margins than other group companies
9. Unreasonable expenses paid to associated enterprises
10. A sudden and significant drop in profits after a preferential tax treatment period, such as the expiration of a tax holiday period.

The interviewees were asked to express their relative concerns about International Transfer Pricing abuses by foreign investment enterprises under the above listed circumstances. 'Foreign investment enterprises whose production and operational decisions are controlled by associated enterprises' was commonly considered as their most significant concern. They also reported that 'In addition, we also pay substantial attention to those foreign investment enterprises whose supply of raw materials and sales of finished products are controlled by their overseas parent companies. These transactions may trigger transfer pricing audits when we consider that purchases are overpriced or sales underpriced'. 'Because of the particular concern of pricing abuses in the area of intercompany transfers of tangible goods and properties, we are devoting increasing resources to auditing such sorts of transactions'.

Other important concerns expressed included 'foreign investment enterprises that have losses, but continuously expand the scale of their operations', 'foreign investment enterprises with a fluctuating patterns of profits or losses, that is, foreign investment enterprises that have a profit or loss every other year or in an irregular pattern', and 'foreign investment enterprises with transactions with associated enterprises established in tax havens'.

In conclusion, foreign investment enterprises which are controlled by associated enterprises and consistently report substantial losses are particularly vulnerable to transfer pricing audits by tax authorities. In addition, foreign investment enterprises continually reporting profit and loss fluctuations from year to year and those transacting with related enterprises in tax havens are also vulnerable to transfer pricing audits.

Based on the four case studies' results, a Questionnaire was sent to eighty Chinese tax authorities to check how concerned they were about International Transfer Pricing abuses by each of the ten types of foreign investment enterprises with its related party transactions. Thirty-eight returns were obtained. The results obtained from the thirty-eight respondent tax authorities from this survey are shown in Table 14.1.

The mean for each variable was based on a scale from 1 = very possible, to 5 = impossible. For research convenience, the original Likert-like code was reversed to 1 = impossible, to 5 = very possible, high means indicating a greater concern for International Transfer Pricing abuses.

Table 14.1   Concerns about International Transfer Pricing Abuses Cited by Tax Authorities According to the Types of Company

The Types of Company	Mean	Standard Deviation
VAR 1 Production and operational decisions are controlled by associated enterprises	4.68	.525
VAR 4 Lower profits or losses for an extended period, but continuously expands the scale of its operations	4.53	.603
VAR 10 Sudden and significant drop in profits after a preferential tax treatment period, such as the expiration of a tax holiday period	4.42	.683
VAR 6 Transactions with associated enterprises established in tax havens	4.34	.815
VAR 7 Lower profitability than enterprises in the same industry	4.34	2.507
VAR 2 Large transaction amounts with associated enterprises	4.32	.525
VAR 9 Unreasonable expenses paid to associated enterprises	4.16	.973
VAR 3 Long periods of losses – for more than two consecutive years	4.08	.673
VAR 5 Fluctuating profit patters, with frequent interchanging of profits and losses	3.97	.716
VAR 8 Lower profit margins than other group companies	3.79	.741

It can be seen that 'production and operational decisions are controlled by associated enterprises' was indicated by the respondents as the most significant concern for possible International Transfer Pricing abuses. Other significant concerns included 'lower profits or losses for an extended period, but continuously expands the scale of its operations', 'sudden and significant drop in profits after a preferential tax treatment period, such as the expiration of a tax holiday period', 'transactions with associated enterprises established in tax havens', and 'lower profitability than enterprises in the same industry'.

Three variables were indicated as being of relatively large concern by the respondent tax authorities. They are 'large transaction amounts with associated enterprises', 'unreasonable expenses paid to associated enterprises', and 'long periods of losses – for more than two consecutive years'.

Variables that were of moderate concern included 'fluctuating profit patterns, with frequent interchanging of profits and losses', and 'lower profit margins than other group companies'.

Foreign investment enterprises typically engage in a wide range of related party transactions with overseas associates. Circular 59 classifies four major categories of reportable transactions with associated enterprises as follows.

1. purchases and sales, transfers and use of tangible assets
2. transfers and use of intangible assets
3. financing
4. provision of services.

The interviewees were asked to express their relative concern about the International Transfer Pricing abuses of foreign investment enterprises via the four types of transactions. The typical response was that 'One of the most common forms of International Transfer Pricing abuses in China is when a foreign investment enterprise makes excessive payments to its overseas affiliates for importing materials or equipment, and when the same foreign investment enterprise underprices its sales or exports of finished products to the overseas associates'.

For that reason 'purchases and sales, transfers and use of tangible goods' was chosen as their most significant concern. Consequently, tax authorities would select transactions generally with the following features as targets for investigation, as quoted by the respondents:

– When machinery and equipment are supplied by foreign affiliates to foreign investment enterprise
– When the foreign investment enterprise's raw materials are supplied by its foreign affiliates
– When the foreign investment enterprise's products are sold to its foreign affiliates.

The results from the thirty-eight respondent tax authorities are shown in Table 14.2.

The mean for each variable was based on a scale from 1 = very possible, to 5 = impossible. For an easier understanding, the original Likert-like code was reversed to 1 = impossible, to 5 = very possible, high means indicating a greater concern for International Transfer Pricing abuses.

It can be observed that 'the transfer of tangible goods' and 'the transfer of intangibles' were cited by the respondents as of great concern for

Table 14.2   Concerns About International Transfer Pricing Abuses Cited by Tax Authorities According to the Type of Transaction Between Related Parties.

International Transfers	Mean	Standard Deviation
Tangible goods	4.68	.620
Intangibles	4.24	.820
Financing	3.92	.941
Services	3.82	1.062

potential International Transfer Pricing abuses, whereas 'the transfer of financing' and 'the transfer of services' were cited by the respondents as being of moderate concern for potential International Transfer Pricing abuses. This result is consistent with Chan and Chow (1997a, 2001) who found that predominant tax audits (95%) were concerned with the buying and selling of goods and materials. Since financing through intercompany loans is not a common practice in foreign investment enterprises, and thin capitalisation is unlikely to be a substitute mechanism for shifting profits out of China, 'the transfer of financing' is not a significant concern of tax authorities for International Transfer Pricing abuses in China.

Enforced adjustment methods

Article 13 of the Chinese Tax Law provides that 'the payment or receipt of charges or fees in business transactions between an enterprise with foreign investment, or an establishment or a place set up in China by a foreign enterprise to engage in production or business operations, and its associated enterprises, shall be made in the same manner as the payment or receipt of charges or fees in business transactions between independent enterprises. Where the payment or receipt of charges or fees is not made in the same manner as in business transactions between independent enterprises and results in a reduction of the taxable income, the tax authorities shall have the right to make a reasonable adjustment'.

Article 54 of the Tax Law stipulates that if the buying and selling between an enterprise and its associated enterprise are not priced at arm's length, the tax authorities may adopt an appropriate method to make adjustments. The pricing methodologies include the comparable uncontrolled price method, the cost plus method and the resale price method.

Owing to the lack of reliable public data in China, the tax authorities in reality also consider 'other methods' to include price transactions as appropriate methods. These are 'profit base' methodologies such as the comparable profit method, profit split method, transactional net margin method, and deemed profit method.

The participants were asked to select one or more pricing method normally used in income adjustment. It appears that the cost plus method and the deemed profit method are most frequently used by the tax authorities during transfer pricing tax audits. The cost plus method involves the cost plus reasonable expenses and profit margin, as quoted. 'In application of the cost plus method, we generally use the cost of the product for both accounting and income tax purposes and apply a reasonable deemed profit margin to arrive at an arm's length price'.

The reason given for the use of the cost plus method as a favourite pricing method was that 'it is simpler to administer and it is understandable. In addition, the data in using that pricing method are more readily available'. The important aspect of the cost plus method is to decide the appropriate mark-ups. In cases where it is difficult to decide mark-ups among comparable enterprises or where there are differences that materially affect the cost plus mark-ups earned in the controlled and uncontrolled transactions, a 'bargaining' usually arises between the tax authorities and the taxpayers to negotiate a mutually acceptable pricing.

The deemed profit method is another popular method used by the tax authorities in circumstances under which the foreign investment enterprise could not provide complete and accurate information associated with costs and expenses and did not calculate taxable income correctly. No detailed guidelines are issued on the application of this method. Tax authorities assess the taxable income of related party transactions by adopting a comparable profit margin. In the absence of comparable transactions, tax authorities consider the deemed profit method as an option.

The comparable uncontrolled price method uses the market price for the transferred goods and services and is often thought of as the 'best pricing method'. The comparable uncontrolled price method is not used as often as expected by the tax authorities because 'the comparable uncontrolled transaction required by using the comparable uncontrolled price method is often difficult to locate or it is not available in the Chinese market at all'.

The results on methods used from the thirty-eight respondent tax authorities are shown in Table 14.3.

Table 14.3 Legally Oriented International Transfer Pricing Methods Enforced by Tax Authorities for Buying and Selling Goods and Materials

Pricing Methods	# of Tax Authorities	Percentage
Cost plus method	32	28.1
Deemed profit method	24	21.1
Comparable uncontrolled price method	23	20.2
Resale price method	17	14.9
Comparable profit method	10	8.8
Profit split method	5	4.4
Transactional net margin method	2	1.8
Other method**	1	.9
Total	114*	100***

Note * 12 tax authorities used more than one International Transfer Pricing method.
** Other method is the global formulary apportionment. *** Percentage totals subject to rounding.

It can be seen that the method most commonly used in income adjustments is 'cost plus method', which was adopted by thirty-two tax authorities (28.1%) in the sample. Other popular methods used are 'deemed profit method', 'the comparable uncontrolled price method', 'the resale price method', and 'the comparable profit method', used respectively by twenty-four (21.1%), twenty-three (20.2%), seventeen (14.9%) and ten (8.8%) of the tax authorities. The least widely used methods by the tax authorities in the sample include 'profit split', 'transactional net margin method', and 'other method', which was the global formulary apportionment.

Constraining factors

Brean (1979) and Lall (1979) both argued that developing countries are more vulnerable to transfer pricing manipulation because of their greater ignorance on matters of International Transfer Pricing. Even if they had strong suspicions that transfer prices were being abused, developing country governments may lack information, expertise and staff to tackle the issue.

The case studies conducted for this book investigated the practical difficulties encountered by the Chinese tax authorities in auditing related party transactions of foreign investment enterprises. The interviewees were asked what factors constrained the International Transfer Pricing monitoring system in China and which therefore eventually hampered tax collection and administration work. The issues identified through interviews with tax officials of the four tax authorities are summarised below.

1. **Lack of Information Exchange with Foreign Tax Authorities and an Appropriate Transfer Pricing, Computerised, Information System.** Foreign investment enterprises often purchase raw materials and machines and equipment from associated enterprises outside China, and then sell finished products to them. The unavailability of pricing information of the overseas companies often gives rise to an 'information gap' which makes the monitoring of International Transfer Pricing difficult. In addition, there is no effective nationwide computerised information-sharing network for tax administration so far. Information exchanges with overseas fiscal authorities may be an alternative for solving the issue. In the interviews, the respondents indicated that only the State Administration of Taxation, the highest tax authority in China, was responsible for the coordination and exchanges with foreign tax authorities in respect of information about transfer pricing, although local tax authorities can pass their pricing enquiries to the State Administration of Taxation for assistance.

   During the interviews, the most often cited issue for transfer pricing monitoring was the lack of information exchanges with foreign tax authorities. The interviewees explained that 'due to the lack of information exchange with foreign fiscal authorities in respect of information about transfer pricing, we cannot access financial information of foreign companies. It is a major challenge for us to determine pricing and income adjustments in cases where the raw materials or machines are purchased or the products are sold overseas by foreign investment enterprises'.

2. **Lack of Well-Defined Transfer Pricing Legislation, Regulations, and an Institutional Framework for Transfer Pricing Auditing.** The tax authorities lacked enforcement power to deal with transfer pricing issues. Over the past decade, the Chinese government has made great efforts to counter International Transfer Pricing abuses through developing increasingly complex transfer pricing regulations. Yet, compared with the transfer pricing regulations of developed economies, the Chinese transfer pricing legislation is considered rudimentary and still needs to

become more sophisticated. The current Chinese transfer pricing rules neither introduce guidelines on appropriate documentation in order to assist taxpayers in managing the compliance requirements nor cover the pricing of intangibles or services or cost sharing arrangements. Moreover, although there are general non-compliance penalty provisions in the tax law, there is no provision in the transfer pricing regulations to impose specific penalties on transfer pricing cases.

3. **Lack of Well-Trained Personnel to Conduct Tax Auditing and Transfer Pricing Surveillance.** The inland city tax bureau lags behind its counterparts located in the coastal cities in terms of training and technical competence. 'Compared with coastal tax authorities, our tax authority (i.e., the inland city tax authority) has relatively less ability to deal with transfer pricing manipulation issues by audit activity'.

4. **Shortage of Adequate Resources.** The inland city tax bureau was not adequately resourced for tax audits on transfer pricing. 'It is only in recent years that a separate division has been set up fully to concentrate on tax audits on transfer pricing for our tax authority'. 'With inadequate staff resources, our tax authority is deterred from undertaking large scale audits.

5. **Lack of Expertise and Experience to Tackle Transfer Pricing Issues.** Circular 59 requires an actual audit coverage of at least 30% of the identified audit targets for each year. However, due to a shortage of manpower and the lack of operational funds, it is difficult for the tax authorities to achieve this coverage. Although the Chinese tax authorities have recently allocated more resources to transfer pricing audits and investigations, they still suffer from a shortage of trained personnel and lack of adequate data gathering and processing facilities. These problems are likely to continue to impede efforts to deal with the complex issue of transfer pricing in the country.

The results regarding constraining factors from the thirty-eight respondent tax authorities are shown in Table 14.4.

According to the number of tax authorities which checked each item of the Questionnaire, it can be seen that most of them – thirty-five, or 20.7% – considered 'lack of information exchange with foreign tax authorities' as the most important factor constraining the Chinese International Transfer Pricing monitoring system. This is followed in

Table 14.4 Factors Constraining the International Transfer Pricing Monitoring System in China

Factors	Number	Percentage
Lack of information exchange with foreign tax authorities	35	20.7
Lack of an appropriate transfer pricing computerised information system	30	17.8
Lack technical competence	24	14.2
Lack of well-defined transfer pricing legislation and regulations	24	14.2
Insufficient staff resources	21	12.4
Lack of well-defined institutional framework of transfer pricing auditing	16	9.5
Lack expertise and experience	14	8.3
Others	5	3.0

Note: Most tax authorities cited more than one factor.

order by 'lack of an appropriate transfer pricing computerised information system', 'lack technical competence', 'lack of well-defined transfer pricing legislation and regulations', 'insufficient staff resources', 'lack of well-defined institutional framework for transfer pricing auditing', 'lack expertise and experience', and 'others', cited respectively by thirty (17.8%), twenty-four (14.2%), twenty-four (14.2%), twenty-one (12.4%), sixteen (9.5%), fourteen (8.3%) and five (3.0%) of the tax authorities in the sample.

Summary

China is a latecomer to the International Transfer Pricing arena. Compared with the transfer pricing regulations of developed economies, the Chinese transfer pricing legislation is considered rudimentary. In China, the efficiency of tax audits is constrained by both internal staff resource scantiness and the lack of a sound institutional framework to deal with the issue.

As the volume of multinational enterprises doing business in China continues to grow, and the Chinese government continues to draw on the experience of the developed economies in enforcing its own transfer pricing rules, it can be anticipated that the tax authorities in China will intensify their investigations of related party transactions over time to prevent the loss of future income. Foreign investment enterprises need to prepare now, more than ever, to support their transfer pricing tax positions when managing their financial affairs involving substantial dealings with associated enterprises.

15
On Avoiding Audit

Introduction

International Transfer Pricing has significant tax planning implications for multinational enterprises. The increasing scrutiny of related party transactions by tax authorities may cause multinational enterprises to face more tax risks and the possibility of double taxation. It seems timely now for multinationals to seek effective ways to manage their transfer pricing audit risks to avoid potential double taxation. Waiting until the tax authorities commence audits is too late.

This chapter reports the effects of tax audits on multinational transfer pricing policies from the survey results and the mechanisms these companies use to minimise tax uncertainty. This chapter also introduces several approaches for avoiding or minimising transfer pricing audit controversies for proactive, risk-aversive multinational enterprises.

Policy effects of tax audits

The opportunities for multinational tax avoidance by shifting profits between jurisdictions are increasing as the world economy becomes more integrated. International Transfer Pricing is the primary method for multinationals to shift profits for tax avoidance purposes. As International Transfer Pricing manipulations have an adverse effect on the tax bases of the countries involved, the practice has captured the attention of governmental tax authorities to an increasing extent.

Consequently, the tax authorities of many countries have improved their scrutiny of the International Transfer Pricing policies of multinational enterprises. They promulgate detailed legislation and supporting regulations requiring multinational enterprises to use the arm's length standard for transfer pricing between related parties. An aggressive tax audit on a company can result in pricing adjustments, potential double taxation, and penalties. Predictably, the increasing scrutiny leads multinational enterprises to adopt some innovative approaches, such as the use of advance pricing agreements to minimise controversy with tax authorities.

In investigating the possible effects of International Transfer Pricing audits on multinational transfer pricing policies and the mechanisms multinational enterprises use to minimise tax uncertainty, it was expected that there would be correspondence between the tax auditing of International Transfer Pricing and the method used for it on the one hand, and, on the other, between the tax auditing of International Transfer Pricing and the company's status regarding advanced pricing agreements.

Australian Companies – Preferred Methods. The data in Table 15.1 show that Australian companies which have been subjected to International Transfer Pricing tax audits, tend to use market oriented transfer prices. A chi-square test on the data, as presented in Table 15.2, reveals that the relationship is significant at the .1 level. For Australian multinationals, there is a significant relationship between tax audits and the market oriented transfer pricing methods used.

New Zealand Companies – Preferred Methods. The data in Table 15.3 show that the respondent New Zealand companies which have been subjected to International Transfer Pricing tax audits, tend to use market oriented transfer prices. A chi-square test on the data, the results for which are shown in Table 15.4, indicate, however, that the relationship is not significant even at a .1 level. Therefore, for New Zealand multinationals, the data do not reveal a significant relationship between tax audits and the transfer method used.

Table 15.1 Australian Respondent Companies Subjected to Audit and Their Preferred Methods for International Transfer Pricing

	Market Based Method		Non-market Based Method		Subtotals	
	No. of Firms	%	No. of Firms	%	No. of Firm	%
Audit	10	58.8	7	41.2	17	100
No audit	13	31.0	29	69.0	42	100

Table 15.2   Chi-Square Test on the Data for Australian Respondent Companies Subjected to Audit and Their Preferred Methods for International Transfer Pricing

	International Transfer Pricing Methods
Chi-Square value	2.867*
Significance. (2-tailed)	.09
Degree of freedom	1
N	59

* Significant at the .1 level.

Table 15.3   New Zealand Respondent Companies Subjected to Audit and Their Preferred Methods for International Transfer Pricing

	Market Based Method		Non-market Based Method		Subtotals	
	No. of Firms	%	No. of Firms	%	No. of Firm	%
Audit	6	50.0	6	50.0	12	100
No audit	25	44.6	31	55.4	56	100

Table 15.4   Chi-Square Test on the Data for New Zealand Respondent Companies Subjected to Audit and Their Preferred Methods for International Transfer Pricing

	International Transfer Pricing Methods
Chi-Square value	.00
Degree of freedom	1
Significance. (2-tailed)	.985
N	68

Chinese Companies – Preferred Methods. The data in Table 15.5 show that the Chinese respondent companies which have been subjected to International Transfer Pricing tax audits tend to use market oriented transfer prices. A chi-square test as reported in Table 15.6, however, shows that the relationship is not significant even at the .1 level. Therefore, for Chinese multinationals, the data show that there is no significant relationship between tax audits and the market oriented transfer pricing methods used.

Table 15.5   Chinese Respondent Companies Subjected to Audit and Their Preferred Method for International Transfer Pricing

	Market Based Method		Non-market Based Method		Subtotals	
	No. of Firms	%	No. of Firms	%	No. of Firm	%
Audit	11	73.3	4	26.7	15	100
No audit	16	59.3	11	40.7	27	100

Table 15.6   Chi-Square test on the Data for Chinese Respondent Companies Subjected to Audit and Their Preferred Methods for International Transfer Pricing

	International Transfer Pricing Methods
Chi-Square value	.332
Significance. (2-tailed)	.585
Degree of freedom	1
N	42

Advance Pricing Agreements. An advance pricing agreement, under which taxpayers and the tax authority establish agreed guidelines for setting transfer pricing for a number of years, is one avenue by which taxpayers may achieve certainty for their transfer pricing policies and avoid the cost of transfer pricing auditing and inspections. The survey respondents were asked to state their status regarding advance pricing agreements. The responses are shown in Table 15.7. Overall, seven respondents (4.0%) had concluded an advance pricing agreement with local tax authorities. Three respondents (1.7%) were currently negotiating with the local tax authorities for an advance pricing agreement. Sixteen respondents (9.1%) would consider an advance pricing agreement in the future. Ninety-six respondents (54.5%) had no plans to apply for an advance pricing agreement, and the remaining fifty-four respondents (30.7%) had not considered the issue at all.

Australian Companies – Advance Pricing Agreements. The data in Table 15.8 suggest that Australian companies that had been subjected to International Transfer Pricing tax audits are more likely to have signed an advance pricing agreement with the Australian Tax Office or would consider an advance pricing agreement in the future to

Table 15.7   Status of Respondent Companies over Advance Pricing Agreements

Status regarding advance pricing agreement	Australia		New Zealand		China		Overall	
	No. of Firms	%	No. of Firms	%	No. of Firms	%	No. of Firms	%
Have concluded an advance pricing agreement with the local tax authority	4	6.9	2	2.7	1	2.3	7	4.0
Are currently negotiating with the local tax authority for an advance pricing agreement	1	1.7	0	0	2	4.7	3	1.7
Plan to apply for an advance pricing agreement with the local tax authority	3	5.2	5	6.7	8	18.6	16	9.1
Have no plans to apply to the local tax authority	38	65.5	37	49.3	21	48.8	96	54.5
Not considered the issue	12	20.7	31	41.3	11	25.6	54	30.7
Total	58	100*	75	100*	43	100*	176	100*

Note: * Percentage totals subject to rounding.

Table 15.8   Experience of Audit and Their Status Over Advance Pricing Agreements for Australian Respondent Companies

Company's Status Regarding Advance Pricing Agreement	Currently Using/ Considering		Not Considering		Subtotals	
	No. of Firms	%	No. of Firms	%	No. of Firms	%
Audit	5	45.4	6	54.6	11	100
No audit	3	8.6	32	91.4	35	100

Table 15.9   Chi-Square Test on the Data for The Experience of Audit and Their Status Over Advance Pricing Agreements for Australian Respondent Companies

	Advance Pricing Agreement
Chi-Square value	5.566**
Significance. (2-tailed)	.018
Degree of freedom	1
N	46

Note: ** Significant at the .05 level.

Table 15.10   Experience of Audit and Their Status Over Advance Pricing Agreements for New Zealand Respondent Companies

Company's Status Regarding Advance Pricing Agreement	Currently Using/ Considering		Not Considering		Subtotals	
	No. of Firms	%	No. of Firms	%	No. of Firms	%
Audit	3	37.5	5	62.5	8	100
No audit	4	11.4	31	88.6	35	100

Table 15.11   Chi-Square Test on the Data for The Experience of Audit and Their Status Over Advance Pricing Agreements for New Zealand Respondent Companies

	Advance Pricing Agreement
Chi-Square value	1.616
Significance. (2-tailed)	.204
Degree of freedom	1
N	43

minimise tax uncertainty. The chi-square test results show in Table 15.9 that the relationship is significant at the .05 level. Therefore, for Australian multinationals, the data indicate a significant relationship between tax audits and a company's status regarding advance pricing agreements.

New Zealand Companies – Advance Pricing Agreements. The data in Table 15.10 suggest that New Zealand companies, which had been subjected to International Transfer Pricing tax audits, are more likely to have signed an advance pricing agreement with the Inland Revenue Department or would consider an advance pricing agreement in the future to minimise tax uncertainty. A chi-square test shows in Table 15.11, however, that the relationship is not significant even at the .1 level. Therefore, for New Zealand multinationals, the data point to no significant relationship between tax audits and a company's status over advance pricing agreements.

Chinese Companies – Advance Pricing Agreements. The data in Table 15.12 suggest that Chinese companies which had been subjected to International Transfer Pricing tax audits are more likely to have signed an advance pricing agreement with the Chinese tax authorities or would consider an advance pricing agreement in the future to minimise tax uncertainty. A chi-square test shows in Table 15.13, however, that the relationship is not significant even at the .1 level. Therefore, for Chinese multinationals, the data indicate that there is no significant relationship between tax auditing and company's status regarding advance pricing agreements.

In conclusion, it appears that the tax audit experiences of Australian multinationals are associated with corporate internal pricing strategies. That is, Australian companies, which had been subjected to International Transfer Pricing tax audits, are more likely to use market based methods or to have an advance pricing agreement with the Australian Tax Office or would consider an advance pricing agreement in the future to minimise tax uncertainty.

Though data regarding International Transfer Pricing tax auditing and the orientation of transfer prices and the use of advance pricing agreements are not significant for New Zealand and Chinese samples, the data are in the same direction as those for Australian samples.

The logical interpretation of these results is that prior audit experience influences these practices – the choice of market based pricing method and the use of advance pricing agreements – and not vice versa. Firms that have been subjected to transfer pricing audits are alert to the need to satisfy tax authorities by using market based pricing and

Table 15.12   Experience of Audit and Their Status Over Advance Pricing Agreements for Chinese Respondent Companies

Company's Status Regarding Advance Pricing Agreement	Currently Using/ Considering		Not Considering		Subtotals	
	No. of Firms	%	No. of Firms	%	No. of Firms	%
Audit	5	41.7	7	58.3	12	100
No audit	6	30	14	70	20	100

Table 15.13   Chi-Square Test on the Data for The Experience of Audit and Their Status Over Advance Pricing Agreements for Chinese Respondent Companies

	Advance Pricing Agreement
Chi-Square value	.083
Significance. (2-tailed)	.773
Degree of freedom	1
N	32

are more likely to apply for advance pricing agreements to defend their transfer pricing policies.

Risk management

As more and more countries are focusing their legislative, regulative and enforcement efforts on International Transfer Pricing practices, the chances that multinational enterprises will have to face a transfer pricing audit are increasing. A survey by Ernst and Young in 2003 discovered that 86% of multinational parent company respondents and 93% of subsidiary respondents considered transfer pricing as the most important international tax issue. Audits on related party transactions by tax authorities were becoming more frequent, and 40% of respondent firms that reported transfer pricing adjustments had suffered double taxation.

It is timely now for taxpayers to seek effective ways to manage the transfer pricing audit risks to avoid potential transfer pricing adjustments, double taxation and penalties. Waiting until the tax authorities commence an audit is too late. Recommendations to taxpayers on how to reduce the risk of a transfer pricing investigation are as follows.

Establishing an appropriate transfer pricing policy. In determining whether or not to audit a taxpayer for transfer pricing compliance, the New Zealand Inland Revenue considers that the following factors are significant.

- An advance pricing agreement is in existence
- The taxpayer's involvement in negotiating transfer prices
- The economic and commercial basis on which controlled transfer prices are calculated
- The taxpayer's co-operation with the tax authorities
- The existence of documentation
- The taxpayer's tax compliance record.

To counter any harmful tax audits, the above factors need to be borne in mind when enacting a transfer pricing policy. In addition, the taxpayer must be aware that the ultimate purpose of developing pricing policy is to demonstrate to the tax authorities that the transfer prices comply with the arm's length principle. Finally, as the substance of transactions is changing constantly, transfer prices must also change to remain arm's length. The transfer pricing policy must be regularly reviewed and amended to ensure that it remains effective.

Preparing and maintaining sufficient documentation to support transfer pricing policy. To avoid disputes or penalties, preparing and maintaining sufficient documentation is crucial. To prove to the tax authorities that the transfer pricing policy is the arm's length, the documentation should be able to demonstrate that the taxpayer has selected the most reliable method and applied it in an appropriate manner in respect of all transfer pricing arrangements. In other words, if the transfer pricing policy is sufficiently documented and made available to the tax authorities, then the tax authorities would have little choice but to accept the policy. Accordingly, the risk of a detailed transfer pricing audit and the likelihood of transfer pricing adjustments can be avoided or mitigated.

Applying for Advance Pricing Agreements. One proactive way to reduce transfer pricing risks imposed by tax authorities, and possible adjustments, is by applying for advance pricing agreements. An advance pricing agreement is a binding legal agreement between the taxpayer and the tax authority. The advance pricing agreement programme provides an important mechanism for taxpayers to obtain certainty that their transfer pricing policies and procedures meet the requirements of the arm's length standard. There are three types of advance pricing agreements: unilateral advance pricing agreements, bilateral advance pricing agreements and multinational advance pricing agreements.

In 2001 the Inland Revenue Department of New Zealand and the Australian Taxation Office reached an agreement over advance pricing agreements for the purpose of eliminating the taxpayer's risk of double taxation and to provide tax certainty for international transactions between New Zealand and Australia (Ferrers, 2001). In the same year, Australia's largest gaming and technology company – the Aristocrat International Pty Ltd – signed the first bilateral advance pricing agreement simultaneously between New Zealand and Australia on the pricing of its dealings with its New Zealand subsidiary – Aristocrat Technologies NZ Ltd.

Summary

In recent years, many governments have been increasing their vigilance in response to their concern over tax abuses by International Transfer Pricing. Consequently, they have generated transfer pricing legislation and a series of guidelines to deal with the issue.

Moreover, the tax authorities have adopted an increasingly aggressive attitude towards the audit of taxpayers' transfer pricing practices.

These actions have imposed intense pressures upon taxpayers. To stay out of trouble, taxpayers need to take positive steps to consider the practical issues relating to the actual operation of the transfer pricing legislation, and the ways for managing their transfer pricing audit risks in their particular business environment. These have been specifically outlined in the chapter.

16
Foreign Enterprises in China

Introduction

The operational context for foreign companies trading in China consists of structures and practices which contrast with those with which such companies are likely to be familiar in their own countries. A different psychology pervades the network of administrative ways and means which are used to control this vast country. China holds out impressive inducements to foreign enterprises to set up in business in China but they are expected to conform to Chinese protocol in the legal and financial spheres. This chapter overviews some of the variables involved.

Laws and provisions

Step by step, China has set up a relatively complete legal system to encourage foreign multinationals to invest in China with confidence. In 1979 the National People's Congress issued the law of the People's Republic of China on equity joint ventures between Chinese and foreign firms. During the years since then, the Chinese government has established laws and statutes governing the foundation, operation, termination and liquidation of such enterprises. They include the three following basic laws.

- The law of the People's Republic of China on Chinese-foreign equity joint ventures
- The law of the People's Republic of China on Chinese-foreign contractual joint ventures
- The law of the People's Republic of China on wholly foreign-owned enterprises.

Detailed rules for the implementation of the three basic laws include:

- The company law of the People's Republic of China
- The income tax law of the People's Republic of China for enterprises with foreign investment and foreign enterprises
- Interim provisions for guiding foreign investment
- Industrial catalogue for foreign investment
- Interim provisions concerning the investment within China of foreign-invested enterprises
- Provisions regarding the merger and separation of foreign-invested enterprises, and liquidation measures for enterprises with foreign investment.

Laws relating to foreign investment include:

- Contract Law
- Labour Law
- Patent Law and Intellectual Property Law.

These provide legal bases from which to guarantee the independent operational rights of foreign enterprises and to protect the legitimate rights and interests of overseas investors.

With the advent of China to the World Trade Organisation (WTO), the Chinese government is in the process of harmonising existing legislation with the rules of the WTO. It has abrogated some redundant laws and regulations, and plans to revise existing laws and regulations that are out of step with the rules of the WTO. In 2000 China revised the Law of the People's Republic of China on Chinese-foreign contractual joint ventures and the Law of the People's Republic of China on wholly foreign-owned enterprises. In 2001 the Law of the People's Republic of China on Chinese-foreign equity joint ventures was also revised.

Financial modifications

Foreign Exchange Controls. Foreign exchange controls and risks are regarded as one of the important factors inducing multinational enterprises to resort to transfer pricing manipulation to circumvent such controls. In past decades, foreign exchange currency controls in China have been relaxed in some respects. On January 1, 1994, the People's Bank of China initiated an extensive reform of China's foreign exchange system. The People's Bank of China unified China's official and swap market exchange rates, announced the gradual withdrawal of foreign exchange certificates from circulation, and made a number of other changes in the rules governing the use of foreign exchange. These rules at the time were intended to facilitate China's long-term goal of making the renminbi fully convertible.

The renminbi is presently convertible on the current account, but not on the capital account. Chinese importers can buy foreign currencies to fund their overseas purchases, while exporters must exchange almost all the foreign currency they earn for renminbi. Approved foreign companies can buy renminbi to make direct inward investments in China, but are not allowed to buy or sell the local currency to fund investments in China's fledgling securities markets (Barale and Jones, 1994).

China's savers are forbidden from buying foreign currencies to make investments abroad. The renminbi's exchange rate has been fixed at 8.28 to the United States dollar. Economists have argued that the renminbi should become more flexible. The Chinese government intends to open its capital account and embrace full renminbi convertibility as early as five years after joining the World Trade Organisation – a fundamental change of policy and practice.

Meanwhile, the Chinese government will rely on an exchange system that allows the renminbi exchange rate to be determined, at least in part, by the forces of supply and demand. In addition, the Chinese government does not impose restrictions on the payment of dividends, royalties and interests in foreign exchange to affiliates, provided that foreign investment enterprises have enough foreign exchange available for such remittances.

On the one hand, the more liberal policies on foreign exchange control implemented in China since 1994 to prepare for the full convertibility of the renminbi have to some extent eased the foreign exchange problems of foreign investment enterprises. The relatively stable exchange rates of the renminbi since the unification of the swap and official rates in 1994 also reduce the foreign exchange risks for business operations in China (Chan and Chow, 1998).

On the other hand, all foreign investment enterprises are required to achieve at least a balance between their foreign exchange revenues and expenditures according to China's foreign exchange control regulations. The balancing requirement, the restrictions on access to foreign exchange, and the repatriation of profits subject to the availability of foreign exchange, all increase the financial risks for business operations in China.

Until the renminbi becomes fully convertible, foreign currency controls and risks will continue to be a significant inducement for foreign investment enterprises to transfer profits out of China (Chan and Chow, 1998).

Tariff Reductions. The customs duty is an important source for the financial revenue of the Chinese central government. China joined the World Trade Organisation in December 2001. The average tariff level of all World Trade Organisation members is now about 6%. It stands at 3% in developed economies and 10% in developing countries.

Between 1992 and 2004, China cut its customs tariffs on several occasions. These tariff rate cuts are in line with its commitment to reduce average import tariffs to 10% by 2005 and to 9.8% by 2010, as part of its World Trade Organisation membership obligations. The steps so far taken are as follows.

- At the beginning of 1992, duties on 225 items of import commodities were cut. The average tariff dropped down to 43.2%
- In 1993, the duties on 3,371 items of imports were reduced, leading the average tariff down to 36.4%
- In 1995, 4,997 items were adjusted, accounting for 76% of all import tariffs, with the overall tariff average down to 23%
- In 1997, the tariffs were again widely reduced, with the average tariff declining by 6% points to 17%
- By 2001, the average tariff of China had been lowered to 15.3%
- At the beginning of 2002, China continued to reduce its average tariff rate. It fell from 15.3% to 12% on more than 5,000 imported items. The reductions in 2002 included a cut in the tariff for crude and refined oil to 6.1%, while tariffs on vehicles and electronics were cut to 17.4% and 10.7%, respectively. China also wiped out quota licenses on fertiliser, cotton, wool and grain.
- At the beginning of 2004, China began cutting its average tariff rate down to 10.4%.

Although a specific figure for tariff cuts has not been set for next time, China will continue to cut its tariff rates according to its commitments to the World Trade Organisation (Tariff cuts on imported goods, 2002; Tariff cut to boost foreign trade, 2001; Tariff rate cuts to continue, 2003).

Company taxation

The current Chinese tax system was virtually established on the basis of the 1994 tax reform. In that reform, a new tax sharing system between central and local governments was eventually established. Under the tax sharing system, taxes are classified into three types:

1. tax assigned to the central government
2. tax shared by the central and local government
3. tax assigned to the local government (Cho, 1998).

The State Administration of Taxation deals with tax policy but, in general, it does not collect tax revenue itself. Instead, provincial (municipal) and city (county) level tax bureaux are responsible for the day-to-day work of assessment and collection throughout the country.

The State Administration of Taxation deals with tax policy and reports to the State Council, the cabinet of the central government. The State Administration of Taxation also supervises provincial level tax bureaux in implementing taxation regulations and policies. Under the State Administration of Taxation, the provincial (municipal) and city (county) tax bureaux form a hierarchy, with each level reporting to the level directly above it. Meanwhile, the local tax bureaux are also supervised by their local governments.

In alignment with the tax sharing system, provincial (municipal) and city (county) tax bureaux are separated into two sets of administrative institutions, namely, the state tax bureaux and the local tax bureaux. Taxes assigned to the central government are collected by the state tax bureaux. On the other hand, local tax bureaux are responsible for the collection of taxes assigned to the local government.

Under the current tax law, foreign investment enterprises are subject to the following categories of taxes: Corporate Income Tax, Value-Added Tax, Consumption Tax, Business Tax, Real Property Gains Tax, Resource Tax, Stamp Duty, Animal Slaughter Tax, Urban Land and House Tax, and Vehicle and Vessel License Plate Tax.

Among these taxes, corporate income tax is of particular interest to the Chinese tax authorities for transfer pricing tax audits. The tax law stipulates that 30% of corporate income tax from foreign investment enterprises is collected by the state tax bureaux and is subsequently assigned to the central government, and a local surtax of 3% is levied by the local tax bureaux as tax revenue of the local governments (Chan and Chow, 1998).

Table 16.1 presents the proportions of company income tax collected from foreign investment enterprises to national industrial and commercial tax for the years 1992–2002. One can observe that, during the past decade, company income tax from foreign investment enterprises has increased from RMB12.23 billion to RMB348.70 billion.

Table 16.1 Proportions of Corporate Tax from Foreign Investment Enterprises to National Industrial and Commercial Tax for the Years 1992–2002 (RMB billion)

Year	National Industrial and Commercial Tax	CorporateTax for Foreign Investment Enterprises	Percentage
1992	287.61	12.23	4.25
1993	397.05	22.66	5.71
1994	472.87	40.26	8.51
1995	551.55	60.45	10.96
1996	643.60	76.41	11.87
1997	754.80	99.30	13.16
1998	855.17	123.00	14.38
1999	1031.19	164.89	15.99
2000	1266.50	221.70	17.5
2001	1516.50	288.30	19.01
2002	1700.40	348.70	20.52

Source: Ministry of Commerce of the People's Republic of China, 2004g.

Accordingly, the proportion of company income tax from foreign investment enterprises to national industrial and commercial tax has also increased from 4.25% to 20.52%.

Foreign investment enterprises are now subject to an average 20% corporate income tax rate, while the domestic rate is 33%. These attractive rates have helped to make China the largest recipient of foreign investment in the world and allowed it to compete with neighbouring economies. When it joined the World Trade Organisation in 2001, the Chinese government promised to introduce a unified corporate tax law within five years. A unified tax rate of between 24% and 28% would be imposed.

To attract foreign investment, a package of special preferential tax treatments is offered. These treatments include a two-year tax holiday starting at the first profit-making year, and a 50% tax reduction for the following three years, as shown in Table 16.2. Therefore, the motivation of foreign investment enterprises for tax-induced transfer pricing in China, especially in a tax-exemption and tax-reduction period, should be low during the tax concession period. After these periods, foreign investment enterprises are subject to the standard corporate income tax rate of 33%. Except for Hong Kong which has a low rate of

Table 16.2   Corporate Income Tax Incentives and Tax Holidays for Foreign Investment Enterprises in China

Incentive	Scope of Application
Tax Reduction	
A reduced income tax rate of 15%	• foreign investment enterprises in SEZs and in PNDZ • foreign investment enterprises of production nature in ETDZs • foreign investment enterprises with investment over US $30 million • foreign investment enterprises engaged in infrastructure development and advanced technology
A reduced income tax rate of 24%	• foreign investment enterprises of production nature in Coastal Open Economic Zones or Open Cities, or in old urban districts where SEZs and ETDZs are located
Tax Holiday and Tax Reduction	
• Exemption from taxation for the first two profit making years and 50% tax reduction for the following three years	• foreign investment enterprises of production nature scheduled to operate for a period less than 10 years
• A 50% tax reduction for additional three years after five year tax holiday	• foreign investment enterprises with advanced production technology
• A 50% income tax reduction for the year of export	• foreign investment enterprises exporting at least 70% of its total production
Reinvestment Incentives	
• A 40% refund of tax paid on the amount reinvested	• foreign investment enterprises reinvesting their share of profit
• A 100% refund of tax paid on the amount reinvested in technology or export-oriented enterprise	• foreign investment enterprises reinvesting their share of profit in an export-oriented or technologically advanced enterprise
Export Incentives	
• A reduced income tax rate of 10%	• foreign investment enterprises in SEZs and ETDZs or foreign investment enterprises subject to 15 % income tax rate exporting at least 70% of total production
• A 50% income tax reduction for the year of export	• foreign investment enterprises subject to income tax rates other than 15% exporting at least 70% of total production

Source: National People's Congress, PRC (1991).
SEZ = Special Economic Zones.
ETDZs = Economic and Technology Development Zones.
PNDZ = Pudong New Development Zone, Shanghai.

Table 16.3   Corporate Tax Rates of Some of China's Main Trading Partners

Parent Country/Region	Corporate Tax Rate
Hong Kong	16.0%
United States	35.0%
Japan	30.0%
Taiwan	25.0%
Korea	27.0%
Malaysia	28.0%
Singapore	24.5%
United Kingdom	30.0%
Germany	25.0%

Source: Ernst and Young Worldwide Corporate Tax Guide (2002).

16%, this is close to the corporate tax rates in China's major trading partners, as may be seen in Table 16.3.

One of the changes the Chinese government is considering is the phasing out of the preferential tax policies in the special economic zones and replacing them with a system of tax incentives available to both domestic and foreign companies involved in specific industrial sectors. These changes will affect China's attractiveness to foreign companies, but they will not be a deterrent since investors consider other advantages and costs as well as tax issues. The increase in the corporate tax rate will have some negative impact. But most multinationals that have invested heavily in China did so because of the available competitive labour and infrastructure costs.

Hong Kong has long been the leading source of foreign direct investment in China. Hong Kong is also China's major trading partner. Many Hong Kong-sourced investments are not actually owned by bona fide Hong Kong residents. A number of western multinational companies form joint ventures with Hong Kong firms to invest in China to utilise the experience and expertise of Hong Kong managers in the China market. In addition, many Taiwanese companies, instead of investing directly, invest in China via Hong Kong for political reasons (Chan and Chow, 1998, pp. 24–25).

Hong Kong adopts a system of source-based taxation whereby corporate taxes are charged only on income sourced in Hong Kong. Profits or revenues repatriated by foreign subsidiaries are exempt from Hong

Kong taxation (Chan and Chow, 1998. pp. 38–39). Hong Kong, given its fairly relaxed approach to international transfer pricing and low tax rates, offers Hong Kong investors the opportunity to adopt structures which divert profits away from their Chinese affiliated companies or subsidiaries (Sun, 1999).

Withholding Tax on Repatriation of Income. The Chinese Enterprise Income Law imposes a withholding tax of 20% on foreign enterprises without establishments in China but which derive interest, rental, royalty and other income from China, or at the rate specified in tax treaties. In 1997, China entered into bilateral tax treaties on income and capital with some forty-six countries. Under the terms of such bilateral tax treaties, a lower withholding tax rate of 10% would normally apply on interest and royalty payments between enterprises in China and the contracting state. Furthermore, the 10% reduced withholding tax rate also applies to interest and royalty income earned by foreign investors if the payer of such income is located in Special Economic Zones, Coastal Open Cities, Coastal Open Economic Zones, Designated Provincial Capitals, Economic Technology Development Zones, Shanghai Putong New Areas, and Tax Bonded Areas (Cho, 1998).

Summary

This chapter presents an overview of the legal and financial system within which foreign enterprises must operate to base their operations in China. This archival information is of particular interest to foreign companies already established in business in China or are preparing to undertake business in the country. The next and last chapter presents the extent of business opportunities in, as well as the practical difficulties to be faced, in the Chinese market.

17
Pacific Trade Prospects

Introduction

This book presents the results of a study of International Transfer Pricing practices and audits in respect of Australia, New Zealand and China, as three prominent economies of the Pacific Region. The data base for it represents a large variety of company sizes, types of industry and business operations. A number of the respondent firms reported having a significant amount of intercompany transfers crossing international boundaries, implying that International Transfer Pricing is an important issue for those companies.

Of the three countries involved, China has enjoyed steady economic growth over recent decades. With its new infrastructure, low labour costs, huge domestic consumer market, and fast-growing economy, China has been and increasingly is the market where multinational enterprises want to be. Although its production is only one fifth of that of the newly enlarged European Union, its potential, if distant of realisation, remains that of the leading economy of the entire world.

With China's entrance into the World Trade Organisation in 2001, foreign companies have been establishing themselves in the country at a fast rate. Many multinational enterprises are prospering in China. However, the Chinese political system still perpetuates uncertainties. Chinese culture remains distinct from that of western countries. Foreign investors, therefore, have to undertake a great deal of learning to become familiar enough with the unique Chinese system and culture to guarantee successful business operations in the China market, bearing in mind the absence of homogeneity in it. It is convenient to speak of it as one market but in reality it consists of a diverse range of provinces each of which has its own particular market profile.

Trade opportunities

The Pacific Rim is regarded as the fastest growing economic region in the world, with Australia, New Zealand and China lying prominently in the area. As the largest developing country in the world, China has become more and more important in the international economic community since it implemented its economic reform and open door policy in 1978.

There is a potentially enormous consumer market in China. It is estimated that, measured by total GDP, China is likely to become the second largest economy in the world by 2010. In the past decade, the rapid economic growth in China has been accompanied by a large inflow of foreign direct investment. As China entered the World Trade Organisation in 2001, foreign direct investment was expected to reach US$100 billion per year. The emerging China market offers huge business opportunities to foreign investors.

Historically, Australia and New Zealand have had close cultural and business ties with the United Kingdom. However, increasingly the two countries have come to recognise that their economic future is linked more closely with developments in Asia. Particularly, both the Australian and New Zealand governments have recognised the importance of the emerging Chinese market to their economic development. As a result, the trade and investment relationship between Australia, New Zealand and China has grown rapidly over the past decade. This trade is set to develop much further.

China is now the world's fastest growing major economy, with current GDP growing at around 9.1% per annum. It is currently Australia and New Zealand's third and fourth largest trading partner respectively. Free trade agreements between China and Australia on the one hand, and between China and New Zealand on the other, are actively being canvassed and expected.

A free trade agreement with China would benefit businesses already exporting there and would create richer opportunities for Australian and New Zealand companies. Built on the already extensive trade in commodities, dairy and agricultural products, and manufactured goods, considerable opportunities exist for enhanced trade in services for Australian and New Zealand firms, including banking, education, tourism, insurance, health and telecommunications. Australian and New Zealand governments believe that a free trade agreement with China would unlock significant trade and investment potential for their economies. With a reduction of tariffs and quota restrictions through free trade agreements and a consequently improved price competitiveness, there is the potential for at least a modest expansion of opportunities for Australian and New Zealand exporters in the world's largest consumer market.

It is worth noting, however, that a free trade agreement may be a two-edged sword. Free trade agreements with China appear to be overwhelmingly in the Australian and New Zealand national interests. On other hand, a free trade agreement could be a nightmare for some struggling local manufacturers in those two countries. For instance, their textiles, clothing, toys, and footwear market shares may be further eroded by low labour cost Chinese companies as a result of reductions in tariffs.

One survival solution under a free trade regime for companies might be to set up or expand existing operations in China. The establishment of trustworthy and trusted relationships are the necessary precursor for such initiatives, coterminous with gaining an understanding of the trading practices and the legal and financial framework within which they must take place. Sooner or later with such intercompany dealings between an Australian or New Zealand parent company and its Chinese subsidiary, the question of International Transfer Pricing tax issues then arises, and centres around the level of risks borne by – and the economic profit which should accrue to – both the parent firm and its Chinese subsidiary.

As companies expand globally, the primary challenge they face is the cultural barrier rather than economic or political barriers. Arpan (1972, p. 10) assumed that differences in the perceived importance of trade variables are a function of different cultural influences and that cultural differences lead to differences in international intercorporate pricing systems.

Cultural factors

Culture can be defined inclusively as the characteristic perceptions, rituals, affiliations, artefacts and values of a defined population. Selective definitions focus more exclusively on the intellectual sphere. For example, Hofstede (1993, p. 89) defines culture as 'the collective programming of the mind which distinguishes one group or category of people from another'. He divides culture into five dimensions that include power distance, individualism, uncertainty avoidance, masculinity and Confucian dynamism (Hofstede and Bond, 1984; 1988). Chinese values, embodied in an ideology now called neo-Confucianism, is a mixture of Buddhist and Confucian doctrines. In this intellectual environment, mental sets are encouraged for people 'to seek their own moral self-development while fulfilling their social duties' (Iqbal et al., 1997, p. 14).

In contrast, Australia and New Zealand, in developing their economies initially from a position heavily influenced by their British colonial history, have imbibed the norms and practices of a European and particularly British nature. Hofstede included them both in the Anglo-Saxon cultural category. An emphasis on an individual's self-interest is often cited as a cornerstone of this culture (Hofstede and Bond, 1984; 1988). In many respects, these two nations strongly tend to indicate similar features as opposed to Chinese eastern culture. Australia and New Zealand have enacted a free market system. Under this system, property rights are protected by laws, the foreign currency is convertible, and the political situation has a relatively predictable, if not certain, quality about it in the two countries, compared with that of China.

In the case of China, two entrenched ways of conducting business exist. The first, called 'Guan Xi', meaning relationships, is a dominating factor. In China, business has to be built on a good relationship with people, such as clients, suppliers, and government officials – so calling for the establishment of a 'Guan Xi'. The second is best described by the familiar word in western culture for describing business bribes. 'Kickbacks' are routinely paid by suppliers to their buyers, the cost of them being passed along to the company in the form of higher prices for inputs. Western people may view this behaviour as corruption and regard it is unacceptable but Chinese people consider it as normal.

Coupled with such cultural differences, foreign investors are faced with a variety of conditions in the China business environment which might be in contrast to those of their usual operating experiences. These include:

- a shaky legal system which lacks the sophistication of western countries over property rights and the recognition of impersonal legal identity
- broken contracts with impunity
- bad debts – not being paid for deliveries – and the lack of effective redress in the legal system
- corruption which the central government recognises and punishes but is powerless to prevent
- rambling bureaucracy in the hands of many inexpert hands and subject to poor procedures
- a growing problem with counterfeiting of everything from CDs to currency.

Quintessence

With the development of the global economy and the increasing world-wide reach of multinational enterprises, the operations of multinationals are increasingly influenced by national culture. Business decisions in general and International Transfer Pricing decisions in particular are subject to the powerful influence of the time honoured local ways and means of commercial activity and personal business conduct. Owing to the significant differences between Chinese and western cultures and their respective political and economic systems, the practices of International Transfer Pricing are likely to be different in the Chinese context.

In the research for this book, the extent to which environmental variables influence the International Transfer Pricing practices of Chinese companies is explored and compared with that of Australian and New Zealand firms.

The results of the research reveal statistically significant differences between the transfer pricing methods used by Chinese companies and their Australian and New Zealand counterparts. Statistically significant differences are also found between the two sets of companies regarding the degree of emphasis they place on environmental factors affecting their International Transfer Pricing policies.

The Chinese companies place more emphasis than the Australian and New Zealand firms on nearly all of the seventeen environmental variables. The Chinese multinationals engage in a relatively wider range of intercompany transactions and business operations in China and are subject to more economic, political and social risks, owing to the particular vagaries of the Chinese business environment (Chan and Chow, 1998). Predictably, the incentives and motives driving transfer pricing manoeuvres are therefore stronger for the Chinese firms than for the Australian and New Zealand companies.

High correlations exist between the order rankings of the environmental variables of each pairing of national groups. Specifically, the highest correlation exists between the rankings of variables by the Australian and New Zealand respondents. This means that there is substantial agreement between these two groups on the relative importance of the variables. The findings, which are consistent with those reported in Tang (1979; 1981) and Oyelere et al. (1999) suggest that despite national differences, there is a high degree of consistency in their perception of the risks and opportunities inherent in the overall business environment with regards to their International Transfer Pricing decisions.

One obvious issue for multinational enterprises is what needs to be done to minimise the likelihood that host country tax authorities will attempt to adjust their transfer prices. Predictably, the tax audit experiences of multinationals are associated with corporate internal pricing strategies. Australian companies, which have been subject to International Transfer Pricing tax audits, are more likely to use market based methods or to have an advance pricing agreement with the Australian Tax Office or would consider an advance pricing agreement in the future to minimise tax uncertainty.

Although the data regarding International Transfer Pricing tax auditing and the orientation of transfer prices and the use of advance pricing agreements are insignificant for the New Zealand and Chinese samples, they are in the same direction as those of the Australian samples. The logical interpretation of these results is that prior audit experience determines these practices – the choice of market based pricing method and the use of advance pricing agreements, and not vice versa.

Market based methods are based on the arm's length principle. By using market prices, the multinationals are acting almost as though they were independent companies. Thus, it is easier to defend their positions to foreign governments and tax authorities, who are very sensitive to arbitrary pricing (Evans et al., 1999). Those firms that have been subject to transfer pricing audits are more likely to be alert to the need to satisfy tax authorities by using market based pricing and be more likely to apply for advance pricing agreements to defend their transfer pricing policies.

The study also finds that a number of corporate attributes are associated with the potential risk of tax audits. Jensen and Meckling (1976) contended that larger firms encountered more government scrutiny. This book shows that the Australian Taxation Office and the Inland Revenue Department of New Zealand tend to audit large-sized multinationals. In contrast, the Chinese tax authorities focus their tax audit efforts on relatively small-sized firms.

Large firms in non competitive environments, however, whose internal transfer prices are not readily compared with market prices, can maintain complex transfer pricing systems aimed in part at tax-avoidance. Small companies facing more competition, whose transfer prices the tax officers can readily check against market prices, do not have the opportunity to find such manoeuvres to their tax advantage (Caves, 1996).

The Australian and New Zealand tax authorities therefore focus their tax audit efforts on large firms that lack arm's length bases for setting transfer prices. However, as the audits of large companies require sophisticated techniques, Chinese tax authorities claim that they lack sufficient staff resources and experience to tackle large multinationals over transfer pricing issues. In the future, however, Chinese tax authorities will pay more attention to the intercompany transactions of large-sized multinationals. Seven factors were identified as constraining the current Chinese International Transfer Pricing monitoring system.

Finally, tax authority transfer pricing auditing is an important concern in transfer pricing decisions for Australian and New Zealand companies. In contrast, it is relatively unimportant to the Chinese firms. This is perhaps because the Australian and New Zealand tax authorities are more aggressive than their Chinese counterparts in administering and enforcing their transfer pricing rules. This study supports published literature (Brean, 1979; Lall, 1979) that the tax authorities of developing economies have suffered from their relative inexperience and insufficient resources, making their economies more vulnerable to transfer pricing manipulation than that of developed countries.

International Transfer Pricing is the pricing process of goods and services transferred between related companies located in different countries. A number of environmental variables affecting multinational transfer pricing have been identified in previous studies. While the existing literature provides documentary evidence that various environmental factors affect International Transfer Pricing decisions, most of them were limited to a single national basis, or, by comparison, across two or more developed national jurisdictions.

Limited studies have been completed on the International Transfer Pricing practices of multinational enterprises that operate in developing countries as compared to those operating in developed countries. The research project for this book aimed to investigate and contrast multinational transfer pricing practices in cross-national contexts – China in relation to Australia and New Zealand. It also investigated the likelihood that the multinationals involved would experience a tax audit by the taxation authorities, and the mechanisms these companies use to minimise tax uncertainty.

The subject of the book therefore is relevant for both academics and practitioners such as managers, accounting and tax professionals who are interested in, and/or are dealing with International Transfer Pricing.

Multinational enterprises use a large variety of pricing methods dealing with intercompany transfers crossing international boundaries. Contingency theory can be employed to explain a firm's choice of transfer pricing method. The contingent theory approach states that companies choose the International Transfer Pricing systems that are perceived as optimal for their particular situation. (Borkowski, 1980). The findings of the study for this book indicate that the transfer pricing systems used differ between Australia and New Zealand on one hand, and China, on the other. The results of this research support the contingency theory approach, in which a multinational chooses the pricing method that best fits its needs in the operating environment. Researches may in future develop different transfer pricing theories and concepts within the context of the different social, economic and legal environments of developing and developed nations.

Implications for Transfer Pricing Regulations. This research has significant implications for Australian, New Zealand and Chinese transfer pricing legislation. Tax authorities can develop regulations which better reflect the economic, social and political realities of cross-border transfers. In addition, the study adds knowledge to International Transfer Pricing practices in both developing and developed nations, and forms a sound basis for further studies on International Transfer Pricing practices in Australia, New Zealand and China.

Implications for Multinational Enterprises. The findings of this study have implications for managers of foreign-owned companies in formulating their transfer pricing policies in Australia, New Zealand and China. One of the objectives of the research was to derive some guidelines about managing transfer pricing that would be useful in practice. The empirical research has provided generalisable conclusions regarding the environmental determinants of International Transfer Pricing policies in Australia, New Zealand and China. Multinational enterprises operating in the three countries always have to explore how to tailor their International Transfer Pricing strategies to 'fit' certain environmental contexts.

The findings also provide a valuable reference for potential foreign investors or designers of transfer pricing systems in planning their investment and operations in the three countries. The respondent companies to the survey covered a wide range of sizes, industries and business operations. With such a diverse set of companies, the findings from this survey should allow companies to benchmark their inter-company pricing strategies against those of other firms of similar size and orientation in Australia, New Zealand and China.

Bibliography

Abdallah, W. M. (2004). Critical Concerns in Transfer Pricing and Practice. Westport CT: Praeger.

Abdel-Khalik, A. and Lusk, E. (1974). Transfer pricing – A synthesis. *The Accounting Review*, 49 (January), 8–23.

Acklesberg, R. and Yukl, G. (1979). Negotiated transfer pricing and conflict resolution in organisations. *Decision Sciences*, 10 (July), 387–98.

Al-Eryani, M. F., Alam, P., and Akhter, S. H. (1990). Transfer pricing determinants of US multinationals. *Journal of International Business Studies*, 21(3), 409–25.

Aliber, R. Z. (1970). A theory of direct foreign investment. In C. P. Kindleberger (ed.), *The international corporations: A symposium*, pp. 17–34. Cambridge, Mass: MIT Press.

Anthony, R. N. and Govindarajan, V. (eds) (1998). *Management control systems* (9th ed.). Boston: McGraw-Hill.

Arpan, J. S. (1972). *International intracorporate pricing: Non-American systems and views*. NY: Praeger Publishers.

Atkinson, M. and Tyrrall, D. (1999). *International transfer pricing: A practical guide for finance directors*. London: Financial Times Management/Pearson Education.

Australian Bureau of Statistics (ed.) (1999, 2000, 2001, 2002, 2003). *Yearbook Australia*. Canberra, Australia: Author.

Barale, L. A. and Jones, T. E. (1994). Getting strict with foreign exchange. [Electronic version]. *China Business Review*, 21(5), 52–6.

Bartelsman, E. J. (2000). *Why pay more? Corporate tax avoidance through transfer pricing in OECD countries*. London: Centre for Economic Policy Research.

Bean, D. (1979). Multinational firms, transfer pricing, and the tax policy of less developed countries. *Malayan Economic Review*, 24, 34–45.

Belkaoui, A. (1991). *Multinational management accounting*. NY: Quorum Books.

Benvignati, A. M. (1985). An empirical investigation of international transfer pricing by US manufacturing firms. In A. M. Rugman & L. Eden (eds), *Multinationals and transfer pricing* (pp. 193–211). NY: St Martin's Press.

Borkowski, S. C. (1980). *An investigation into the divergence of theory and practice regarding transfer pricing methods*. Ann Arbor, MI: University Microfilms International.

Borkowski, S. C. (1990). Environmental and organizational factors affecting transfer pricing: A survey. *Journal of Management Accounting Research*, 2(Fall), 78–99.

Borkowski, S. C. (1992). Choosing a transfer pricing method: A study of the domestic and international decision-making process. *Journal of International Accounting, Auditing & Taxation*, 1(1), 33–49.

Borkowski, S. C. (1996a). Advance pricing (dis)agreements: Differences in tax authority and transnational corporation opinions. *International Tax Journal*, 22(3), 23–34.

Borkowski, S. C. (1996b). An analysis (meta-and otherwise) of multinational transfer pricing research. *International Journal of Accounting*, 31(1), 39–53.

Borkowski, S. C. (1997a). Factors motivating transfer pricing choices of Japanese and United States transnational corporations. *Journal of International Accounting, Auditing & Taxation*, 6(1), 25–47.

Borkowski, S. C. (1997b). The transfer pricing concerns of developed and developing countries. *International Journal of Accounting*, 32(3), 321–36.

Borkowski, S. C. (1997c). Factors affecting transfer pricing and income shifting between Canadian and U.S. transnational corporations. *International Journal of Accounting*, 32(4), 391–415.

Borkowski, S. C. (2001). Transfer pricing of intangible property harmony and discord across five countries. *International Journal of Accounting*, 36(3), 349–74.

Brean, D. J. (1979). Multinational firms, transfer pricing, and the tax policy of less developed countries. *Malayan Economic Review*, 24(October), 34–45.

Bruns, W. J. and Kaplan, R. S. (eds) (1987). *Accounting and management: Field study perspectives*. Boston: Harvard School Press.

Buckley, A. (ed.) (1992). *Multinational finance* (3rd ed.). NY: Prentice-Hall.

Buckley, P. J. and Hughes, J. F. (2001). Incentives to transfer profits: A Japanese perspective. *Applied Economics*, 33(15), 2009–15.

Burns, J. O. (1980). Transfer pricing in US multinational corporations. *Journal of International Business Studies*, 11(2), 23–39.

Campos, G. (1996). Transfer pricing survey of major trading nations. *International Bureau of Fiscal Documentation Bulletin*, 55(5), 212–22.

Caves, R. (ed.) (1996). *Multinational enterprise and economic analysis* (2nd ed.). Cambridge, England: Cambridge University Press.

CCH Australia (ed.). (2004). *Australian master tax guide* (35 ed.). Milsons Point, Australia: Author.

CCH New Zealand (ed.). (2004). *New Zealand master tax guide*. Auckland, New Zealand: Commerce Clearing House.

Chan, K. H. and Chow, L. (1995). A tax perspective on international transfer pricing for business operations in China. *Hong Kong Accountant*, (January/February), 48–55.

Chan, K. H. and Chow, L. (1997a). International transfer pricing for business operation in China: Inducements, regulation and practice. *Journal of Business Finance and Accounting*, 24(9/10), 1269–89.

Chan, K. H. and Chow, L. (1997b). An empirical study of tax audits in China on international transfer pricing. *Journal of Accounting & Economics*, 23(1), 83–112.

Chan, K. and Chow, L. (1998). *International transfer pricing in China*. Hong Kong: Sweet & Maxwell Asia.

Chan, K. H. and Chow, L. (2001). Corporate environments and international transfer pricing: An empirical study of China in a developing economy framework. *Journal of Accounting and Business Research*, 31(2), 103–18.

Cho, S. (ed.) (1998). *Taxation reforms in China*. Hong Kong: Hong Kong Polytechnic University.

Clews, G. and Howe, B. (2001). *An introduction to transfer pricing in New Zealand.* Retrieved October 10, 2002 from http//www.rmmb.co.nz/papers/tpnz.html.

Cohen, S. S. (1995). *Transfer pricing and taxation of international income in developing countries.* NY: United Nations Secretariat.

Cooper, D. R. and Schindler, P. S. (eds) (1998). *Business research methods* (6th ed.). Boston: McGraw-Hill.

Coopers & Lybrand. (1997). *International transfer pricing: 1997–98.* London: CCH Editions.

Cravens, D. (1982). *Strategic marketing.* Homewood, IL: Irwin.

Cravens, K. S. and Shearon, W. T. (1996). An outcome-based assessment of international transfer pricing policy. *International Journal of Accounting,* 31(4), 419–43.

Creswell, J. W. (1994). *Research design: Qualitative & quantitative approaches.* Thousand Oaks, CA: Sage publications.

Cunningham, G. (1978). *An accounting research framework for multinational enterprises.* Ann Arbor, MI: UMI Research Press.

Drury, J. C. (1997). Studies in management accounting practice: Issues arising from survey findings. In I. Lapsley & R. Wilson (eds). Explorations in financial control (pp. 99–122). London: Thomson.

Dun and Bradstreet Corporation. (2001, 2002, 2003). Who's Who. High Wycombe, Bucks, UK: Author.

Dunning, J. H. (1980). Toward an eclectic theory of international production. Journal of International Business Studies, 11(Spring/Summer), 9–31.

Dunning, J. H. and Rugman, A. M. (1985). The influence of Hymer's dissertation on the theory of foreign direct investment. American Economic Review, 75(May), 228–32.

Easson, A. J. (1991). International tax reform and the inter-nation allocation of tax revenue. Wellington, New Zealand: Institute of Policy Studies.

Eccles, R. G. (1985). The transfer pricing problem: A theory for practice. Lexington, MA: Lexington Books.

Eden, L. (1985). The microeconomics of transfer pricing. In A. M. Rugman & L. Eden (eds), Multinationals and transfer pricing (pp. 13–46). NY: St Martin's Press.

Emmanuel, C. R. and Mehafdi, M. (1994). Transfer pricing. London: Academic Press.

Ernst and Young (1999). *Transfer pricing 1999 global survey.* London: Ernst & Young International.

Ernst and Young (2001). *Transfer pricing 2001 global survey.* London: Ernst & Young International.

Ernst and Young (2002). *Worldwide corporate tax guide.* NY: Ernst & Young Global Limited.

Ernst and Young (2003). *Transfer pricing 2003 global survey.* London: Ernst & Young International.

Ernst and Young (2004). *Transfer pricing global reference guide.* London: Ernst & Young International.

Evans, T. G., Taylor, M. E. and Rolfe, R. J. (eds) (1999). *International accounting and reporting* (3rd ed.). Houston, TX: Dame Publications.

Ferrers, T. (2001). Correspondents: Tax territories talk turkey. *Chartered Accountants Journal,* 80(11), 72.

Fisher, J. (1995). Contingency-based research on management control systems: Categorization by level of complexity. *Journal of Accounting Literature*, 14, 24–53.

Foreign investment companies operating in China (ed.) (2001). GuangDong, China: GuangDong World Publishing (in Chinese). Foreign investment companies operating in China (ed.) (2001). GuangDong, China: GuangDong World Publishing (in Chinese).

Garrison, R. H. and Noreen. E. W. (eds) (2000). *Managerial accounting* (9th ed.). Boston: McGraw-Hill.

Ghosh, D. and Crain, T. L. (1993). A transfer pricing decision model for multinationals. *International Journal of Accounting Education & Research*, 28(2), 170–81.

Gresik, T. A. (2001). The taxing task of taxing transnationals [review]. *Journal of Economic Literature*, 39(3), 800–38.

Grubert, H. and Mutti, J. (1991). Taxes, tariffs and transfer pricing in multinational corporate decision-making. *Review of Economics and Statistics*, 73(2), 285–93.

Grubert, H. and Slemrod, J. (1998). The effect of taxes on investment and income shifting to Puerto Rico. *Review of Economics and Statistics*, 80(3), 365–73.

Guo, Y. (2000). China: Transfer pricing. [Electronic version] *International Tax Review*, (1), 45–51.

Hansen, D. R. and Mowen, M. M. (eds) (2000). *Management accounting* (5th ed). Cincinnati, OH: South Western Publishing.

Harrison, J. and Glyn-Jones, A. (1999). *Transfer pricing handbook: A practical guide for New Zealand business*. Auckland, New Zealand: CCH New Zealand.

Hines, J. R. and Rice, E. M. (1994). Fiscal paradise: Foreign tax havens and American business. *Journal of Economics*, 109(1), 149–82.

Hirshleifer, J. (1956). On the economies of transfer pricing. *Journal of Business*, July, 172–84.

Hoare, J. and Hainsworth, S. (2000), Transfer Pricing. *Chartered Accountants Journal*, April, 66–7.

Hofstede, G. (1993). Cultural constraints in management theories. *Academy of Management Executive*, 7(1), 81–93.

Hofstede, G. and Bond, M. (1984). Hofstede's cultural dimensions: An independent validation using Rokeach's value survey. *Journal of Cross-Cultural Psychology*, 15(4), 417–33.

Hofstede, G. and Bond, M. (1988). The confucian connection: From cultural roots to economic growth. *Organisational Dynamics*, Spring, 5–21.

Holland, T. (2000). The day of the renminbi. *Far Eastern Economic Review*, 163(48), 76–80.

Horngren, C., Foster, G. and Datar, S. (eds) (1999). *Cost accounting: A management emphasis* (9th ed.). Upper Saddle River, NJ: Prentice-Hall.

Horngren, C., Foster, G. and Datar, S. (eds) (2000). *Cost accounting: A managerial emphasis* (10th ed.). Upper Saddle River, NJ: Prentice-Hall.

Huang, M. and Yu, H. (1997). China: Transfer pricing. [Electronic version] *International Tax Review*, April, 21–6.

International Monetary Fund. (2003). *Balance of payments statistics yearbook*. WA: Author.

Iqbal, M. Z., Melcher, T.U. and Elmallab, A. A. (1997). *International accounting: A global perspective*. Cincinnati, OH: South-Western College Publishing.

Ismail, B. (1982). Transfer pricing under demand uncertainty. *Review of Business and Economic Research*, 18(1), 1–14.

Itagaki, T. (1985). The equivalence of duties and quotas in the multinational enterprise. In A. M. Rugman & L. Eden (eds), *Multinationals and transfer pricing* (pp. 117–31). NY: St Martin's Press.

Jacob, J. (1996). Taxes and transfer pricing: Income shifting and the volume of intrafirm transfers. *Journal of Accounting Research*, 34(2), 301–12.

Jensen, M. C. and Meckling, W. (1976). The theory of the firm: Managerial behaviour, agency costs and ownership structure. *Journal of Financial Economics*, 3, 305–60.

Kanodia, C. (1979). Risk sharing and transfer price systems under uncertainty. *Journal of Accounting Research*, Spring, 74–98.

Kaplan, R. S. (1982). *Advanced management accounting*. Englewood Cliffs, NJ: Prentice-Hall.

Lall, S. (1973). Transfer pricing by multinational manufacturing firms. *Oxford Bulletin of Economics and Statistics*, 35(August), 173–95.

Lall, S. (1979). Transfer pricing and developing countries: Some problems of investigation. *World Development*, 7, 64–71.

Lamminmaki, D. and Drury, C. (2001). A comparison of New Zealand and British product-costing practices. *International Journal of Accounting*, 36(3), 329–47.

Lecraw, D. J. (1985). Some evidence on transfer pricing by multinational corporations. In A. M. Rugman & L. Eden (eds), *Multinationals and transfer pricing* (pp. 223–40). NY: St Martin's Press.

Leitch, A. R. and Barrett, S. K. (1992). Multinational transfer pricing: Objectives and constraints. *Journal of Accounting Literature*, 11, 47–92.

Lin, L., Lefebvre, C. and Kantor, J. (1993). Economic determinants of international transfer pricing and the related accounting issues, with particular reference to Asia Pacific countries. *International Journal of Accounting*, 28(1), 49–70.

Ministry of Commerce of the People's Republic of China (2004a). *Top fifteen sources of direct foreign investments in China*. Beijing: Ministry of Commerce of the People's Republic of China (in Chinese). Retrieved January 15, 2004 from http://www.mofcom.gov.cn

Ministry of Commerce of the People's Republic of China (2004b). *Trends in total exports and imports and the imports and exports of foreign investment enterprises in China*. Beijing: Ministry of Commerce of the People's Republic of China (in Chinese). Retrieved January 15, 2004 from http://www.mofcom.gov.cn

Ministry of Commerce of the People's Republic of China (2004c). *The industrial output value of foreign investment enterprises as a proportion of national gross industrial output value in China*. Beijing: Ministry of Commerce of the People's Republic of China (in Chinese). Retrieved January 15, 2004 from http://www.mofcom.gov.cn

Ministry of Commerce of the People's Republic of China (2004d). *Foreign direct Investment in China. Beijing: Ministry of Commerce of the People's Republic of China* (in Chinese). Retrieved January 15, 2004 from http://www.mofcom.gov.cn

Ministry of Commerce of the People's Republic of China (2004e). *Forms of foreign direct investment until December 2002*. Beijing: Ministry of Commerce of the People's Republic of China (in Chinese). Retrieved January 15, 2004 from http://www.mofcom.gov.cn

Ministry of Commerce of the People's Republic of China (2004f). *Foreign direct investment from the top fifteen countries/regions until December 2002*. Beijing: Ministry of Commerce of the People's Republic of China (in Chinese). Retrieved January 15, 2004 from http://www.mofcom.gov.cn

Ministry of Commerce of the People's Republic of China (2004g). *Proportions of corporate tax from foreign investment enterprises to national industrial and commercial tax for the years 1992–2002*. Beijing: Ministry of Commerce of the People's Republic of China (in Chinese). Retrieved January 15, 2004 http://www.mofcom.gov.cn

National Bureau of Statistics (2002). *China statistical yearbook*. Beijing, China: China Statistical Publishing House (in Chinese).

National People's Congress, PRC (1991). *Tax collection and administration law of the People's Republic of China*. Beijing, China: Author (in Chinese).

Natke, P. A. (1985). A comparison of import pricing by foreign and domestic firms in Brazil. In A. M. Rugman & L. Eden (eds), *Multinationals and transfer pricing* (pp. 212–22). NY: St Martin's Press.

New Zealand transfer pricing guidelines (2000). Wellington, New Zealand: New Zealand Inland Revenue Department.

Nobes, C. and Parker, R. H. (2000) (eds). *Comparative international accounting* (6th ed.). Harlow, England: Financial Times.

Organisation for Economic Cooperation and Development (OECD), Committee on Fiscal Affairs (1995). *Transfer pricing guidelines for multinational enterprises and tax administrations*. Paris: OECD Publications.

Otley, D. T. (1980). The contingency theory of management accounting: Achievement and progress. *Accounting, Organisations and Society*, 5(4), 413–28.

Oyelere, P. B. and Emmanuel, C. R. (1998). International transfer pricing and income shifting: Evidence from the UK. *European Accounting Review*, 7(4), 623–35.

Oyelere, P. B., Emmanuel, C. R. and Forker, J. J. (1999). *Environmental factors affecting the international transfer pricing decisions of multinational enterprises: A foreign-controlled versus UK-controlled companies' comparison*. Commerce Division Discussion Paper, Lincoln University, Lincoln, New Zealand.

Patton, M., Insley, J., Happell, T., Feil, M. and Know, P. (1994). Transfer pricing: Australia wants its fair share of tax, too. [Electronic version]. *Tax Management International Journal*, 23(5).

Plasschaert, S. R. (1979). *Transfer pricing and multinational corporations: An overview of concepts, mechanisms and regulations*. Westmead, England: Saxon House.

Plasschaert, S. R. (1985). Transfer pricing problems in developing countries. In A. M. Rugman & L. Eden (eds), *Multinational and Transfer Pricing* (pp. 247–66). NY: St Martin's Press.

Porter, M. E. (1980). *Competitive strategy: Techniques for analysing industries and competitors*, NY: The Freepress.

Porter, M. E. (1985). *Competitive advantage*. NY: The Freepress.

PriceWaterhouse (1984). *Transfer pricing practices of American industry*. NY: Author.

Radebaugh, L. H. and Gray, S. J. (eds) (1997). *International accounting and multinational enterprises*. (4th ed.). NY: John Wiley & Sons.

Rahman, M. Z. and Scapens, R. W. (1986). Transfer pricing by multinationals: Some evidence from Bangladesh. *Journal of Business Finance & Accounting*, 13(3), 383–91.

Rich, C. and Harrison, J. (1997). New Zealand joins transfer pricing fray. [Electronic version] *International Tax Review*, 8(5), 7–10.

Richardson, S. A., Dohrenwend, B. S. and Klein, D. (1965). *Interviewing: Its forms and functions*. NY: Basic Books Incorporated.

Riley, P. and Diamond, G. (1998). Australia: Transfer pricing ruling. [Electronic version] *International Tax Review*, 9(1), 51–2.

Robbins, S. M. and Stobaugh, R. B. (1973). *Money in the multinational enterprise: A study of financial policy*. NY: Basic Books, Inc.

Rolfe, C. (ed.) (1997). *International transfer pricing: 1997–98*. London: CCH Editions Limited.

Root, F. R. (1978). *International trade and investment*. Cincinnati, OH: South-Western Publishing.

Rugman, A. M. (1981). *Inside the multinationals: The economics of internal markets*. NY: Colombia University Press.

Rugman, A. M. (1985a). Transfer pricing in the Canadian petroleum industry. In A. M. Rugman & L. Eden (eds), *Multinationals and Transfer Pricing* (pp. 173–91). NY: St Martin's Press.

Rugman, A. M. (1985b). The determinants of intra-industry direct foreign investment. In A. Erdilek (ed.), *Multinationals as mutual invaders: Intra-industry direct foreign investment* (pp. 38–59). London & Sydney: Croom Helm Ltd.

Rugman, A. M. and Eden, L. (1985). Introduction. In A. M. Rugman & L. Eden (eds), *Multinationals and transfer pricing* (pp. 1–10). NY: St Martin's Press.

Rushinek, A. and Rushinek, S. F. (1988). Multinational transfer-pricing factors: Tax, custom duties, antitrust/dumping legislation, inflation, interest, competition, profit/dividend, and financial reporting. *International Journal of Accounting*, 23(Spring), 95–111.

Statistics New Zealand (ed.) (1997). *Australian and New Zealand standard industrial classification (New Zealand version)*. Wellington: Author.

Statistics New Zealand (ed.) (1999, 2000, 2002). *New Zealand official yearbook*. Wellington: Author.

Statistics New Zealand (2001). *Balance of payments: Sources and methods-Reference reports*. Wellington: Statistical New Zealand. Retrieved June 22, 2001 from http://www.stats.govt.nz

Su, X. L. (1998). Tax administration and transfer pricing issues in China. In S. Cho (ed.), *Taxation reforms in China* (pp. 90–99). Hong Kong: The Hong Kong Polytechnic University.

Sun, H. S. (1999). DFI, foreign trade and transfer pricing. *Journal of Contemporary Asia*, 29(3), 362–82.

Tang, R. Y. (1979). *Transfer pricing in the United States and Japan*. NY: Praeger Publishers.

Tang, R. (1981). *Multinational transfer pricing: Canadian and British perspectives*. Toronto, Canada: Butterworths.

Tang, R. (1982). Environmental variables of multinational transfer pricing: A U.K. perspective. *Journal of Business Finance & Accounting*, 9(2), 179–89.

Tang, R. (1993). *Transfer pricing in the 1990s: Tax and management perspectives*. Westport, CT: Quorum Books.

Tang, R. and Chan, K. (1979). Environmental variables of international transfer pricing: A Japan-United States comparison. *Abacus*, 5(June), 3–12.

Tariff cuts on imported goods (2002). *Far Eastern Economic Review*, 165(13), 25.

Tariff cut to boost foreign trade (2001, 12 December). *China Daily*. Retrieved September 15, 2004 from http://www.china.org.cn/english/BAT/23486.htm.

Tariff rate cuts to continue. (2003, 9 December). *China Daily*. Retrieved September 11, 2004 from http://www.chinadaily.com.cn/en/doc/2003-12/09/content_288808.htm.

The Far East and Australasia: Regional survey of the world (35th ed.) (2004). London: Europa Publications.

The world top 500 multinational companies operating in China (2nd ed.) (2003). ShangDong, China: People's publisher of ShangDong (in Chinese).

Vaitsos, C. V. (1974). *Intercountry income distribution and transnational enterprises*. Oxford, England: Clarendon Press.

Wallace, R. S. and Mellor, C. J. (1988). Nonresponse bias in mail accounting surveys: A pedagogical note. *The British Accounting Review*, 20, 131–39.

Ward, K. (1992). *Strategic management accounting*. Oxford, England: Butterworth-Heinemann.

Watson, D. J. and Baumler, J. V. (1975). Transfer Pricing: a behavioural context. *The Accounting Review*, July, 466–74.

Wu, F. H. and Sharp, D. (1979). An empirical study of transfer pricing practices. *International Journal of Accounting*, 14(Spring), 71–99.

Yin, R. K. (ed.) (1992). *Case study research: Design and methods* (2nd ed.). London: Sage Publications.

Yunker, P. (1983). A survey study of subsidiary autonomy, performance evaluation and transfer pricing in multinational corporations. *Columbia Journal of World Business*, 19(Fall), 51–64.

Zhu, C. J. (1997). Economic system. *Asia Pacific Journal of Human Resources*, 35(3), 19–44.

Index